LOOKING FOR ERIC

MAINSTREAM / SPORT

LOOKING FOR ERIC

IN SEARCH OF THE LEEDS GREATS

RICK BROADBENT

MAINSTREAM
PUBLISHING

EDINBURGH AND LONDON

Copyright © Rick Broadbent, 2000
All rights reserved
The moral right of the author has been asserted

First published in Great Britain in 2000 by
MAINSTREAM PUBLISHING COMPANY (EDINBURGH) LTD
7 Albany Street
Edinburgh EH1 3UG

ISBN 1 84018 696 8

This edition, 2002

A catalogue record for this book is available from the British Library

Typeset in Allise and Berkeley Book
Printed and bound in Great Britain by Cox & Wyman Ltd

CONTENTS

For Debs (getting married on the day Leeds beat Manchester United was the best of omens) and for Mum and Dad.

ACKNOWLEDGEMENTS

This book could not have been possible without the goodwill of the players featured, so I wish to thank Gordon Strachan, Eddie Gray, Tony Currie, Peter Lorimer, John Charles, Bobby Collins, Norman Hunter, Jack Charlton, Lucas Radebe, Allan Clarke, Johnny Giles, Stephen McPhail, Michael Bridges, Nigel Martyn and Dominic Matteo. I would also like to thank David Batty for his courtesy and Peter Ridsdale.

It has also been a family affair and I am indebted to Gaynor and Debs for their heroic photo shoot for the cover, Greg for keeping all his old programmes, Dan for the Harry Kewell article, Mum for her contacts and memories, and Don for the fish and chips! I must also thank Dad for taking me to Leeds in the first place when York City was technically closer and I knew no better. It could have been so different.

Paul Eubanks and Phil Vasili were a great help regarding Albert Johanneson and, though my dealings with agents were mixed, I should thank Simon Bayliff, Phil Graham and especially Matt Kleinman and Gary Blumberg.

Peter Lorimer was kind enough to give me the phone numbers of several players, while my friend, David Anderson of the Press Association, was also a great aid with his suggestions, while keeping me informed of Eric's attendance at Manchester United games. Dave's wife, Audrey, also spared the time to translate a letter into French for me, for which I am grateful.

In France I was lucky enough to come across Yves Ciccullo and Raphael, both of whom provided useful background on Eric. Vittorio Fioravanti did the same regarding John Charles.

Thanks go to Andrew Varley for letting me browse through his picture library; the staff at the National Newspaper Library in Colindale; and to all at Mainstream, especially Bill Campbell for getting back to me so quickly.

Finally, I am, as ever, blessed to have Debs and Erin as my assistants.

When this book was first published in 2000, David O'Leary was still at Leeds United and, hence, there are numerous references to him being the current manager. I have left these references in this revised edition because I felt that doctoring the text would dilute the passion and colour of the interviewees' comments.

RB, August 2002.

PROLOGUE — Waiting for Eric

Eric was different. Anyone could see that. Maybe it was those thick, black eyebrows which resembled slugs on steroids and were forever raised in quizzical superiority. Or maybe it was the way he insisted on wearing his collar up and puffing out his chest like a peacock in full display. Whatever it was, no other player has caused eager-to-please fans to turn up to Leeds' training ground dressed in full combat gear, only to realise their hero had actually said he was heavily influenced by the poet Rimbaud rather than Rambo. And, of course, no other player would ever seek vengeance on a foul-mouthed supporter by launching into a kung fu kick and then citing metaphysical meanderings about seagulls and trawlers as his defence.

Eric was different, all right. And as he stood on the hastily-constructed podium outside Leeds Town Hall he blew kisses to the massed ranks of Leeds fans, who had begun to gather early that morning to pay homage to the newly-crowned Division One champions. Then, like his team-mates before him, Eric took the microphone and a baited hush hung over the crowd. I caught the eyes of a heavily-tattooed skinhead, a painted Tricolour segmenting his face, and I felt an unlikely bond. For all the affection in which we held this Frenchman, who had been unknown to all but the saddest of Europhile anoraks just a few months earlier, we had rarely heard him speak. It was said he didn't *parle anglais*, but you sensed that was an expedient excuse he employed to avoid being interviewed. Now Eric took centre-stage once more and, in tones dripping with continental charm, said simply: 'I don't know why, but I love you.'

The feeling was mutual, but like all great love affairs it turned sour. You suspected it had to end in tears. Though he had provided the impetus which propelled Leeds to the 1992 title – their first since the end of the Revie era in 1974 – you always sensed there was little common ground between him and the prince of dourness, Howard Wilkinson. In retrospect, it seems amazing that it should have been Wilkinson who signed Cantona in the first place. The Yorkshireman was the arch pragmatist, a man who exuded the passion of a stuffed fish on a morphine drip; while Cantona was all flair, flicks and finesse, the wayward lovechild of Frank Worthington and Sacha Distel. It was the unlikeliest of marriages and it was no surprise when it ended in divorce. The vultures were quick to circle. Alex Ferguson bought him for a pittance, Leeds went into characteristic decline and Manchester United became the benchmark for the rest of the country. Some Leeds fans were unforgiving and there were vile attacks on the Cantona family home, but I could only remember those fleeting moments together with fondness. Eric was different, but Leeds were good again and, by Christ, it had been a long time coming.

I first became a true Leeds fans in 1975. I can vividly recall sitting around the kitchen table in a Cornish holiday cottage with my parents and brothers, listening to the European Cup Final on a crackly transistor radio. When Leeds lost, my dad and elder brother cried. I was six and figured this football thing must really be something, to reduce a grown man and an anguished adolescent to tears. Later I would wonder how it was that we ended up in a remote Cornish village without a television, if it really meant that much to them, but for now I was hooked. Line and sinker.

I became an avid fan, delighting in Eddie Gray's dropped shoulder and Billy Bremner's bellicosity. I would stick with them from my vantage point in the North-East stand as Tony Currie kept Leeds alive in the late 1970s. And I did not desert them in the 1980s when the team was dreadful, my dad stopped my season ticket ('you can pay yourself if you want to watch that rubbish') and Elland Road was an ugly place where the National Front fascists would dole out their propaganda alongside the man with the enamel badges and rosettes. But as any football fan of any denomination knows, you are lumbered with your team through thick and the more prevalent thin. And the beauty of it is, there is always hope. However bad it gets, you know there is the chance that the pendulum will swing the other way and that for every Jimmy Adamson – the faintly comical pipe-smoking Leeds manager whom I recall as an incoherent Harold Wilson wannabe – there will be a David O'Leary. For every Paris 1975 there will be a Bournemouth 1990; and for every David McNiven, gliding around a ploughed field like a drunk on roller-skates, there will be an Eric.

As 1999 drew to a close and a new millennium beckoned, I decided to pay homage to some of the greatest Leeds players by tracking them down and hearing first hand what they thought about it all. I knew this would not be easy – indeed, in some cases, impossible. Billy Bremner was sadly no more and Albert

Johanneson had died in alcoholic squalor in a Leeds tower block several years earlier. Eric, meanwhile, had turned his back on football and was carving out a new career as a film star. Ironically, Vinnie Jones, one of the least artistic players to ever walk the Elland Road turf, had eclipsed him in that respect by starring in the critically-acclaimed *Lock, Stock and Two Smoking Barrels*. Finding Eric and getting him to talk about his former career would be the hardest quest of all. But I decided I had to do it. Having watched from the outside for a quarter of a century, I wanted to know the inside story. So I drew up my list of targets.

I am not suggesting it is a definitive list of Leeds legends, but each subject played a special role in the development of the club and each one captured the affection of the fans. Watching them had been a vicarious experience, we felt we were part of them, we owned them. Now I wanted to find out where the heroes had gone. Had it just been a job – or had they lived, breathed, slept, eaten, loved and hated Leeds United in equal measures, just as I had done?

GORDON STRACHAN – Ginger Spice

There's nobody fitter at his age, except maybe Raquel Welch.
RON ATKINSON, 1996

ordon Strachan stands up from behind his desk at the Sky Blue Lodge, Coventry City's modest training ground, and walks over to a window. 'Here, have a look at this,' he says with an impish glimmer in his eye. He points to a pitch where a group of tracksuited youngsters are knocking a ball around. 'They're our apprentices,' he says. 'They don't know it yet, but they're going to be working their bollocks off today. You see, we've just found out they were all nightclubbing last night.' He laughs. 'Treat them like a parent,' he says. 'Small tellings-off with lots of love.'

It is no surprise that Strachan the manager should relish playing the father-figure, because Strachan the player did the same. When he arrived at Leeds in 1989, one of the first things he did was to put teenage prodigy David Batty back on the straight and narrow. 'Batts had been around the club for a year or so and he was going through a rough period where he wasn't sure about life,' recalls Strachan. 'It's the sort of thing a lot of 19-year-olds do, but when I got there he was unhappy and was mumbling about getting a transfer and being ready to move on. I told him to shut up and get on with it.' It worked, as did almost everything Strachan attempted during his time at Elland Road. Part man, part Duracell bunny, this pint-sized colossus was the most telling factor in turning Leeds from comatose giants back into a genuine footballing force.

He was also the first to respond to my request for an interview. Given his commitments as a Premiership manager, albeit only Coventry, I had expected to have to badger him to agree, but days after sending out a letter I got a one-line reply:

> Dear Rick, I'd be happy to meet you one morning. Please give my
> secretary a ring to arrange the details. I look forward to seeing you.
> Yours sincerely,
> Gordon Strachan (Team Manager).

He had signed it himself and I felt mightily encouraged. The interview was arranged and so it was that I turned up at his office that December morning for my first meeting with a legend.

The first thing I notice about Gordon Strachan is that he is tiny. Perhaps that is why the fiery aggression and acidic wit became such key components of the Strachan persona – as defence mechanisms. He fetches me a cup of tea and we walk to his office, the wee man whistling Cher's 'If I could Turn Back Time', which seems strangely significant.

Strachan was the man who, as much as anyone, helped make Leeds great again. Howard Wilkinson had his five-year plan, but the chances are it would not have got off the ground had he not taken a punt and signed a 32-year-old winger who was surplus to requirements at Manchester United. Though he was out of favour at Old Trafford, the signing of Strachan gave the first hint that Leeds might actually be going places. A fading star he may have been, but Leeds had become the graveyard of journeymen and the benchmark for mediocrity. The sons of Revie – Allan Clarke, Eddie Gray and Billy Bremner – had all received precious little backing as they attempted to bridge the gap between player and manager (in Gray's case the bridge had been a hyphen), but now Howard Wilkinson was in charge and the wind of change was blowing through Elland Road. The pictures of the Revie team, which decorated the Elland Road corridors and provided proof that it had been different once, were now taken down. Nostalgia was quite literally a thing of the past.

However, it was the signing of Strachan for £300,000 in 1989 which really signalled Wilkinson's intent. The fact he was a Manchester United man only added to the kudos in getting a player who clearly had some small inkling of ability. 'My time at Manchester United was up,' says Strachan. 'Ferguson and myself had been together too long and, because of that, I wasn't at my best. We lost to Nottingham Forest in the quarter-final of the FA Cup and Ferguson came running after me and asked me if I wanted to talk to Ron Atkinson at Sheffield Wednesday. Leeds were also interested, but I knew Big Ron and so I was thinking about going to Sheffield. Out of courtesy I went to see Howard too and I liked the fella. It was the first time for ages that I felt someone believed in me. I'd also be lying if I said it had nothing to do with the money. They made me a great offer and I'd have been daft to turn it down. But Howard rescued me. Going to Leeds saved my career.'

Though they had first worked together at Aberdeen a decade earlier, the relationship with Ferguson had recently plumbed new depths when I met Strachan. Ferguson had just savaged him in his controversial biography, *Managing My Life*, a *Sunday Times* bestseller and all-encompassing settling of scores and personal vendettas. Strachan, claimed Ferguson, was a man not to be trusted. He also said he would not expose his back to him in a hurry and that the manner in which Strachan could 'go against his word without a qualm was sickening'. So had Strachan been dishonest over the Leeds move? 'That's one man's opinion,' he says. 'One man in all my time in football. I've heard about his book, but I haven't read it. He can be that way, though. He's a difficult man to like. I said I was bored and he's mentioned it a couple of times since. The thing is you can only do so much at a club and then, it's like David Bowie, you have to reinvent yourself.'

Thankfully, Strachan would reinvent himself as chief alchemist at Elland Road rather than an androgynous space cadet with a pierrot face, ten-inch heels and a backing band from Mars. However, he quickly realised there were manifold problems at a club now famous only for its hooligans. 'My first couple of games I thought "what have I done?" I got the man of the match award on my début at Portsmouth and I'm given 24 cans of beer. I said "I can't go walking out to the car with that. There are people out there watching me and I'm a professional footballer. It won't look good if I stick a crate of booze in the boot." There are standards that you should aspire to, but that was the kind of mentality we had at Leeds in those days. One of the reasons Howard brought me in was to make the club more professional and leaving Portsmouth with a car full of booze would have been a bad start. The rest of that season was a struggle.'

There was a more serious problem to deal with, too. Various cliques led to an internecine atmosphere in the dressing-room and a lack of unity on the pitch. 'Howard decided to clear the decks in the summer,' says Strachan. 'He had to do it. Too many players were living off the back of the old Leeds team and trying to live up to their image of a hard side. They were promoting this nastiness, which was not a real tribute to the side of the '70s because, though they could look after themselves, the Revie side could also play football. In the '80s some Leeds players were living off the history of the club, they were no use to anyone and they had to go.'

Among those to depart was John Sheridan, one of the few shining lights amid the immutable '80s gloom. A classy and mercurial player, the shock at Sheridan's departure was hardly tempered by the arrival of Vinnie Jones, Wimbledon's walking provocation. I was at university at the time and my friends marked the occasion by buying me a t-shirt with the archetypal British bulldog on the front and the legend VINNIE JONES FAN CLUB on the back. It was meant as a joke, as I presumed the signing was. Football may be a funny old game, but spending twice as much money on Jones than on Strachan seemed to be a move from the Salvador Dali School of Football Management.

Strachan and history put me right. 'I have to admit I laughed when I first heard about it, but Vinnie was a breath of fresh air,' smiles Strachan. 'I didn't have the right to complain about dropping down a division and playing with people like that. In my last year at Old Trafford, I'd not done myself justice so I no longer had the right to be sitting at the table next to Bryan Robson. This was my choice.

'Vinnie and I were like chalk and cheese, but we got on great together and we had the same sense of humour. I was good for him and he was good for me. We didn't want him to be a monster, though. In a pre-season game against Anderlecht one of their players ended up with a bloody nose. That's what Vinnie thought he was here for. I'd said, "Put the fear of god into them, but don't try injuring anybody." We soon realised he could actually pass the ball, though, and it was his best year as a footballer.'

Having finished tenth the previous season, Leeds began the new campaign with hopes at a rare high. Along with Jones, Wilkinson had recruited Mel Sterland, Chris Fairclough, John Hendrie and John McClelland, but the season started in the worst possible manner as Leeds were demolished 5–2 at Newcastle. The next few games provided little evidence to justify the pre-season optimism. With talk of John Aldridge being a possible transfer target, television cameras caught one fan screaming at Wilkinson: 'Forget Aldridge, you need Marco van bloody Basten.'

However, soon the tide turned. 'We kicked off a 16-game unbeaten run and played some good football, what I'd call power football,' says Strachan, who had immediately endeared himself to the Elland Road support. Any fears that a Manchester United man might be unwelcome at Leeds had been hastily vanquished, though Strachan admitted he had no idea about the rivalry between the two clubs.

'All the time I'd been at United, Leeds were in the Second Division,' he said. 'I hadn't even been to Elland Road until the day I signed. It was only later, when we played Manchester United, that I realised there was this incredible hatred. When I arrived I thought people were just looking at me and thinking "here's this little fella from Manchester United". I didn't realise it was Manchester United who we hate intensely. I don't know how I got away with it.'

Had he been a failure, he may not have done, but Strachan's effervescence, his energy and aggression – lined with the soft underbelly of an Andrex puppy – made him a huge favourite. When Leeds won 2–0 at Middlesbrough in December they went to the top of the Second Division. Batty, having heeded Strachan's words, was by now a regular; Gary Speed was chomping at the bit as he awaited his chance; and the attacking options were strengthened when Lee Chapman was signed for £400,000 from Nottingham Forest. Like Jones, Chapman was one of those deceptively effective players. His mincing stride and clumsy movements put one in mind of a constipated Frankenstein's monster, but he scored goals aplenty and was the best striker Leeds had had for a decade. 'He was another one who peaked at Leeds,' says Strachan. 'We played to his strengths. At Nottingham Forest they were playing balls into his feet and one-twos, but that wasn't his game. If you put the ball to him early he would hold on to it, you could support him, get the ball wide, cross it and he'd score. It was easy. Football is a simple game, it's the players that make it complicated.'

It was simple enough against title rivals Sheffield United at Elland Road. With Strachan at his cheeky, imperious best and Speed scoring the breakaway goal which kick-started his Leeds career, United won 4–0. Yet in typically masochistic style, Leeds then lost their unbeaten home record to Barnsley to set up a nervous finale with Sheffield and Newcastle both having a chance to pip Leeds to promotion. It came down to the penultimate weekend of the season. Leeds were home to Leicester, knowing a win would secure the title depending upon their rivals' results. Gary McAllister, soon to be a Leeds player himself, pricked the bubble of exultation that had greeted Mel Sterland's opener as he fired home an equaliser for Leicester. Time was running out. And then up popped Strachan to strike a left-footed shot into the top corner to seal the win. Elland Road went apoplectic. The misery that had started when Leeds were relegated in 1982, continued through mindless riots at Birmingham and Bradford and sealed the fates of three Revie heroes, now appeared to be over. 'I've been in stadiums all over the world, but I don't think I'll ever feel an atmosphere like that again,' recalls Strachan. 'There was a oneness with the team and supporters: you get that once or twice in your career, they're in there with you, making the pass, feeling the tackles, the hurt.'

As the whistle sounded, the fans invaded the pitch in jubilation. Everyone believed promotion had been secured, even the players. 'Vinnie came into the changing rooms and told us we were up,' says Strachan. 'Me and Mervyn Day immediately burst into tears. It was something we'd worked so hard to achieve and, for Mervyn, it was close to the end of his career. Then somebody else came in and said it's all off. Newcastle had beaten West Ham. I felt like battering Vinnie for being so stupid, but he'd slunk away into the background. We had one game left against Bournemouth on Easter Monday and it was not easy to pick ourselves up after the emotion of the Leicester game. You wanted to play Bournemouth there and then, that evening. It was a long week and it dragged on and on.'

By the time I arrived at my girlfriend's house in Bournemouth the night before the game, the Leeds fans had already left their inexorable mark on the sleepy Dorset town. Everybody seemed to have a tale about these depraved northern Vikings who had been on a lager-fuelled crusade of rape and pillage. I began to feel embarrassed about the Leeds United car sticker on my clapped-out Peugeot in the drive. One person my girlfriend knew had been punched in the face by a Leeds fan the previous night. Someone else's beach hut had been burnt. Garden fences had been uprooted as a maelstrom of madness drowned out any goodwill that had been built since Birmingham.

On the day of the game the violence showed no signs of relenting. For the true fans it was sickening. Scarcely a year after 94 football supporters had been killed in the Hillsborough disaster, a minority of Leeds followers showed a collective need for a frontal lobotomy. This should have been one of the greatest days in the club's history, but the news bulletins were filled with condemning reports of football hooligans running riot on the south coast. One Bournemouth player, Paul Miller, had his car attacked as he drove to the ground and it was with mixed emotions that I took my seat in the main stand at a sun-drenched Dean Court. Behind me sat Trevor Brooking, doing radio commentary for the BBC. 'How do you think it will go today?' I asked him. Brooking looked at me with that pained, lipless expression that has since become his forte on *Match of the Day*. The thinking man's iguana. 'I'm more concerned about what's going on outside,' he said. He had a point.

'We knew there was trouble,' says Strachan. 'The dressing-room was very small and David Batty was sat by the window, looking out at what was happening and telling us. I was able to switch off from it all, because you have to if you are a professional. I still think about it every now and then and it spoilt the day a bit. I don't understand it. You would need to be a lecturer in sociology or behaviour to get to the bottom of it, but it's black and white to me.'

Leeds made sure of the championship thanks to a single goal from Chapman. The players sprinted off and the fans streamed on. At one point I had Glynn Snodin, the Leeds defender who was injured at the time, on my shoulders. I found my brother, who had been in another part of the ground, and hugged him. We had done it. Those years spent watching unmitigated dross had suddenly been erased from the memory bank and replaced by something altogether more frightening and baffling – success.

'The violence doesn't really ruin my memories,' says Strachan. 'I'm all consumed with the fun days I had at Leeds. It wasn't an easy game to handle down there. It was a long, long morning in our hotel in Poole, but the feeling of elation was fantastic. There was a lot of singing and dancing going on, but I just sat at the front of the bus. The sun was setting on a beautiful day and I had a warm glow of self-satisfaction inside.'

Although Leeds would clinch the last-ever Division One title two years later, Strachan says winning promotion was his greatest achievement at Leeds. 'That was something somebody asked me to do,' he explains. 'I had been asked to get us promoted, but nobody ever said "Can you win the Division One title for us?" When somebody asks you to do a specific job and you deliver, you feel great. It was my greatest pride and joy. I've still got the pictures dotted around the house.'

For Wilkinson, however, it was merely the first stage of a carefully-drafted plan. The second stage saw no room for sentiment and John Lukic, Chris Whyte and McAllister were all recruited. Two of the fans' favourites, Vinnie Jones and Mervyn Day, were suddenly out of the frame. 'I was surprised Howard changed things so quickly,' says Strachan. 'I thought Vinnie could have stayed on in the squad because we didn't have a great amount of midfield players, but the trouble with Vinnie was that he had become so big he was now a celebrity. You just couldn't have had him on the bench, because with his celebrity status he wouldn't have been able to handle it.'

And so McAllister arrived for £1 million after Brian Clough's abstruseness had dissuaded him from joining Nottingham Forest. Hugely gifted with the sort of artistic skills not seen in a Leeds midfield since the days of Tony Currie, McAllister was the antithesis of Jones (who was now destined to go through life with a Leeds tattoo on his leg, the sad epitaph to a lost love affair).

'McAllister couldn't have been more different from Vinnie,' admits Strachan. 'Verbally he used to abuse the other players a lot, because he couldn't understand why people couldn't read what he was going to do. They weren't on his wavelength to start with, but he calmed it down and got the respect of the other lads.'

Success came instantly. Says Strachan: 'On the first day of the season, we were 3–0 up at Everton and I thought "This is going to be a doddle." But they got two goals back and we were hanging on for grim death.' Nevertheless, Leeds enjoyed a great first season back in the top flight, making the semi-final of the Rumbelows Cup, losing to Manchester United over two legs, and finishing in a very respectable and equally unexpected fourth place. 'We thought it was going to be a struggle that season and had no inkling that we would do as well as we did,' continues Strachan. 'Fourth was a fantastic effort.'

Wilkinson had worked a miracle at Elland Road, but was still not content to rest on his laurels. The troublesome left-back spot was filled by Tony Dorigo, Chelsea's £1.3 million Aussie, while Southampton's Rod Wallace arrived as a £1.6 million foil for Chapman. 'Dorigo gave us pace and was a great signing,' recalls Strachan. 'He should have won more caps for England, but the game was too easy for him. Maybe it was the way he looked, his hair all neatly in place, the fact he was never dirty. I was very happy with his effort, but I always felt he had another ten per cent to give.' With England midfielder Steve Hodge snapped up from Nottingham Forest for £900,000, the team-building was over. Leeds were ready for their title assault.

A superb start to the season saw Leeds go ten games before they finally lost to a Mark Bright goal at Crystal Palace. Despite that defeat, the gauntlet had been thrown down to Manchester United, who were seeking their first championship for a quarter of a century. The question was, could Strachan still inspire those around him at the ripe old age of 34? The answer was an unequivocal yes. The 1992 campaign was the apotheosis of Strachan's career, as the man discarded by United three years earlier became their nemesis.

The nation was watching too. In the pre-Sky era, live television audiences saw Leeds thrash Aston Villa 4–1 and Sheffield Wednesday 6–1. The midfield of Strachan, Batty, McAllister and Speed became revered as the best in the country, while Chapman and Wallace were forging an effective alliance up front.

'How good was that midfield? It was good enough to win the league and that is all it can be measured in. People try to compare teams from different eras, but you can't do that.' Nevertheless, I put it to Strachan that it was even better than the current Leeds midfield, a heady cocktail of precocious youngsters like Lee Bowyer, Harry Kewell and Stephen McPhail, and the new father figure, David Batty. He refuses to be drawn. 'So much has changed,' he says. 'The rules have changed. There's more room to play in the middle of the park now. The back-pass rule has changed the face of the game. All you can say is we were the best at the time and we deserved the title because we worked harder than anybody else. That's a fact. We worked harder than anyone in training and it showed on the pitch. We were fitter. Howard would put us through the ringer.'

By the time Strachan turned 35 in February 1992 it seemed that both he and Leeds might have finally hit the wall. Wilkinson decided the side needed a boost and opted to take Eric Cantona on loan from Nîmes, while Sheffield Wednesday dithered. Cantona's reputation preceded him, but had little to do with his footballing ability. He was an enigmatic maverick, a free spirit with disciplinary problems who seemed unlikely to acclimatise to Wilkinson's authoritarian approach. This was the Cantona who had been banned from the French national side for calling the manager 'a shitbag' and had, in fact, quit the game in disillusionment before being offered a chance of resurrection at Hillsborough.

The 25-year-old hardly made the most auspicious of starts. His début at Oldham on 8 February coincided with Leeds' second defeat of the season and the start of a dismal run in which they won just three of their next twelve games. A 4–0 trouncing at Maine Road left the other Manchester club top of the table with three games in hand. Just as had been the case so often in the Revie era, Leeds looked as though they would have to settle for second best.

'Eric helped,' says Strachan. 'He scored a few goals and gave us a bit extra, although, to be honest, you can over-emphasise his influence. I mean, I don't recall him scoring too many clinchers or setting anybody up for the winner. I didn't know about his reputation when he came, I just thought he was a big, quiet fella. His English wasn't great, but even if it had been perfect I don't think he would have mixed too well. It wasn't that he was aloof – you only think that if you let it affect you that way – he was just quiet. He was always approachable. It's different when you approach someone and they look down on you, but Eric wasn't like that. Nobody had any problems with him personally. It was, just, well . . .' I know, Gordon, I know. Eric was different.

Cantona was initially used predominantly as a substitute and was soon showing fleeting moments of mesmerising skill. 'The sign of a great player is if he can do the simple things well,' says Strachan. 'Eric did them brilliantly. When he passed me the ball it was to my right foot, because he knew I wanted to hit it first time. Lots of players don't appreciate things like that, but Eric did.'

Against Chelsea, Cantona scored a wondergoal, juggling the ball with sublime dexterity before firing an exocet into the top corner. Leeds won 3–0, had a supersub of David Fairclough proportions sitting on the bench, and then Manchester United began to falter in the home straight: their draw against ten-man Manchester City and defeats by Nottingham Forest and bottom-of-the-table West Ham meant the games in hand had been erased for no gain and Leeds were back in the box seat.

And so they came to Sheffield on a blustery Sunday morning. If Leeds won and Manchester and their team of Devon Lochs lost at Liverpool that afternoon, the championship would come to Elland Road a week before the end of the season. The bizarre victory which ensued suggested someone upstairs had already decided the outcome. 'I hated that game,' says Strachan. 'I was in agony with a back problem. I shouldn't have played, but I tried for 45 minutes of excruciating pain.'

Leeds fell behind to a goal from the Wimbledon throwback Alan Cork, but equalised through Wallace's deflected strike. Then fate began not so much to smile on Leeds as to laugh hysterically. The Blades' keeper, Mel Rees, suffered an injury and could only hobble around throughout the second half. That enabled a looping cross to evade him and Jon Newsome stooped to conquer with an easy header. However, the celebrations were short-lived as back came Sheffield. A cross from John Pemberton, later a popular Leeds player himself, struck the hapless Chapman and cannoned into the net. Depression enveloped sections of Bramall Lane. Were Leeds about to be undone by an own goal from their most prolific scorer? However, as the tension mounted, Cantona broke with the ball. He was challenged by Brian Gayle and the ball bounced into the air. Then it happened. Surely the most unspectacular goal to ever clinch the championship. As Rees left his goal with a semi-arthritic shuffle, Gayle headed the ball over him and into his own net. In the absence of a genuine hero, Cantona and Wallace hugged each other. Gayle (a dead-ringer for the comedian Craig Charles, only funnier on this occasion) anxiously sought a scapegoat and looked close to tears. Leeds had won 3–2.

Though Manchester United still had to play that afternoon, you sensed that was that. When you win a game thanks in no small part to an own goal, a deflection and a one-legged goalkeeper, you can safely assume luck is on your side. With a home game to come against struggling Norwich, you felt Leeds would still win the title even if Manchester United refrained from their choking tendencies to earn a victory against arch rivals Liverpool. 'I'd rather Everton won the title than Manchester,' said Liverpool keeper Bruce Grobbelaar, suggesting footballers as well as celestial bodies were rooting for Leeds.

Liverpool won their televised game 2–0. It was over. With typical gracelessness, Manchester United would claim they had thrown the title away, a view with which many journalists were happy to concur. 'The ones who say they lost it rather than us winning it are probably Manchester United fans,' says Strachan. 'We showed great determination and kept plugging away. Everybody else had the chance to do that, but they couldn't. It's about the amount of points you get, not when you get them. There were some great games and we played some great football. Nobody can dispute that.'

In some ways the finale to the Second Division Championship had been more satisfying, as Leeds had actually won the game that clinched the title. This one was a passive victory. Wilkinson did not bother to watch the Manchester United game, preferring to concentrate on his Sunday lunch. Strachan went swimming with his wife at the Holiday Inn in Leeds. 'The game was on in the bar and the kids were watching it and kept telling me the score,' he says. 'Then it finished and we'd done it. There was no massive celebration for me. Lee Chapman had live cameras in his house and David Batty was there. I think Chappy was already thinking about his TV career then. But I just went to a friend's and, as I drove there, I passed the chairman's house. I thought I'd pop in and see him and we just sat there having a cup of tea. That was how I celebrated the championship. He looked very smug, but I think he was pleased to see me.'

Apart from the Charity Shield victory over Liverpool the following August, that was to be Strachan's last honour as a player. Yet he showed no signs of wilting. He had already been crowned Footballer of the Year – rubbing salt into Ferguson's gaping wounds – and the years of conditioning and attention to his diet were paying off. He became known as Bananaman, for his love of fruit. 'I always looked after myself,' he says. 'Maybe I was more advanced than other players, but you have to have standards.'

Leeds, however, were creaking and seemed intent on substantiating every football cliché going. Defending the title was certainly proving more problematic than winning it and teams were now raising their game for the visit of the champions. Leeds went the entire season without winning an away game: they slumped to a dismal 17th in the inaugural Premiership and, when they went to Anfield, the Kop gave its own damning verdict by chanting 'you're not champions any more.' And then there was the European Cup. Leeds got past Stuttgart in the opening round, but needed the Germans to field an ineligible player to do so. After demolishing Stuttgart 4–1 at Elland Road on a heady night, Gary Speed's volleyed goal from Eric's knock-down an enduring memory, it seemed Leeds had gone out on away goals. However, UEFA called for a third game on neutral ground in Barcelona and goals from Strachan and Carl Shutt were enough to send Leeds through in an eerie Nou Camp.

Then came the 'Battle of Britain' against Rangers, a game hyped to the heavens. The first leg was in Scotland. 'It was a crazy game,' says Strachan. 'We started fantastic. Gary McAllister scored a brilliant goal after about two minutes and we should have been two or three up in 20 minutes. I scored a good goal that wasn't offside, but it was ruled out, and then big Lukic punches the ball in his own net and it all went pear-shaped.' Leeds lost 2–1, but hopes were high for the second leg – only for them to lose by the same scoreline. 'They came to Elland Road and Mark Hateley scored a wondergoal. I mean, Mark Hateley! God! That was the best goal he'll ever score! That was it, the season came crashing down around us.'

It got worse too. Cantona, by now the darling of the terraces, was transferred to Manchester United for a mere £1.2 million in November. It was a move which sowed the seeds of Wilkinson's downfall, but Strachan insists the Leeds boss had no choice. 'It's like the nursery rhyme,' he says. 'When Eric was good he was very, very good; but when he was bad he was horrid. Eric had made up his mind that he wanted to go. He decided he could not play with Chappy and his form went.

'When things went well for Eric he was brilliant. When they went badly he made life a misery for everybody. People have written a lot about it and they try to analyse it, but it's quite simple. Some people are selfish and Eric would get fed up if he felt things weren't right for him. He would terrorise those about him. If you ask any of the players who were there at the time they will tell you that his training sessions were awful. Whatever Howard Wilkinson would say, Eric would do the opposite. Howard had to do something. Now it looks like a cheap transfer fee, but I don't think anybody really expected him to go on and be such a dominant figure at Old Trafford. He just went to the right place at the right time.'

Strachan believes there were several factors responsible for the dramatic turnaround in Leeds' fortunes. 'There was a bit of a hangover from the year before,' he says. 'The determination changed a bit, maybe there wasn't the same hunger. There was more talk about cars, houses, clothes and boot deals, which angered me, but the major factor was the back-pass rule. It changed everything. Suddenly everybody had to be top notch on the ball and it really hit us hard. Manchester United had Garry Pallister and Steve Bruce and they could play the ball better than Chris Fairclough and Chris Whyte.'

It sounds like the sort of excuse British Rail might come up with. In fact, I'm half surprised when he doesn't follow it up by suggesting there were too many leaves on the training pitch. It also does little to explain why Leeds had one of the best home records and worst away ones. Could Lukic handle the back pass at Elland Road but nowhere else? Well, he couldn't handle it anywhere, of course. That was the whole basis of the new rule. I'm confused and decide Strachan probably knows best.

Leeds did come to terms with it the following season, but an era had ended. Sterland retired, Whyte and Chapman moved to the lower divisions and then Wilkinson made the move which would fatally undermine him in the eyes of the fans, by agreeing to sell local hero Batty to Blackburn. Nevertheless, Leeds finished fifth in what would be Strachan's last full season at the club. Most onlookers felt Strachan was being groomed as a future manager of the club and it was another shattering blow when he departed for the comparative wastelands of Coventry mid-way through the 1994–95 season. Again, many were quick to point the finger at Wilkinson, who seemed to be masochistically dismantling the dynasty he had been building. But this time he was blameless. Strachan explains: 'I didn't want to go anywhere else and, going on to the coaching staff, I thought I would be there for a long time. I was happy and life was good. I was playing in the reserves and it was one of the most enjoyable times of my career. I loved playing with the youngsters like Whelan. We played 13 games and won 11 and I was having fun. But then I got the offer to come here with the guarantee of becoming manager one day and Leeds didn't try very hard to keep me.'

In fact, Leeds did less than that: they even convinced Strachan that he was no longer wanted. 'The clincher came when they asked me to go and work in the community. I thought that was quite insulting. You know, I'd helped them win titles and they were asking me to go out at night and work in the community for a few extra quid. That was embarrassing and helped me to make up my mind. It wasn't Howard's doing, it came from higher up. I got on great with Howard and still do. We speak all the time. But I decided to go to Coventry with Big Ron and I'm glad I did.'

You cannot help feeling that, even with David O'Leary working wonders, Leeds' loss was Coventry's gain. Strachan insists he is not an obsessive, but his passion for the game remains undimmed. 'It's a different culture now from five years ago,' he says, sitting back in a chair which dwarfs him and putting his hands on his head. 'There's so much money, but as long as I've got good pros around me who can teach the kids by not setting bad examples then I'm OK.' He pauses for a moment and then picks a hole in his own argument. 'Then again, I've got Carlton Palmer here . . .'

He flashes me another of those impish grins. 'I use my humour to keep them under control.' That and running their bollocks off when they've been nightclubbing. 'That's my best weapon. There isn't much humour around in football these days. There are a lot of negative people around now and it's my way of combating them. We could do with more humour. I don't think there are enough characters around and we don't breed characters as kids anymore. Life is a lot easier for the youngsters now. When life was hard you had to be a character just to survive.'

Our meeting concluded, I thank him, take a quick photograph and leave him in reflective mode. I walk out of his office and squeeze past the local press men, who are patiently waiting for team news ahead of the forthcoming FA Cup tie against Norwich. From within Strachan's office, there comes singing. It is the refrain to 'If I Could Turn Back Time'.

If only, Gordon. If only.

TONY CURRIE – Kiss and Tell

There is no salvation without the artist.
ERIC CANTONA

t is 1975. Glitter bands and platform heels provide an antidote to the sinking pound and rising unemployment. On the football field, Norman Hunter and Chopper Harris take great delight in gouging great lumps out of each other as football becomes a brutalised battleground. And then there are the *contra* rebels, those maverick dissidents who insist on staying true to their own ideals. At Bramall Lane, one such footballing eccentric is in full flow. With his long blond locks and rock star looks, Tony Currie knows he possesses more creativity in his bouffant sideburns than most of his peers put together. Currie collides with Leicester City's ebullient Alan Birchenall and they collapse in a heap. As they get up, Birchenall says: 'Come on TC, give us a kiss.' Currie obliges. The photograph is sent around the world. A German gay magazine prints the picture. Traditionalists are astounded. Nobody can recall Matthews and Finney copping off in such a fashion. 'That's all they remember me for,' says Birch, who now works as a public relations officer for Leicester City. By contrast, TC is remembered for so much more.

In some ways that famous photograph epitomises Tony Currie. Forever bucking against convention, blowing kisses to the crowd, evading malevolent tackles with the arrogant air of a sequinned matador, he became football's answer to P.T. Barnum. When he asked to leave Leeds in 1979 because of his wife's depression, the then manager Jimmy Adamson sensed it was the beginning of the end. 'They'll lynch me,' he told Currie before pouring himself a large whisky. 'Then he asked me if I wanted one, but I said I'd better not,' recalls Currie. 'I walked out and he might have been drinking all day after that. I knew how he felt. It broke my bloody heart to leave Leeds.'

Born on New Year's Day in 1950, Currie was already established as a star by the time he moved to Leeds. A Londoner, he started his career at Watford, but was quickly snapped up by Sheffield United for £27,500. By the age of 22 he had helped Sheffield to promotion and he was an England international. The world was at his mercurially gifted feet. Further north, Jimmy Armfield had the insuperable task of trying to emulate Don Revie, who had left Leeds after 13 years to succeed Sir Alf Ramsey as England manager. In 1975 Armfield had almost managed to bring unprecedented glory to the club, but the European Cup campaign had ended in controversy – felled at the final hurdle by an unsympathetic referee, Gerd Muller and riotous fans. Now Armfield was clinging to the last vestiges of the Revie dynasty. Age was catching up with Leeds. Johnny Giles had already gone to West Bromwich Albion and Billy Bremner was soon to follow him out of Elland Road. Armfield was flogging a dying thoroughbred and knew he needed some fresh blood. Currie was an obvious choice.

As I walk from my car in the Bramall Lane car park, a line of fans are queuing outside the main stand. It is the day of the AGM and there is much to talk about. Sheffield United are a club in crisis. Phone-ins are routinely flooded with calls from irate fans demanding changes at the top. There is even heretical talk of a merger with arch-rivals, Sheffield Wednesday, a move as universally popular as trying to install Salman Rushdie as the president of Baghdad Book Club.

A couple of teenagers, whom I take to be apprentices, are loafing around outside the reception. I cannot help thinking of the banjo-playing sequence in *Deliverance* and consider that the future of football is not particularly bright if these two shell-suited striplings are the best we can manage. 'Do you know where the office for football in the community is?' I ask. One of them points over his shoulder. I thank him and wonder whether he or the fans in line will ever again see a player as good as Tony Currie in this heart of depressed South Yorkshire.

The 49-year-old version sits behind his desk in a tiny office within the main stand. Yellowing papers are arranged in a haphazard mess and Currie, still reasonably trim and wearing a Sheffield United training top, looks flustered. 'Up to my eyeballs,' he says. I cannot help feeling a little sad. The morning papers are full of talk about Roy Keane's new contract being worth £50,000 a week and here is Tony Currie, far more talented, scratching out a living by visiting schools and hosting bazaars in his role as community organiser.

'I don't have any regrets,' he tells me without too much conviction. 'I don't wish I'd been born 20 years later. Well, the money would have been nice. I mean I'd be a millionaire now. But I wouldn't have wanted to be like Beckham. I wouldn't have wanted to be followed around everywhere you go. He obviously loves it and what he gets is his own fault. Falling in love with a Spice Girl hasn't helped, but even if he hadn't done, he would still be idolised and recognised and followed all over the place. Bestie had it in our day and I felt sorry for him. I had it in Sheffield. I couldn't go out without someone wanting to pin me up against a wall and fire questions at me. I never got any peace and it must have been 100 times worse for Bestie.'

Talk of Best seems to make Currie thoughtful and he eases into a discussion of how he joined Leeds back in 1976. 'They'd wanted me for a little while. They were looking for someone to replace John Giles and in my last season at Sheffield we were down by Christmas. We'd got four points in thirteen games and I had a gentleman's agreement with the chairman saying I could move on if we got relegated. They were very fair, because I'd signed a six-year contract the year before, pledging myself to Sheffield United until I was 30.'

The story of Currie's signing shows a quaint naïvety, which is now extinct in these days of agents and entourages. 'I was on an end-of-season trip in Gibraltar with the team and I was told to go and report to John Harris, the manager, when I got back. Nobody told me why and I didn't ask, because you didn't in those days. You just got on with it. So I went to John Harris's house when I got back and I still didn't ask any questions. Forty-five minutes later we were driving into Leeds United. I still didn't ask John what was going on. I didn't want to. Maybe I was scared.

'Even when we drove through those gates I didn't think the club would let me go. It hadn't sunk in what was happening. Then John Harris let me go in and see Jimmy Armfield and, by the time I'd come out, I'd signed. I think John was a bit taken aback because I'd done it and they'd lost me.'

The story underlines the paradox at the heart of the Currie legend. On the one hand he was the arrogant show-off, supremely confident and happy to ridicule opponents with his superior skills. On the other he was the quiet loner, a 'strange fish' as Stan Bowles called him.

'Some of the boys might have thought, "who's this big-headed bugger?" – but that wasn't me. I was like that on the field because I knew what I could do. I didn't feel any pressure replacing Johnny Giles, because I knew I had ability. I wasn't like Duncan McKenzie. He used to strut about, but Duncan wasn't a team man and I was. It was a myth that I was lazy.

'I was an introvert off the pitch, but throw a ball at my feet and I switched on. It was my stage. I loved showing people what I could do. Hitting a ball 70 yards and have it land at someone's feet is an art and there's not many people who can do it. I loved doing the long balls, the little chips, the spin backs. There were a lot of hard men around in those days, but it wasn't a case of them targeting me for being fancy. They knew my ability and they knew if they could stop Currie they'd stop Leeds ticking. It was the same when we played any team. We'd always want to cripple Johnny Giles, although it was quite an achievement if you could get over the top higher than Johnny.'

Ironically, Currie's first game for Leeds was against West Bromwich Albion, Giles's new home. The press billed it as a showdown between the two. 'I shall not be tempted to go out and prove who is best,' Currie told the *Yorkshire Post*. 'Giles used to move around all over the field and that is what I'll be doing. I don't mind playing on the left as long as I have a free role like Giles to spray the ball around. Giles was so consistent at passing the ball any distance, but I can do that. I can hit anything I want.' He then showed the cocky side of the dichotomy. 'I'll be sick if I don't get a goal,' he said. 'I've scored on all my débuts apart from the one for England – and that doesn't count because they took me off too early!'

The game ended 2–2. Currie did not score, but he did do enough to win over those who had questioned the wisdom of splashing out £240,000 on a fancy dan. The *Yorkshire Post*'s Barry Foster wrote:

> Leeds looked less like a team than at any other time Giles has graced Elland Road, with only Tony Currie displaying the class of the old Leeds. He must have wondered where all the stars had gone. He did everything right, but had so little help from his teammates. He gave total commitment for 90 minutes, his shooting being a particularly forceful part of his game, but even in the days of John Charles, Leeds found one man could not do it all on his own all the time.

Currie still remembers the game. 'I can still see Alastair Robertson putting one of his studs into me and how I didn't break my leg I'll never know. There was a great big hole in my leg in the perfect shape of a stud and I went off and got it stitched. He'd gone through my shin-pad and I swore I'd get him back for that.' He is quick to stress the latter point, bristling at the suggestion that he was all flair and flares, steelless silk from Sheffield. 'I could handle myself,' he says. 'Don't you worry. I weren't a soft touch. I can tell you that. You couldn't be, in those days, or you'd never survive.'

He has always struggled to disprove that popular opinion. In his Sheffield days his form attracted a string of clubs but, as well as admiration, the big boys had their reservations. Bill Shankly was one: the Liverpool manager once made the damning comment that he imagined Currie lived in a bungalow, as 'he'd nae want to be bothered with all that climbing stairs'.

Currie feels his reputation as a showman did sometimes work against him, especially when it came to England. He ended up with 17 caps and he still feels aggrieved that Don Revie exiled him to the international wilderness (even though Ron Greenwood later recalled him). 'People always talk about my work-rate, but that's a load of crap,' he says. 'I worked hard, but I'm sure my reputation didn't help me. Revie didn't like my style of playing. He played me once in three years. He capped 90-odd players in his time, but I had one chance against Switzerland in 1975 and that was it. End of story. I was in every squad of his, but I never got a look in. People picked up on it. They'd say Currie is a weed or he doesn't tackle, so I'd go out, run my bollocks off and let it affect my game. I should have ignored it, but I couldn't. I hate it when people say I was lazy, because it wasn't true. I was a perfectionist. I wanted to be the greatest player to ever pass a ball.'

Currie thought the move to Leeds would further his England aspirations. At the time he had already won seven caps and had made an impression on the public consciousness during the infamous defeat by Poland in 1974 – when he led the unsuccessful siege of Jan Tomaszewski's goal. However, Currie's belief would be derailed by an ironic twist. His move to Elland Road only came about because Revie had departed and Armfield was now in charge. Yet Revie was now the England manager and this enigmatic figure, whose paternalistic Leeds regime had included in-house bingo sessions, short haircuts, sex-education lessons and lectures on etiquette, was hardly going to be a huge fan of a long-haired maverick with a reputation for nightclubbing, alcohol and groupies. Currie is adamant that this reputation was unjustified. 'It was just the hair,' he says. 'Everyone thought they knew what I was like, just from the way I looked and played. I weren't like that at all. I was a family man.'

One man prepared to believe him was Don Howe, then the Leeds assistant manager and later an Arsenal and England stalwart. 'The word "great" must not be overused,' he told reporters as they assembled at the club's training ground. 'We are too ready to describe good players as great ones and there are only a very few of them; but I know Tony Currie has the ability to become real quality.' Howe was also quick to back up Currie's self-assessment of his work ethic. 'There is nothing wrong with Tony's application or work-rate, either in training or matches. He works tremendously hard. When I think of the great midfielders, I always think of Johnny Giles first. He was the best I've ever seen, a man with all the attributes that a midfielder needs, and Tony will rank alongside him one day.'

Currie believes he was a victim of style and he admits he is not the only one. The players with whom Currie is routinely linked, because of their idiosyncratic approach to the game, were similarly short-changed by England. Stan Bowles won five caps, Rodney Marsh got nine. Frank Worthington – Leicester City's epicurean answer to Elvis Presley – managed eight and Peter Osgood had to make do with four, two of which were as a substitute. The sophistic argument was that these romantics had the style but not the substance for the international arena. However, such a ready dismissal of the ingenious was disingenuous. 'I got bitter about it,' admits Currie. 'It affected me, but it was the same with Glenn Hoddle. He got 50-odd caps but he should have got 100. It took England two or three years before they decided he was up to it. All pro footballers could see he was the man for the job, but they'd bring him on as a sub, like they did with Gascoigne to start with, and it was obvious he should have been on from the beginning. Maybe people have something against flair. It doesn't mean you're airy-fairy, though, because you can pass the ball. England had some good players in my time. There was Mick Channon and Martin Chivers, but who's to say the likes of Marsh, Bowles and Worthington wouldn't have been better? It just needed a brave man to pick us all. Unfortunately, we didn't have that man.'

Revie's England reign ended in ignominy when he quit to take up a £60,000 a year job in the United Arab Emirates, leaving the FA to read about it in the papers. Hell hath no fury like a midfielder scorned and Currie pulls no punches as he gives his opinion of Leeds' best-loved manager. 'He was a selfish man,' he says. 'It didn't surprise me when he did that. It summed him up. He wanted to be close to the players, but he treated us like schoolboys.'

However, if Currie's international career had hit a hiatus, his Leeds form was the stuff of domestic bliss. Under Armfield and Howe, he added the consistency to his undoubted talents and became the undisputed darling of Elland Road. A few games into his Leeds career and Barry Foster was even more taken with Currie. 'Leeds' £240,000 investment in flair, finesse and an eye-catching future is only self-discipline away from being a midfield player regarded among the best soccer has ever produced,' he wrote.

'I loved Jimmy,' says Currie, 'but I don't think many players at Leeds had as much respect for him as they should have done. Maybe it was because he was coming in on the back of Revie. But I thought Jimmy and Don [Howe] were a good partnership, and Jimmy did buy the likes of me, Ray Hankin and Brian Flynn.'

With the physical stature of a stunted Subbuteo player, little Brian Flynn made Gordon Strachan look like a souped-up Adonis, but the diminutive Welshman could play and he and Currie struck up an effective partnership. 'Flynny was great,' he says. 'He had the lot. He knew his capabilities and we developed a great understanding. He was always looking for me to give me the ball and he was always there to help out if there was trouble.'

With Currie, Flynn, Gordon McQueen, Joe Jordan and Ray Hankin, Leeds looked to have the talent to bridge the void left by the departure of some of the Revie heroes. They would prove to be nearly men, however. In 1976 they finished fifth. The following season they made the FA Cup semi-final, but lost to Manchester United at Hillsborough. In 1978 it was a similar story as they went out of the League Cup at the semi-final stage to Brian Clough's Nottingham Forest. For Clough, a victim of player power during 44 days of acrimony as Leeds manager, it was the sweetest of revenges. The 1979 season inspired feelings of *déjà vu* as Leeds threw away a 2–0 lead in the first leg of the League Cup semi-final at home to Southampton and then lost 1–0 in the return. By now Armfield had gone. The Leeds board were impatient for success and Armfield, affable, personable and dispensable, bit the bullet.

'To be honest, I think he would have gone earlier if it hadn't been for some of the players,' says Currie. 'We saved his job for a number of months. A few of us had a word with the chairman and said "come on, give him a bit longer". It's funny really, because the same thing happened when I was at QPR. Tommy Docherty was the manager and he was about to get the sack, so six of us went to see Jim Gregory and we saved his job for about a month, too.'

Such philanthropy did not extend to all Currie's managers. With Armfield gone, Leeds turned to the highly-respected former Celtic chief, Jock Stein – the most successful club manager in the history of the game – but he was to last even less time than Clough as he quit to take up the Scotland manager's job after just 43 days in charge. The hotseat at Leeds had spontaneously combusted and had been replaced by an ejector seat.

'I thought what Jock Stein did was disgraceful,' says Currie. 'To come in and use a club like Leeds as a stepping-stone was shocking. I mean, his name was being bandied about and it was obvious he was going to get the Scottish job. I thought what he did was wrong, but he didn't have a job at the time because he had retired from Celtic and he didn't want to be out of work.

'As a man he was fine. He loved me and he was one of the old-style managers that talked to individuals more than he did the whole team. He was very similar to Shankly, although Bill was a lot more outrageous and outgoing, and John Harris at Sheffield had the same sort of Scottish calm.'

When Stein left, Leeds turned to Jimmy Adamson. Looking from the outside it was hard to imagine that Adamson could be a good manager. Whenever he appeared on television he would be chewing on a pipe and spouting semi-coherent manager-babble in an unique northern accent which made him the stuff of parody. I used to think the same about Jack Charlton. How could he possibly be so successful as the Republic of Ireland manager when he couldn't even remember the players' names? Jack was a no-frills, down-to-earth, brass-tacks northerner. Devoid of pretence or extravagance, this was a man who believed a prima donna was a top-notch kebab. He was easy to like. His habit of referring to Bobby Charlton, arguably England's most famous ever footballer, as 'our kid' was endearing. It was just hard to believe a man who once said, 'I kept getting Pat McGinlay confused with Charlie Nicholas, no not Nicholas, the other one, what's he called, Paul wotsit, McStay . . .' could be a managerial genius.

Adamson was just as enigmatic. 'Jimmy was all right, but he was an oddball,' says Currie. 'I had a lot of respect for him, but he was pretty strange. The way he spoke was baffling. You had to listen very carefully to work out what he was talking about. He'd say something and mean another. It was like a bloody riddle. But when I did eventually decipher what he was saying, I thought it was actually quite good.'

He did not share the same feelings for Adamson's sidekick, however. 'He had a fella called Dave Merrington as his number two,' he recalls. 'An unbelievable bloke. He was one of them that would throw teacups and go mad. One day in the dressing-room at half-time he was giving the lads a right going-over and I looked at Hank and took the mickey behind his back. On the Monday I found I'd been stitched up by the youth team coach who'd seen me do it. Merrington got hold of me and shoved me up against the wall. He's a big chap and he's my coach, so I'm not going to do anything because it would get me in lumber. He threatened me and said, "if you ever do that again I'll do you." I just looked at him and said absolutely nothing. He was a nutcase and the players all thought so. He was very conscientious and had his own ideas, but the bloke was a bloody idiot.'

After just three years at Elland Road, Currie's time was coming to an end. His wife, Linda, was depressed and yearned to move back to London. On 10 August 1979 Currie signed for Queens Park Rangers for £400,000 (then a club record). Leeds' fans were plunged into a combined state of shock and mourning. It made the front page of the *Yorkshire Post*. The rumour-mill began working overtime as people sought a reason for the departure of a man who had repeatedly stated his love of the club. No doubt fearing a backlash, the Leeds chairman Manny Cussins claimed the club were innocent. 'We have not sold Currie just for the sake of making money,' he said. 'We did not want to sell him and have only done so under pressure from the player and under protest.' Having washed his hands, he left Adamson to placate the lynch-mob. 'We are very disappointed,' he spluttered. 'We know he is a crowd-puller and a good player, but you have to be compassionate and he wanted to move back to London because of his domestic situation.'

Linda Currie, herself, also wasted little time in going public with the reasons behind her husband's transfer. 'I never really liked it in Leeds from the start,' she said. 'I could not make friends and could not settle. You have to put up with gossip when you are in the public eye, but there were all sorts of things going round. There were stories about wife-swapping and us splitting up and people were quite nasty. I put it down to jealousy. Rumours about Tony being a heavy drinker and it affecting his game and our marriage breaking down were all untrue. Every footballer has a tipple on a Saturday after a match. Tony didn't want to leave Leeds; he was loyal to the club. People who know that wonder why he left, but what they can't seem to understand is that he loves his wife and children more than football and he left for us.'

Currie added: 'I don't know anything about a drink problem or the other stories, but I can assure you they are nonsense. I left for my wife's sake. She had an illness and my football and our life were under strain.'

The only man who appeared to be delighted by his departure was QPR's new manager, Tommy Docherty. 'I only bet on certainties and there is no gamble here,' he declared. 'Our man is world class. Compare his fee with that being asked by Ray Wilkins. Ray is a fabulous player, but he's a long way from being as good as Tony. It's up to me to give the punters what they want and Tony will put thousands on the gate at Loftus Road.'

Now Currie has mixed feelings about his exit, not least because his altruistic attitude to his wife was quickly rewarded with a divorce. The streets of London, it seemed, were not paved with marital gold any more than the ones in Yorkshire. 'I had a great time at the club and leaving wasn't my fault,' he says. 'I regret it, but there was nothing I could do about it. Even though I asked for the move I thought they let me go too easy. Why didn't they say, "I know you've got to go back to London, but come up two days a week"? People do that now. Clubs bend over backwards for their players, but I wasn't given any alternative. I went and I was the main schemer. We had a very good team at that point. We had Frankie Gray, Arthur Graham, Hank, Carl Harris, Paul Hart, myself and Flynny. Cor dear. I just don't understand why they did not try to hang on to me. After that season they had a bad year and it was a decade before they replaced me. They bought Alex Sabella, but he was a waste of time: fancy, but not a team man. Not until they got Gary McAllister did they finally get a quality replacement for me. They could have given me some options, but I didn't get one. Not one. It's a shame because that team might have done something.'

Even now, 20 years after the event, Currie can feel the frustration at seeing that

Leeds team under-achieving and his departure accelerating the descent which would end in relegation three years later. 'Jimmy Adamson once said to me, "a player with your class and skill should never fall below 80 per cent in any game you play." I knew exactly what he meant and told him not to worry. I don't feel I let anyone down in my time at Leeds. People say I never achieved what I should have done, but I actually achieved exactly what I wanted to. OK, I'd have liked to play 100 times for England, but that was out of my hands. People got a hell of a lot of pleasure out of seeing me play and I've still got the letters to prove it.'

Nevertheless, you cannot help feeling Currie was born in the wrong age. Though his style nestled perfectly into the hedonistic exuberance of the 1970s, he was too late for the great Revie side and too early for the '90s revival. 'Leeds were still a big club when I joined,' he says, 'but John [Giles] had gone and the others were all in their 30s and on their way out. I only played four games with Billy Bremner, which was a shame, and just one season with Allan Clarke, who was one of the best-ever strikers. But they had some good younger players like Joe Jordan and Gordon McQueen and maybe it would have been different if they'd stayed. It was another bad mistake by the club letting them go to Manchester United and I think it was a mistake for them too. I mean they hardly set the world on fire there, did they?

'Then there was Don [Howe]. They were naïve in letting him go too, because he and Jimmy Armfield were a great team. Don was the hard man and a very good coach, while Jimmy was the softly-spoken manager. They were different personalities but it worked. When Arsenal came in for Don they let him go just like that, which was bloody ridiculous.'

Currie would never win a major trophy. The closest he came was the 1982 FA Cup Final, when his foul on Graham Roberts led to the penalty from which Glenn Hoddle won the replay for Spurs. The irony was tangible. As Hoddle hit unprecedented heights and wrote himself into Spurs folklore, his predecessor in the line to the throne of the entertainers was mistiming his way to football oblivion. A bad tackle at Wembley was scant reward for a career blessed with footballing peaks of Himalayan proportions and moments of theatrical slapstick.

The time he sat on the ball after nutmegging an opponent; the kisses to the crowd after a shimmying slalom through the centre; his habit of applauding the fans whenever he scored a wondergoal, as against Southampton on 25 November 1978 – remember that one?

I'm not like Nick Hornby. He can recall the dates and times of famous moments in Arsenal's history down to the nanosecond. I am not blessed with such a photographic memory. I just recall isolated snapshots. Caught up in the hysteria of it all, it was an incandescent blur of white passion and noise watching Leeds as a boy. But then I do remember that goal against Southampton. Currie intercepted a pass from Baker and waltzed past Nicholl before unleashing a physics-defying banana shot which sailed past Gennoe in the visitors' goal. It was the same day my dad bought me my yellow Leeds scarf and the sun was shining.

Starsky and Hutch was the top show on television. Pass the anorak will you, Nick?

As I see myself and Currie applauding each other in reverent mutuality, I find it somewhat surprising when he now tells me: 'I actually cut out a lot of the showmanship at Leeds, because I wanted to win things. At Sheffield we never had the squad to achieve that, but at Leeds we came close. In my three years there I became a much better player, because when you've got better players around you they drag you up higher. They all wanted to be winners and I wanted to be the best of them. You have to remember that Leeds had always liked a bit of showmanship. Billy and John were like that. Take that game when they murdered Southampton and they were taking the mick with their flicks and backheels.' He lets out a laugh. 'That was brilliant, but even so, they'd still never had anyone like me before.'

Life after Leeds saw Currie's career and life embark on an inexorable downward spiral. Perhaps the fact he turned up for his medical at Loftus Road on crutches was a portentous moment. Injuries jeopardised his ability. The 1982 Cup final, and the enjoyment he gained from working with Terry Venables, were the solitary pluses from an ill-fated return to his roots. 'Venables was the best I've worked with,' he says. 'He should still be the England manager in my opinion. He was so positive and confident in what he was saying. He *knew* he was right. He put everything across so easily and didn't blind you with bloody science. He was very astute. You could see his mind ticking over with ideas all the time.'

Nevertheless, it was Venables who let Currie go when QPR won promotion in 1983. For Currie it was a rude awakening to the realities of life. He was past his best and no longer the prize catch. The man who had been chastised for being happy to be the 'big fish in the small pond' at Sheffield United was now a floundering minnow. QPR could manage quite happily without the fading skills of a paling playmaker. The man who had likened his art to the theatre found the stage had gone. The curtain came down and Currie traded the London Palladium for grim working men's clubs. A summer season in Canada was followed by bit-part roles at Torquay, Southend and Chesham and, when it was clear that his knees would stand no more, he took a job as a cab driver to pay the bills.

By now Currie was living with his mother in her council house and he was drinking heavily. He readily admits that it was not unusual for him to get through four bottles of whisky a week, but he denies he was ever an alcoholic. 'I'd lost my wife and my career and I didn't have a job,' he says. 'I was 33 years old and on the scrapheap. It was really 1983 when my drinking got bad, but I wasn't hooked. I'd do a bottle one day and then not touch the bloody stuff the next. I never wanted to see it again, but then after a day off I'd have some more. I was drinking to forget what was happening. I suppose that's why most people drink. It wasn't a problem, though. You drink to put things out of your mind and that's fine. I wasn't addicted. It wasn't that hard for me to get off it.'

Having quit the fags and booze, Currie landed his current job at Sheffield United in 1987. Not surprisingly, his inability to manage his own life meant few chairmen felt sentimental enough to let him manage their clubs. News travels fast in the insular world of football and the word was out. Tony Currie was on his uppers.

'After I packed in playing I never thought about managing, although I wish I had, now,' he says. 'I did have the chance to go to Wigan once. One of the directors who used to be at Sheffield ended up as their chairman and he asked me to be their player-manager. But I'd just got divorced and I didn't want to leave the children. I didn't want to leave London, and Wigan seemed like a thousand miles away.' Suddenly, Currie looks wistfully into the distance. 'If I'd done that, who knows? Things might be different. I might be England manager now.'

Instead he is more concerned with the profits from the Saturday club and the birthday parties which Sheffield United host. If he is envious of today's multi-million-pound megastars he hides it well, though you sense there is a rich vein of simmering regret somewhere not too far beneath the unscarred surface.

'Everyone says the game's better and players are fitter now, but I can't see it,' he says. 'We used to have to trudge through inches of mud from November. They don't do that now and they don't go back in the afternoons and run their wotsits off. Now all the pitches are like Wembley and the players don't have to worry if it's going to hit a bobble. Players are already looking ahead, so they've got improved vision and skills. In my day there were a handful of players in the entire league who were good enough to know what they were going to do with the ball before they got it – and I was one of them.

'Now it's all special diets and personal trainers, but that's just show. What people forget is that it's easier running on grass than ploughing through sludge. There's still great players. Hoddle was excellent and Chris Waddle came on a hell of a lot. If he could have kept his crosses on this side of the pitch instead of in the back of the stand then he would have been untouchable. Then there's Gascoigne. I was so disappointed with him when he smashed his leg to pieces in the Cup final. He still did well at Lazio, though. I would turn on the TV to watch them play on Sunday afternoons and if he wasn't in the team I'd turn it off again. He was another excellent player, but he's never grown up and is a bloody fool. He's made a few million so I suppose he can laugh at a few people, but I imagine there's more laughing at him.'

Two months later and a few hundred people are laughing at Currie at Leicester's De Montfort Hall. For one night only he is back on stage, wearing a football shirt and rekindling memories of yesteryear. It is a nostalgic trawl through time to honour Alan Birchenall's service to Leicester City. A lot of the greats from the club's past are present – players such as Peter Shilton, Gordon Banks and Frank Worthington. The latter receives a huge cheer as he launches into a few one-liners. 'My wife's not really up with the modern music,' he says. 'She thinks Take That is Stan Collymore's chat-up line.' As Collymore signed for Leicester two days earlier, the joke is nothing if not topical. A potted history of the club, penned by an *EastEnders* scriptwriter no less, is then played out against a lame musical backdrop. And then comes the finale. Birch sits on the stage and on walks Currie.

It is not the first time Currie has ventured into the acting world. In 1995 he had a cameo role in the film *When Saturday Comes*, which told the story of a brewery worker who overcame the booze to hit the big time with Sheffield United. Rugged Yorkshireman Sean Bean played the lead and Currie's brief role called for him to offer some encouraging words of advice. His wooden performance was entirely in keeping with what was, in truth, an appalling film. The critics savaged it. 'Risible,' said one, 'like *Rocky* Blu-Tacked to northern England and washed down with Tennent's Extra.' He could almost have been referring to Currie's story with that. At the time I remember wondering why a rising star like Bean – who had stunned the nation's housewives with his bare buttocks in *Lady Chatterley's Lover* and would later be an arch cad in James Bond – would risk his future by starring in what was effectively B-list Mills and Boon meets Manchester United Reserves. But then Bean was a real-life Blades fan and Currie was their best-ever player. I think I understood.

Somewhat gingerly, Currie sits down on the stage. Birch puckers up. Currie reciprocates. The reality of the situation is that two middle-aged has-beens are snogging on stage, but for a magical moment the embarrassment wanes and we are all transported back to 1975. TC nutmegs an opponent, shoots and scores. He blows kisses to the fans and applauds them. He is the ringmaster once again.

Back in the real world, Birch comes up for air. He wipes his mouth and threatens to move back in for more. Amongst everything else, it seems TC is a good kisser, too.

EDDIE GRAY — Better than Best

When I look at Eddie now and see where he is, I think there must be justice in this world. He was treated very badly at Leeds, but now it's come full circle and he's back where he belongs. Everyone loves Eddie.

PETER LORIMER

Jack the gateman mistakes me for Henry Winter, the *Daily Telegraph's* chief football writer. I am told not to worry. 'He can be difficult,' says one of the local journalists who have gathered outside Leeds' Thorp Arch training ground. I assume he means Jack and not Henry Winter. Most of the assorted hacks are waiting for Jack's permission to enter and talk to David O'Leary about life, the universe and Saturday's match at Liverpool. The way Jack keeps shuffling to and from his shed, shaking the head and demanding passes, as if this were some Eastern European check point, makes me think this could be a long wait. Eventually the real Henry Winter turns up. Blond, suave and impeccably turned out, Winter resembles an Aryan version of David Niven. His presence seems to bemuse Jack, who looks accusingly in my direction. I shrug my shoulders. Jack scowls: he retreats, beaten, into his shed and we all walk through.

The Leeds players have just finished training. Lee Bowyer is one of the first changed. He dresses like a member of Oasis in a cagoule and combat trousers. He looks three stone wet through and it is hard to believe he was once accused of wrecking a McDonald's. Bowyer climbs into his silver Porsche and then tears out of the car park at a speed which suggests he is intent on emulating James Dean. It is just a couple of weeks since Bowyer and Jonathan were alleged to have been involved in the violent beating of an Asian youth outside a nightclub in Leeds town centre. Minutes later Woodgate also exits the changing-rooms. The real Henry Winter says 'Keep your chin up' and Woodgate, who looks remarkable bony for an England centre-half, smiles gratefully.

The Leeds press officer is an attractive redhead called Liz. A reporter from the Dublin-based *Daily Star* cannot help but let his eyes follow her as she walks past him. He looks at me incredulously. 'Christ!' he says. 'We've got this 90-year-old fella at the Irish FA!' O'Leary finally appears from within a red-brick building and the *Daily Star* man engages him in conversation. O'Leary has agreed to write a column for the paper. Gary Kelly ambles past. He knows the *Daily Star* man and enquires, 'How's the family?' Oliver Holt of *The Times*, dark and heavily stubbled, like an inflatable Italian waiter, takes Stephen McPhail away for an interview. A Norwegian film crew are chatting to Eirik Bakke, the midfielder who has played such an impressive role in the absence of the perennially-injured David Batty. Only I am left. So I wait. And wait.

And then Liz says, 'He'll see you now.' We walk through the changing-rooms. Nigel Martyn is loafing about with Jason Wilcox, while Harry Kewell signs a shirt. Liz takes me down an anodyne corridor that adds to the prison atmosphere and ushers me into the assistant manager's office. And so we meet – the fake Henry Winter and the real McCoy, Mr Leeds United himself.

Eddie Gray joined Leeds United in 1963. Some 37 years later he is still here. Not bad for someone who at the age of 16 suffered a career-threatening injury from which he never fully recovered. Don Revie, the man who brought Gray to Elland Road, had no doubts about his genius. In 1974 Revie said: 'When I first signed him as a 15-year-old, I felt in my own mind that I had recruited one of the most brilliant prospects who had ever lived. If Eddie had been blessed with any sort of luck at all he would have been a bigger name than even George Best.' Later Revie came up with one of those great quotes that sticks in the mind and makes you wish modern managers were a tad less bland. 'When Eddie Gray walks on snow, he doesn't leave footprints,' he said. Stick that up your 'we're going for three points on Saturday' and swivel.

Gray, himself, is as affable and enthusiastic a man as you could wish to meet in professional football. His thinning hair now lives up to his name, but he is in excellent shape and works out most days. He is late because he has been punishing himself in the club gym, and he sweats as he speaks in his thick Glaswegian brogue.

'When we won the second championship in 1974 I only played seven or eight games,' he says. 'It was my thigh. I first did it when I was 16. I was playing for the reserves and I took a corner against Sheffield Wednesday. It just went. I ruptured a muscle and then there were complications. As a result I never had the opportunity to play to my full potential. The thigh injury restricted me in every way, whether it be pace or striking the ball. I was always aware of it.'

Those who saw Gray play may find this hard to believe. His dipped shoulder and incredible balance remain shining beacons of wing play. He made just shy of 600 appearances for Leeds and scored 66 goals. Scotland capped him a desultory 12 times between 1969 and 1977, which was something of a joke, even allowing for his injuries. That strike against Burnley on a Somme-like Elland Road – when he waltzed his way past a phalanx of desperate defenders, beating one of them twice just for good measure, before slotting home an unstoppable shot – still rates as my favourite Leeds goal. In 1984, aged 36 and his widening girth highlighted by one of the most horrible polyester shirts in Leeds' history (a sort of Damien Hirst-meets-Millets) he was still the most gifted player on the park. And now I am told he never played at full throttle.

Revie knew that, too, and felt the frustration of seeing Gray's talent stifled by injuries. 'I often sit back and wonder why it should happen to someone like him', he said. 'He has always been a fitness fanatic and, off the field, no football manager could wish for a more ideal player. I have never heard him swear or say a wrong word to anyone. It's very sad. Football at its highest level is a game of skill. The player who can do the unusual – even the impossible – is not only worth his weight in gold, but unique. Eddie Gray is like this. He is one of the very few players I have come across who can throw an opposing player completely off balance with just a slight movement of his body. No amount of coaching can ever put this in a player – it is a born talent and, as such, obviously rare.'

Revie was ready to move heaven and earth to sign Gray after being alerted to his talents by Leeds scout John Barr. When Revie and coach Syd Owen first clapped eyes on the hunched-shouldered teenager they were stunned. 'We could hardly believe what we were seeing,' said Owen. However, Leeds were not alone in wanting the young wing wizard and, with Celtic and Rangers heading a list of more than 20 clubs vying for his signature, the chances of him opting for a club that was slumming it in the Second Division seemed slim.

'I don't mean to sound boastful, but I could have gone anywhere in the country,' says Gray. 'Why Leeds? Don just had this great drive and ambition. He also had the will to go and visit the players in their own homes and persuade their parents it was the best thing. He came to my house and persuaded the chairman, Harry Reynolds. Then he went to my school and saw the headmaster. He convinced him to let me finish early, so I came down here in 1963 and I was fine because my mate, Jimmy Lumsden, came with me. In those days Scottish schoolboys weren't allowed to sign professional forms; so I signed as an amateur and they said I was working as a printer. I never did, but you had to say it.'

Lumsden, who never made it at Leeds, reiterated how Revie managed to win over his minions. 'He was a hard man, but when my father died he was fantastic,' he says. 'He spoke to me for an hour and told me to take as much time off as I needed. He sent flowers up to my mother and then got her down here for a week and paid for it. That's how he created the spirit at the club. He looked after people.'

If Gray's career was blighted by bad luck, he did have the good fortune to join Leeds at just the right time. Revie had taken over at the club on 15 March 1961. Success did not come instantly. In his first full season in charge, Leeds endured the worst year in their history and finished 19th in Division Two. Yet neither Gray nor Revie appeared to have any doubts that the revolution was coming.

'I knew that this club was going to be successful,' says Gray. 'There was a tremendous will among the players. Billy Bremner was already an established player, so was Bobby Collins and, not long after I joined, Johnny Giles arrived. I knew what I could do and I wasn't in awe of any of them. People might call it arrogance, but I didn't think there was anybody going to stop me from getting in the team. Jim Storrie, an old Scottish forward we had, came up to me one day and said, "I hear you've been going round saying it won't be long before you get in the team." I said, "That's what I think," and he said, "Good on you, son, that's the way to talk." What you've got to remember is that for a young player with ability, the easiest thing is to get an opportunity. What's hard is to take it and what's harder still is to maintain it over a period of ten to fifteen years. When you are a young kid you need total faith in yourself.

'Take Harry Kewell. When Harry came here from Australia, he was 15 and thousands of miles away from home, but he had no doubts whatsoever that he was going to play for Leeds United and become one of the best players in the country. You'd speak to him then and he'd say, "I'll play for Leeds until I'm 26 and then I'll make my way back to Australia." He probably won't, but that's the belief he had at 15.'

The golden era in Leeds' history began in earnest in 1964 when the Division Two title was secured. It was the start of a glittering reign which included two championships, an FA Cup, a League Cup and two Fairs Cups (the forerunner of the UEFA Cup). In addition Leeds were runners-up in the League on no fewer than five occasions and they lost four major cup finals. However, while that period cemented Leeds' reputation, it also saw them become the most reviled side in the land for what was seen in some quarters as their calculated cynicism. It is an accusation Gray, one man exonerated from such allegations, passionately denies.

'The reason people hated us was we used to do the lot,' he says. 'If the other side wanted to mix it, we'd mix it with them. If they wanted to play football, we'd play football. That's why we were hated. Teams wouldn't bother trying to intimidate us, because they knew we'd do it back to them, with interest; but on our day, with everyone playing to his potential, there would not have been many clubs that have ever played could have beaten us.'

Nevertheless, the great football of the Revie era seems destined to be tainted by the memory of dubious tactics. 'That was just the way the game was then,' insists Gray. 'When we played Chelsea, I knew the first thing the full-back would do would be to kick me up in the air. The referee would walk off these days, because he wouldn't be able to cope. It made the game more interesting, though, and it also made it a lot harder to create. It made you realise that you had to be strong to survive. I got a bad injury when I was 16, but I still played until I was 36. Even the attitude of the supporters influenced things, because they expected it to happen. The supporter nowadays is more cultured in his approach to the game and there is television analysing every elbow or tackle from behind. In those days those sorts of things happened every single week and the refs wouldn't do anything – even when players were getting punched. You must have seen the old clips of the scraps and tackles. Nobody got a red card. You'd have to half kill someone to get sent off.'

Gray then uses a good example to illustrate the point that Leeds were not alone. 'When I first came to the club we had a full-back called Willie Bell. He played for Scotland against Brazil and, when nobody was looking, Pelé stuck the nut on him. Willie had this great big cut over his eye and there was blood all over the place. He'd been headbutted by the great Pelé, but things like that happened. After the game the players would all be in the bar having a drink.'

There is a famous photograph of the time where Spurs' Dave Mackay is holding Billy Bremner by the scruff of his shirt, anger painting his gnarled face, while Bremner's is a blank canvas of innocence. It is often reprinted to illustrate the Leeds side's capacity to irritate, but Gray believes it has long been misinterpreted. 'If you talk to Dave now, he's embarrassed about that photograph. You see, it was just the way the game was. At times players took it to extremes, but the tackles were nothing like as fierce as when I first came here – we were in the Second Division. When we went to Sunderland, Jesus, it was like going to war.'

Gray made his début on 1 January 1966 and showed immediate signs of promise, scoring a goal and helping Leeds to a 3–0 victory over Sheffield Wednesday. Leeds, who had lost to Liverpool in the previous season's FA Cup final, were on their way and the frail-looking winger, whose neck would recede into his body as he prepared to extract maximum humiliation from perplexed defenders, was with them.

The first trophy came in 1968. Leeds met Arsenal in the League Cup final at Wembley and won 1–0, Terry Cooper – the gifted left-back who became famed for his white boots – volleying home Gray's corner after 18 minutes. For three successive nights prior to the final, Cooper had dreamt that he would score the winner at Wembley, and so it proved. However, it was an unedifying contest that did little to help Leeds' public image, although both clubs were equally to blame. There were allegations of cheating, which the mud-slingers would hurl at Leeds for the best part of a decade, gathering pace. The new tactic of getting Jack Charlton to stand in front of the opposing goalkeepers at corners was causing a storm of protests and helped Cooper make his dream come true. In retrospect, it was no surprise Leeds v. Arsenal should be a dreary affair. Both sides have long had a knack of bringing out the psychotic in each other. They are the footballing equivalent of a psychiatrist's ink blots. One look at them and all this submerged angst and bile pours forth and you start imagining headless horsemen, air crashes and Billy Bremner and Bob McNab performing do-it-yourself skin grafts. Nevertheless, a trophy is a trophy (unless it's the Auto Windscreens or Zenith Data Systems). Leeds, Revie and Gray had arrived.

Their success meant the season was becoming incredibly congested. Whereas Manchester United now bleat about their fixture chaos, Leeds just got on with the job in hand. They finished fourth in the League, lost to Everton in the FA Cup semi-final and then beat Ferencvaros to win the Fairs Cup in a game held over until the start of the following season.

In 1968 I was born and Leeds embarked on their greatest-ever season. I would like to think the two events are genetically linked, but as Gray toys with a pen and rests his foot on an outstretched drawer, I realise it probably had more to do with him. 'We had a brilliant record that season,' he says. 'We lost two games all season, which is incredible, really, and we won the title with a record number of points. Burnley thrashed us 5–1 at Turf Moor, but we didn't lose again after that. We ended up having to go to Liverpool on the last day and avoid getting beat. We got a 0–0 draw and it was fantastic. Although we'd already won the League Cup and the Fairs Cup, the club had never won the championship in its history. You can't be considered a great side until you've won the championship and we won two. We also played in four FA Cups in nine years and an awful lot of semi-finals, but we never won as many trophies as we should have done. We were involved every year at the highest level and the competition was tough, but we lost championships by the odd point or on goal difference. Even so, it was better to take part in those games than not at all.'

The most controversial of all the near-misses came in 1971. Leeds were two points clear at the top of the table, but second-placed Arsenal had two games in hand. Leeds' penultimate game was at home to West Bromwich Albion, who had not won away in 16 months, and Revie's men were expected to triumph comfortably. What followed has gone down in history – a day swathed in infamy and passion, which some onlookers and historians have labelled as the moment football hooliganism was born.

West Brom were already 1–0 up when Tony Brown blocked Norman Hunter's attempted pass on the half-way line and broke clear. The linesman flagged, because Colin Suggett was clearly in an offside position in the centre, but referee Ray Tinkler waved play-on. Brown almost stopped himself, before realising the whistle had not gone, and he charged forward, sliding the ball to his left into the path of Jeff Astle, who scored. All hell then broke loose. Leeds players jostled Tinkler and fans, many wearing suits and ties, stormed on to the pitch. The game was held up for five minutes; 23 arrests were made; and Revie walked off the pitch, ruefully shaking his head as if knowing the title had gone. 'I don't blame the fans at all,' he said later of the pitch invasion. Leeds chairman Alderman Percy Woodward agreed. 'There was every justification for it,' he insisted. Even Barry Davies, commentating for the BBC, climbed off the fence and said, 'The Leeds fans are going absolutely mad and they have every right to.' That was the first and last time the Beeb has condoned crowd trouble. Leeds eventually lost 2–1 and Arsenal went on to win the title by a point and do the Double.

Everyone, West Brom boss Alan Ashman included, agreed that Leeds had been robbed. Everyone, that is, apart from Gray. 'I never thought too much about it,' he says. 'Over 42 games the best team always wins the championship and we should never have been in that position for it to be so important. Nothing cost us the league championship but ourselves.' But surely he felt some injustice at being deprived of a second title in such a manner? 'Every team gets bad breaks at some point in the season and, to be honest, I didn't think it was offside anyway.' He smiles a big, broad grin and I am not sure if he is winding me up. Is he seriously saying the most celebrated offside decision in football history was actually a good decision? 'Yes,' he says. 'That's my opinion. I never thought it was offside at the time and, having seen it again on television, I still don't. There's always been a rule about not interfering with play and Suggett wasn't. When Tony Brown knocked the ball past Gary Sprake, Astle broke from behind the ball. It can't have been offside.'

Such a phlegmatic approach no doubt helped Gray cope with the numerous disappointments Leeds were to suffer as they so often became victims of their own success. In 1970 Leeds had been going for the Treble, only to be faced with an incredible five games in eight days during a gridlocked run-in. Inevitably, the wheels fell off. Against Southampton in the league they lost to two own-goals and a dodgy penalty. Even the Press started to sympathise with their *bête noir*, Tom German of *The Times* writing: 'If they lose the championship it is because of the commitments heaped on them by the rewards of their own talents.'

Lose it they duly did. And the European Cup semi-final against Celtic and the FA Cup final replay against Chelsea. The latter was a clash of contrasts. In one corner were the playboys of the western London footballing world, demi-waved drama queens who had a catalogue of celebrity fans. Alan Birchenall, Tony Currie's old snogging partner, played for Chelsea before moving to Leicester City; he summed it up when he told how one of his team-mates 'was on the bog with the door open, reading the programme, when Raquel Welch walks in the changing-room'. In the other corner were Leeds, famed for their bingo, carpet bowls and putting competitions. In the glamour stakes Chelsea were Marilyn Monroe and Leeds were Thora Hird.

The first game against Chelsea at Wembley was one of Gray's finest hours as he tormented David Webb with a quite sublime display of wingcraft. It ended 2–2. Mick Jones put Leeds 2–1 ahead with only seven minutes left, but there was still time for Ian Hutchinson to equalise for Chelsea following a disputed free kick conceded by Jack Charlton. Leeds lost the replay 2–1 after extra-time, Webb having the last laugh by scoring the scrappy winner.

Typically, Gray was in self-deprecating mode as he commented some time afterwards on his Wembley performance. 'Everyone said that the way I played against Chelsea was my best game, but I didn't think I played exceptionally well that day. I've seen people play a lot better.'

Perhaps it was the fact Gray's career was blighted by persistent injuries that made him appreciate Leeds' triumphs and failures with such apparent equanimity. By the time Leeds won their second championship, in 1974, it seemed as though his career might have been over at the tender age of 26. 'I was told I'd never play again,' he says. 'That was it. When Jimmy Armfield came in, the club were waiting to hear from the Foootball League insurers. I was winding up and then Jimmy asked me to do a bit of coaching with the kids.'

It was then that Gray realised where his future ambitions lay. In 1974 he told reporters: 'I'm certainly interested in the coaching and training side of the game and would certainly think about it as a permanent thing if I'm not able to play again.' Gray began coaching the junior players and travelled with them to their Northern Intermediate League matches. 'It's a satisfying job,' he said at the time. 'At Leeds it's always been stressed to us that skill is important, but you can't teach skill. You can only help develop it.'

It seemed that Gray had found his new niche, but he would defy medical opinion and continue to play for another decade. His heart was in performing on the field and he admitted at the time to some black periods when the injuries began to take their toll both mentally and physically. 'The depression at times has been quite bad,' he said in 1974. 'When playing football is the only thing you can do, when you've no other interests, it's not surprising that you get depressed. I try to look on the bright side, though, instead of sitting at home moping. No footballer can feel at his best unless he's fully fit – you feel you're cheating the club if you turn out with an injury. But I've never been able to train flat out for three years now. There's always something holding me back. At times you feel like packing it all in, but you don't really believe that you ever will.'

Support for Gray was not in short supply, as his younger brother Frank was by now on the Leeds books. 'I don't know why the family should produce two top-class footballers,' says the elder star. 'Dad was a good player in junior football, but no one else in the family ever made it to the top. Frank was always more keen than I was. He always seemed to be playing with a ball, no matter where he was.'

Part of the legacy Armfield would leave at Elland Road was the resurrection of Eddie Gray. 'I coached the kids for a while and then Jimmy asked if I'd like to play in a reserve game,' recalls Gray. 'I thought, why not? I gave it a go and did all right. The following Saturday I played in the FA Cup and scored. That was it. I learned how to play with the injury. I came to know what I could do and what I couldn't, how to compensate. I played like that from the ages of 26 to 36.'

Losing Revie to the England job in 1974 signified the end of an era and it was a body-blow to the players he had nurtured from adolescence. 'I wouldn't say Don was friendly with the players, but he was such a dominant figure that it was always going to be hard for anyone else coming in,' says Gray. 'Brian Clough arrived and found it impossible, although it was one of the best moves he made financially [Clough received a reported £98,000 pay-off] and that made him stronger because he didn't have to worry about money any more. His methods didn't work at our club, though they've been proved to be very successful elsewhere.

'But you have to remember that Don had been at the club for 13 years and a lot of the players had grown up with him – people like Billy, Gilesy, Big Jack, Norman Hunter, Paul Madeley and myself.

'We were all led to believe that Johnny Giles was going to take over from Don, but it never happened. So we got Brian Clough and then Jimmy Armfield, who was an entirely different character. He was not so dominant and things went back to the way they had been. After a difficult start for Jimmy, we went to the

European Cup final, but the decline had already started. We got too many managers bringing in too many players to replace irreplaceable players who were household names.'

It was perhaps no surprise that Clough and Armfield failed to take up the baton from Revie. A year before acceding to the Elland Road throne, Clough had launched a scathing attack on Leeds after the FA slapped the club with a £3,000 fine for their disciplinary problems. 'Leeds should have been instantly relegated after being branded one of the dirtiest clubs in Britain,' he had said. 'It's like breathalysing a drunk driver, getting a positive reading, giving him his keys back and telling him to watch it on the way home.' He had also put the boot into Peter Lorimer when attending a dinner held in the Scot's honour. 'He's always falling over and spends too much time protesting when there's nothing to grumble about,' he had railed with characteristic tactlessness.

Armfield was an entirely different figure but equally flawed. A likeable man with a good football knowledge, he found the pressures of emulating Revie hard to live with. Much later, as he reflected on his time at Leeds, he admitted as much: 'The three toughest jobs are football management, lion-taming and mountain-rescue – in that order.'

After Armfield came Jock Stein (fleetingly) and Jimmy Adamson (disastrously). On Adamson's departure in 1980 the Leeds board, eager to curry favour with an increasingly disgruntled bunch of fans who were by now earning a bad reputation, looked to their former stars.

'I sympathised with Allan Clarke,' says Gray. 'We had around fourteen players for ten years, but suddenly they started going, one by one. In the late 1970s we still had Paul Madeley, but the nucleus of the side had gone. It was very difficult for me and things started to get tougher every year. When Allan came in he was beset by problems. He tried to spend a bit of money to rectify the problems, but it never happened and the club got relegated.'

Clarke, the man who had won Leeds the FA Cup with his header against Arsenal in 1972 and become the most expensive player in Britain when he signed from Leicester for £165,000, was sacked. If anything proved that the glory days were over it was the fact the heroes were now being castigated as villains.

And so Leeds looked to Gray, who became the first player-manager in the club's history. 'I enjoyed it, I really did,' he says. 'But financially the club was a shambles. When Billy [Bremner] took over from me, he said it was like shovelling leaves in a gale, and it was. We had no money at all and were literally struggling to pay the wages. The club had gone into a sudden decline, the money hadn't been spent wisely and we were a mess. I had to introduce a lot of young players and, though I wouldn't have done that if they hadn't been up to it, things were tight. We had to sell just to cut the wage bill. When I look back I realise I never had the opportunity to be successful, but at the time you're still caught up in the enjoyment of the game. Now I realise it was an impossible job. In those days it was common for the manager to go to the board meetings and I'd sit there while they said, "We can't afford this and we can't afford that . . . We'll have to cut back here and we'll have to cut back there." I ended up getting the sack in circumstances you wouldn't normally get it. We were unbeaten in seven games and had just won against Walsall in The Milk Cup. I was just glad they gave it to Billy after me. I didn't bear a grudge. I'd rather it went to Billy, who loved the club and had it in his blood, than someone else.'

It seemed that Gray's connection with the club he had graced for 20 years was over. He joined Rochdale as manager and after two seasons went to Hull, where he served a year, before moving to Middlesbrough as a coach. He returned to Elland Road during the Howard Wilkinson era to help coach the prodigiously talented youngsters on the books. Working alongside Paul Hart, he saw his charges lift the FA Youth Cup for the first time in four years. Gray was back where he belonged.

When Dave Williams joined Manchester United in 1997 and with George Graham now in charge, Gray became reserve team manager and he had instant success by leading his side to the Pontins Premier Division title. Graham, himself, departed the following year – the carrot of revenge over Arsenal too strong to dissuade him from joining Spurs – and David O'Leary was appointed the new boss after a campaign to bring in Leicester's Martin O'Neill had failed. O'Leary had no hesitation in immediately installing Gray as his number two.

Now Gray is clearly revelling in his role and he can see manifold similarities between the current side and the Revie legends. 'We never ever thought we would get beat,' he says. 'Maybe it was because we were young, too. People are waiting for the bubble to burst with this side and that happened when Don was here. I remember one night, at Swansea, Don introduced six teenagers: players like Terry Cooper, Paul Reaney, Norman Hunter and Rod Johnson.' He pauses as he notes my blank expression. 'Not a lot of people will remember Rod, but he was one of the shining lights of the side at the time. It just never happened for him. Sometimes that's the case.

'There was a great spirit among the players and we've still got a very strong association. The players still meet up, even though we're all living in different parts of the country now. I see Peter Lorimer, Norman Hunter and Bobby Collins a lot and I play golf quite often with Mick Bates. It was a great atmosphere then and it's the same now. These young boys have grown up together. There's Harry Kewell, Alan Maybury, Matthew Jones, Alan Smith, Jonathon Woodgate, Steven McPhail and Paul Robinson – all of them stayed here at the centre. They lived together and won titles together, so there's this great bond.'

I suggest it must be strange for him to see teenagers earning staggering amounts of money when none of his contemporaries were able to retire to a life of luxury after their playing days. 'David's got a wonderful philosophy with the players,' he says. 'They can earn plenty of money, but there's got to be self-satisfaction at the end of your career. You have to be able to look back and say, "I enjoyed that, I made the best of my ability." People can earn a lot of money in all sorts of walks of life; but you ask any of them if they'd like to play football in front of 40,000 people and win championships and trophies and they'll say yes. You need the desire and that can't come from money alone. You need hunger and the longer you maintain that drive, the longer you are likely to stay at the top. If you're successful, you'll get money anyway. It's a cycle.

'I think the system was wrong in my day. Players got to 30 or 35 and they were finished. But television has brought big money into the game and I don't begrudge them one penny as long as they are performing and enjoying it. The main thing at a football club is to work hard and make sure you earn what you receive.'

The man receiving maximum publicity at Leeds at the time I see Gray is Harry Kewell, the 21-year-old left-sided Australian. Though they are very different styles of player, it is impossible not to draw comparisons between two of the best left-footers the club has ever had. 'Harry? I love watching Harry play,' says Gray. 'He was the first of the young players to get into the side and now he's been joined by a lot of his mates. We had Billy Bremner and Norman Hunter. They were the first to make the breakthrough and then a lot of young players followed. Hopefully, it will take the same path and they'll be just as successful.'

My time is up. Gray has work to do. He shows me out and we make small talk about the previous weekend's FA Cup tie at Aston Villa. Leeds had led 2–1 at half-time and seemed destined to make it to the quarter-finals – only for Benito Carbone to score twice after the break. 'It was too comfortable,' says Gray. 'I said that to them at half-time. There's no such thing in football as a game that's too easy.'

If the Leeds youngsters want anyone to teach them about the harsh realities of football, there can be no better guru than Gray. Here is a man who has been plagued by persistent injuries and yet he is still as fit as the proverbial fiddle. Here is a man who was sacked by the club he loved, only to bounce back and help restore it to the big time. In short, here is a survivor. An hour in his company and I feel uplifted. Work hard, be nice to people and you will get your just deserts. I decide to try this out and so I put on a coathanger grin and hand my plastic pass back to Jack.

'Thanks very much,' I say.

'No problem,' replies Jack with surprising courtesy. And then as I turn my back and walk to the car, buoyed by the fact that the Eddie Gray philosophy appears to work, Jack shouts after me.

'See you again, Henry.'

Ah, the Winter of my discontent.

PETER LORIMER — Hot Shot

Ninety miles an hour.
THE KOP, 1970s

H i – *My name is Sabine and I am big Eric Cantona fan. Do you wish to talk with me? We be friends and I can help you perhaps. Is this OK? What do you want me to do? Do you speak French?'*

I have joined the Eric Cantona Internet mailing list. It is basically a message board for 750 widely dispersed fans of the poetically-challenged Frenchman. As a first step in trying to track him down I decide to ask his legions of fans in cyberspace, so I post a message asking if anybody knows his whereabouts. A bloke in Burnley wishes me luck and then a Swedish traffic warden says he understands he is in Europe, possibly France or maybe Spain. Well, that narrows it down. I decide I'll need more than the best wishes of some over-aged groupie from Lancashire if I am to take advantage of the Scandinavian jobsworth's priceless nugget of information. I decide the Internet is a waste of time.

And then I get an e-mail from Sabine, whom I immediately picture as some hybrid of Brigitte Bardot and Vanessa Paradis, a frustrated artist-turned-can-can-dancer from the Moulin Rouge with a penchant for seagull-spouting ex-strikers. I can safely say that it is the first time a French nymphette has asked to be my friend. *What do you want me to do?* I ponder this question and realise my response needs to be very carefully worded as I need to take my computer in for a PC World service soon. I type in my reply and leave the house. I get in the car and drive to Leeds where Peter Lorimer is expecting me.

The Commercial is one of those pubs which is rather grandiosely called a hotel. It is situated not far from Elland Road in the Leeds suburb of Holbeck. It is here that Peter Lorimer is living out the former footballer's cliché by running a pub. These days footballers own trendy nightclubs, bars and restaurants. They are the *nouveau riche*, the pop icons of the new millennium. Lorimer, the only player to have scored more than 200 goals for Leeds – and still the club's youngest-ever player, having made his début aged 15 years and 289 days – is from another age.

The Commercial's interior bears few trappings of success or the landlord's former glamorous lifestyle. There is a crude oil painting of him, a caricature of some old players and a scarf or two. There is also a current Leeds wallchart behind the bar, where the season's results have been crudely filled in; but that is about it.

Whereas Eddie Gray (with whom Lorimer shares a drink every Wednesday evening when the former's Leeds commitments allow) is still in fine fettle, Lorimer has submitted to the ravages of middle-age spread. That thick mop of jet-black hair is now greying and he shuffles around methodically behind the bar. As he puts the kettle on, a large, ruddy-faced man with a shock of white hair walks in. This albino tomato looks strangely familiar. 'All right Johnny boy,' says Lorimer and I realise this is none other than John Charles, the first true Leeds legend, still considered by many to be the best player to have worn the white shirt – or even any shirt. I introduce myself. He laughs a big, hearty Welsh roar and sits down with a punter called Taffy. They talk about Leeds' forthcoming trip to Roma in the UEFA Cup while I count my blessings. I had planned to ask Lorimer, who is in charge of the Leeds ex-players association, where Charles lived, so I could trace him. This is incredible luck. The way things are going, Vanessa Paradis will have ditched Johnny Depp and will be sitting in my lounge with Monsieur Cantona's home address and bank account details by the time I return.

Lorimer brings me a coffee. It is Tuesday afternoon, but there are still a few regulars drinking pints while the racing cackles away on the television. Life is a lot slower these days for the man once famed for having the hardest shot in football, reputedly clocked at a blistering 90 m.p.h.

Don Revie was not far off that pace when he got stopped for speeding somewhere between Leeds and Dundee in 1962. No doubt his excuse, that he was rushing to Scotland to sign a prodigiously-gifted inside-right, did not wash with the police; but they could not stop him from getting his man.

Lorimer, who had once scored 176 goals for his school in one season, made his début on 29 September 1962 in a 1–1 draw against Southampton. But it was another three years before he managed to establish himself in the first team. By then Leeds were already beginning to make waves. The previous season they had finished as runners-up in the League and the FA Cup, coming agonisingly close to completing the Double in their first season in the top flight. In the 1965–66 season they were second again and had their first taste of European action, beating Torino, SC Leipzig, Valencia and Ujpest Dosza before losing to Real Zaragoza and their 'magnificent five' in the semi-final of the Inter Cities Fairs Cup.

Leeds would play in Europe for each of the next nine years, until they were banned because of their rioting fans in Paris in 1975, and those trips provided Lorimer with some of his most memorable nights in football. 'There were some awful journeys,' he says in a Scottish accent that has a definite Yorkshire inflection after so long south of the border. 'Going to Eastern Europe in those days was a nightmare. It would take days to get there on these bumpy roads and by the time you got home you'd have another game. We didn't complain, because that was how you made your money. It was all in bonuses for winning this or getting to the final of that. One year we played 76 games and it wasn't like it is now. They didn't put games back to help you and it took longer to get everywhere. It makes me laugh when they say they've got it hard now. But even so, those European nights were great experiences.'

All too often they were also covered with controversy. Though Leeds won the Fairs Cup in 1968 and 1971, against Ferencvaros and Juventus respectively, it is their failures that are more firmly embedded in most memory banks. Probably the most infamous was the 1973 European Cup-Winners' Cup final against AC Milan in Greece. Leeds lost 1–0 to a fourth-minute goal from Chiarugi, but that scarcely told the story of a spiteful game. Leeds were denied what appeared to be three clear penalties, while the Italians took cynicism to new depths. Two minutes from time, Norman Hunter reacted to a blatant foul by Rivera and was sent off. At the end the neutral Greek crowd applauded Leeds off the pitch and chanted 'Shame, shame'. The Greek referee, Christos Michas, had cost Leeds the cup and was subsequently banned. The papers called it 'Floodlit Robbery'. Syd Owen told pressmen: 'Don Revie is heartbroken. It is like someone dying in his family. What have we done to deserve this?'

For Lorimer, who had inspired Leeds to 30 shots on goal in the absence of Billy Bremner, Johnny Giles, Allan Clarke and Eddie Gray, it was another night of injustice. 'That referee was proved to be biased,' he tells me. 'It was the same in the European Cup final in 1975. In the changing-room afterwards we knew we'd done our bit, but we'd been beaten by foul means. We were helpless. It was up to UEFA, but they were useless. These days it couldn't happen. There are proper channels for investigations, but at the time UEFA were just a bunch of old fogeys who used to sit around getting pissed at the odd meeting. Sure, there are still poor refereeing decisions nowadays, but they are made by accident. In our day there were other things that went on in the game and we were probably the biggest victims of it. It cost us two major trophies.'

Even the usually docile Jimmy Armfield was riled enough after the European Cup final defeat by Bayern Munich two years later to exclaim: 'Bayern Munich must be the most fortunate European champions ever. We had 85 per cent of the game and should have been awarded two penalties for blatant offences by Franz Beckenbauer. It might sound like sour grapes, but Bayern Munich don't look like European champions to me. The night of 28 May 1975 will stay in my mind for a long time.'

Not long after I met Lorimer, Nottingham Forest revealed they were claiming compensation for being robbed in the UEFA Cup semi-final against Anderlecht some 16 years earlier. 'Lots of Belgian officials kept going into the referee's room before the game and we later found out he'd been paid £18,000,' said former Forest striker Gary Birtles. 'The trouble is, it's not against the law to bribe a sporting official in Belgium.' Birtles's last comment was staggering. He qualified it by saying it was only sporting officials, but this did little to appease me. He was basically saying that if you lived in Belgium and had a few quid to spare you could guarantee an FA Cup final victory for your team of nonagenarians; but woe betide anyone who tried to slip the parish council a backhander to pass their plans for a new patio. Nevertheless, what it did show was that Leeds were not alone in being on the wrong end of some highly dubious incidents on the European stage.

Lorimer insists that, while such malpractice was endemic on the continent in the face of an insouciant governing body, the domestic situation was much cleaner. Yet Leeds would be tainted by allegations of match-fixing themselves in 1977: when Bob Stokoe claimed Revie had tried to bribe him way back in 1962, when Leeds faced the threat of relegation to the Third Division. 'I was manager of Bury and he offered me £500 to take it easy,' claimed Stokoe. 'I said no and then he asked if he could approach my players. I said under no circumstances. After that match I lost all respect for Revie.' When Leeds needed a point from their game at Wolves to complete the Double in 1972, there would be more unproved allegations of attempted match-fixing.

Though Lorimer admits Revie did have his faults, he is adamant that corruption was not one of them. Stokoe's allegation was never proved and one does wonder why it took 15 years to come to light. Like the rest of the Leeds team of that era, Lorimer is still loyal to the man who revolutionised the club. However, he does admit Revie's superstitious disposition was a fault. 'Sometimes you'd think he was barmy,' he says, a wry smile decorating his face as he pictures his former manager's antics. 'He would walk down the street to the same lamppost every day and he'd always wear his lucky suit. It was so worn out that his arse was hanging out of it. Another of his things was that he hated people taking pictures of any of his players on the day of a game. I remember before the FA Cup final against Sunderland, me and Eddie Gray were walking down the stairs of the hotel into the foyer and there was a young journalist there. He took a photograph and Don went mad. He went over and grabbed the camera off him. He threw it against the wall and smashed it, and told the journalist never to take pictures without asking him first. He was absolutely furious. Me and Eddie were just standing there thinking "What the hell's all this about? We're here to play football."'

Revie's superstitions, which trod a fine line between obsessiveness and paranoia, eventually had a knock-on effect on the team. 'It did get to you,' admits Lorimer. 'It filtered through and you'd start to get worried. It made you nervous. It was the same with the dossiers he would produce on our opponents. They were huge, thick things and he used to read them out to us, page after page, analysing every player, every free kick, every corner. It made no difference to him if we were playing Torquay or Manchester United. The lads would be just thinking, "Let's go out and give this lot a good tanking," but by the end of it all, you'd end up thinking, "Crikey, these aren't a bad side." You'd end up with a bit of fear and, though it's no bad thing to have a bit of respect for your opposition, it got to the stage where you'd think you were up against Real Madrid when in reality it was Aldershot.

'That was just him, though. I think he felt he'd be failing in his job if he didn't cover everything. If we were due to play someone in the cup and they had a sloping pitch, he would trawl around town for a local pitch with the same sort of slope and we'd get a bus there and practise on it. It was unbelievable, but maybe that was why we were so successful.'

Whether wearing a threadbare suit worked or not, Revie was hugely successful and revered by his players. After two seconds and two fourth places, Leeds won the championship in 1969. Their tally of 67 points beat Arsenal's 38-year-old record and significantly only three members of the side – Johnny Giles, Mike O'Grady and Mick Jones – had cost any money. The rest – players like Lorimer, goalkeeper Gary Sprake and arguably the most versatile figure to ever play for the club, Paul Madeley – were the product of a peerless scouting system and an effective youth policy. Even so, Leeds were not without their critics, who pointed to their goal tally of 66 as evidence of their inveterate defensiveness.

By the next time they won the title five years later, things had begun to change. 'We were absolutely unstoppable at that time,' says Lorimer, pouring a pint for Taffy who has lost on another horse race. 'We thrashed a lot of sides around then. We got seven against Southampton, six against Chelsea and five against Manchester United. As far as Revie had gone, he'd relaxed a bit by then. He realised that all these massive dossiers, mammoth team-talks and stuff was a bit over the top, and he realised the lads were getting pissed off with it all after more than ten years. The thing is, Revie was terrified of losing. He was a pessimist. But I think he got to the point where he thought these lads are good and can beat most teams – so he'd go through it all a lot quicker, just reminding us of one or two points. "Just go out there and do it."'

Leeds and Lorimer did just that. With Eddie Gray weaving his magic on the left flank, Leeds had a very different sort of player wreaking similar havoc on the right. Lorimer became famed for his goalscoring, not just in terms of his prolificacy, but also in his raw power. If Leeds won a free kick within 30 yards of goal, the Elland Road Kop would almost instinctively break into a chorus of 'Ninety miles an hour', leaving opposing goalkeepers in little doubt as to what the home side were plotting. With Allan Clarke and Mick Jones providing the finishing touches – later aided by the arrival of Joe Jordan, the toothless warrior who proved abscess does make the heart grow fonder – Lorimer also earned a reputation as a creator and made countless assists as Leeds grew through their success into a dynasty.

In 1972 Leeds won their solitary FA Cup and undermined every argument and accusation that had been levelled against them regarding their supposedly rough-house tactics. When Leeds demolished Manchester United 5–1, Brian Glanville of the *Sunday Times* could scarcely contain himself: 'The spectacle was almost that of a matador toying with a weary bull, the delighted roars of the crowd at each new piece of virtuosity the equivalent of the *olés* of the bullring.'

However, that exhibition paled into mediocrity against the gloating mercilessness of the 7–0 destruction of Southampton in March. This was the game in which Barry Davies, commentating for *Match of the Day*, cried: 'It's almost cruel.' It was the game in which Bremner, Giles et al. were transported back to their childhood – young boys pulling the wings off flies. Shortly after I met Lorimer, I was in the back of a cab in the Midlands when the discussion turned to football. The driver was an Aston Villa fan and I told him I was Leeds. 'Leeds, heh?' he said. 'God, remember that Southampton game.' It wasn't the goals so much as the way Leeds kept possession that has preserved its memory: Bremner and Giles pulling out all their party tricks while Southampton players ran around like headless chickens. It was the game which seemed to sum up the best parts of Leeds United, the skill, the arrogance, the forcefulness. Yet, incredibly, Lorimer says the brilliant brutality of the performance came about by mistake.

'That Southampton thrashing was an accident,' he says. 'The only reason we passed the ball about like that was we were feeling sorry for them. We'd already scored six and, to be frank, it was embarrassing. Nobody likes embarrassing fellow pros, whatever anybody thinks, and we knew some of their lads. The message came from the bench, "Just knock it about, don't get any injuries," so we did. Little did we know we were making it more humiliating for them. It's quite funny, really. Of course, you need class players to do that. It's not easy and, if you look at the clip, their players are not stood back watching us. They're trying like mad to get the ball and they weren't mugs, either. They had people like Channon.'

By the time of the second title, the winds of change were beginning to blow through Elland Road. After a record-breaking 772 games and 22 years at the club, Jack Charlton retired and began his highly successful managerial career at Middlesbrough. Meanwhile newcomers like Jordan, Gordon McQueen and Eddie Gray's younger brother, Frank, were breaking through.

'Jack had gone and there were rumours he wanted Terry Cooper to go with him,' recalls Lorimer. 'Then there were rumours about Norman and Gilesy, and I suppose they were getting a bit old. But it was the Press who were trying to break up the team. They'd had enough of us. They were bored and wanted fresh faces. We had a brilliant family spirit – I saw Mrs Revie the other day at a function and 25 years on she still treats us all as if we are her boys! – and we had total trust in each other. It had been built up over years and it meant we were almost telepathic on the pitch, but the Press never liked us. There wasn't much wrong with the side at that time. We won the League in 1974 and should have won the European Cup in 1975, but people wanted the team to break up. Don didn't want to be the one to have to do it. I think he thought, "I've had a great relationship with these lads, I don't want to have to tell them it's over." So the England job came along and he took it. I'm sure in retrospect he wished he hadn't. We all wished him well. It wasn't like he left us in the shit. He bowed out with us at the top. I was pleased for him, even though I'm a Scot and he was going to manage England. Luckily, we beat England when we played them, so that was fine.'

And so to Brian Clough. A committed critic of Leeds and their style, it was not so much a marriage made in heaven as one made in the back seat of a Ford Capri after too many brown ales. In *Clough: The Autobiography*, he recounted his first meeting with the Leeds team. 'I didn't hold back,' he said. 'I told Peter Lorimer he tried to con referees, I told Norman Hunter and Johnny Giles that they were such good players that they didn't need to go around kicking people. And I told Eddie Gray that, with his injury record, if he'd been a racehorse they'd have shot him.'

Clearly, winning friends and influencing people was not high on Clough's list of priorities. Lorimer reflects: 'Cloughie was the wrong man for the job because he hated Leeds, he hated the club and, most of all, he hated Don Revie. There was a bit of jealousy there, I'm sure. Let's be fair, Cloughie was a great manager. To win the League with a club like Derby, and the European Cup twice with a club like Forest, were mega achievements. But to come to a club like Leeds United with 16 internationals and try to humiliate them was committing suicide.

'He said we should throw all our medals in the bin because we'd never won one without cheating. Now you can take the piss out of young lads, but not seasoned pros. People say it was player-power that did for him, but it was the board that came to the players rather than vice versa. They wanted to know why the hell we were second bottom after seven games and going nowhere. They said, "We think it's the manager, are we right?" It was hard not to agree with them, what with Cloughie's attitude. I bore him no malice. I thought he was a funny bloke and I respected what he did at Derby and Forest. But he was a bully and he came in to prove a point.'

Though Jimmy Armfield's reign was was far from inglorious, it was during his tenure that the seeds of decline were sown. 'Jimmy was a nice man, but the job was a bit big for him,' says Lorimer. 'He did the job to the best of his abilities, but the pressures were too much for him. Players started to go and it was sad walking in some mornings and you'd hear someone else was moving. We'd been together for 12 years and then, bang, all that fun and laughter were gone. It was a terrifically happy dressing-room at Leeds during the great days. We had the quiet ones, the pranksters, it all blended really well. There was a wonderful camaraderie which was different from any other club and it was genuine. Revie made everyone a part of the club, right down to the women who washed the kit and the tea ladies. You'd always go and have a natter with them and treated them as you'd want treating. Revie said they were one of the team, not just a washer-up woman. That was how he taught us to be. He wanted us to be honourable towards people.'

The unique atmpsphere in the camp meant some players arriving from outside received a shock to the system. 'The one who got the biggest surprise was Sniffer [Allan Clarke],' says Lorimer. 'He came from Leicester, where he was supposed to be a rebel, and we were expecting problems. We'd heard he'd refused to join the players' pool at Leicester (where money gained from Press interviews was divided equally), but when he came here he thought it was brilliant and he was one of the lads.'

After Armfield and Jock Stein came Jimmy Adamson. 'Where the hell they dug him up from I don't know,' says Lorimer. 'He was a disaster. He had no record and that was that, the club was gone. We started getting little cliques and there was no harmony.'

Lorimer left for Vancouver in 1979 and Leeds' decline continued apace. It would take more than 20 years before they were restored to the domestic footballing summit, and the club would spend eight long years wallowing in the sewage of the Second Division while money was frittered away and the ground was sold. It need never have happened, according to Lorimer. 'It all started to go wrong when they didn't give Gilesy the manager's job,' he says with utter conviction. 'Don had recommended Gilesy for the job and the chairman had actually given him it. But Billy [Bremner] was disappointed because he wanted to be the manager, so he asked the chairman why he hadn't been considered, and the chairman started wondering whether it would create a rift if he gave it to an old player. So he went to John and asked him to wait for a couple of days. John said "I never asked for this job in the first place. Mr Revie approached me and recommended me and I said I'd be honoured to take it, but I never went looking for it." Where John went wrong was, he rang all the lads the day before he was to be announced as the new boss. He said he wanted to let them know beforehand rather than them turning up at the training ground and finding out there.

'To a man we backed him, but the trouble was he rang Billy too and so Billy went to the chairman and that was it. John was embarrassed by the whole thing. Billy didn't mean any malice by it and I think he would have accepted John, he just wondered why he hadn't been asked. I think Don kidded Billy along a bit, too, and said he would be the man, just so he got the best out of him on the pitch. No disrespect to Billy, but John was the best man for the job. I worked with him again in Vancouver and he was a terrific manager. Billy may have been our captain, but John was our general. He conducted the orchestra. By having the courtesy to let his mates know, it backfired on him. If he'd never made those calls Billy would not have said a word and the club might have stayed at the top.'

Ironically Leeds would belatedly look to their old boys when Adamson's spell as manager ended in failure: Clarke, Gray and Bremner all got their chance. However, rekindling former glories on a shoestring budget was a thankless task. During Gray's reign, Lorimer came back from Canada to spend another two years at the club. By that time he was 37, his waist was widening and he lacked the pace and power of yesteryear. Nevertheless, the skills remained undimmed by the passage of time and he played a key role in midfield for Gray's side of youngsters, surpassing John Charles's league goals record during his swan-song.

'They'd been relegated by the time I got back and it was soul-destroying, really,' he says. 'Eddie did a great job, bringing through players like John Sheridan, Denis Irwin, Scott Sellars and Andy Linighan. That was 15 years ago and they are all still playing. The club was totally skint. I suggested a couple of players from Canada, but Eddie said "Peter, we just haven't got any money." I couldn't believe it. When Don left we had £2 million in the bank, a bloody fortune in those days, and we were the best team in the country. Three years down the line and it had gone. The crowds were still good, but the money had filtered away and Eddie was left to pick up the pieces. If you pulled a drunk off the street and said ruin a football club, he couldn't have done it quicker than that board did. They even sold the ground. They didn't know how lucky they had been having someone like Don, who ran things from top to bottom, from boardroom to washroom. That's the way the great managers were then. They wanted to run everything. They wanted to watch the youth team, the reserves, the kids, take training, buy players, see their families, the lot.'

On the day I visit Lorimer the newspapers are draped in stories of a bust-up between Alex Ferguson and David Beckham over the latter's absence from training. A few days earlier the Leicester City team had been thrown out of their Spanish hotel after new signing, Stan Collymore, had let off a fire extinguisher in a piano bar.

'Those things would never have happened under Shankly or Revie,' says Lorimer. 'If you skipped training you'd get blown out, simple as that. Nowadays it's difficult for managers because they are dealing with young players who are all millionaires, so it's difficult to control them. Fine them a week's wages and that doesn't hurt. It's a drop in the ocean. But I tell you, if the Gascoignes and Collymores of this world had been with Revie they would have never had their problems because it would have been knocked out of them as kids.'

Lorimer provides Taffy with another pint and shuffles off to put the kettle on again. It is 15 years since he stopped playing. After his second spell at Leeds he spent a couple of seasons at Whitby Town and had a brief spell with Hapoel Haifa in Israel. He never really fancied trying his hand at management. 'I saw the grief Norman [Hunter] got at Barnsley,' he says. 'People giving loads of abuse to him and swearing at his family. I thought I could do without that.' He still turns out for the Old Boys' team of which he is manager, but it is hardly the same. Behind me John Charles, immaculately turned out in a jacket and tie, is reading *The Sun* and excitedly discussing his impending return to Rome where he used to play in the 1960s. It is a surreal feeling to think I am propping up the bar in a modest Yorkshire pub surrounded by the two greatest goalscorers in the history of Leeds United. Charles played 38 times for Wales, while Lorimer made 21 appearances for Scotland in a six-year international career. The highlight was the 1974 World Cup in West Germany. Lorimer played in all three of Scotland's games: a 2–0 win over Zaire, a 0–0 draw with Brazil and a 1–1 draw with Yugoslavia. It was not enough. Unbeaten and unbowed, Scotland went out after Brazil got the required 3–0 win over Zaire.

The public bar at The Commercial in Sweet Street has become a time machine. As Taffy leaves, disgruntled with his inability to pick a winner, I wonder how these two great footballers have managed to cope without the adulation of 40,000 partisan Yorkshiremen. At times it has clearly been hard. In 1991 the *Daily Mirror* printed a feature on Lorimer, detailing how he had lost all his money to gambling. Charles, too, has struggled to make ends meet. Now, in this small pub off the beaten track, neighbouring some wasteland and an ugly mail order factory, I realise how easy it is for a hero to become forgotten. When they stop wearing the uniform and the floodlights stop shining, they are just flesh and bone like the rest of us.

'Some people are easily forgotten,' agrees Lorimer. 'There was a time, towards the end of the Howard Wilkinson era, when we were not welcome at Elland Road. My lad was 13 at the time and becoming a Leeds fan, so I rang the club and asked for two tickets. They told me I'd have to pay like anyone else. I couldn't bear to do it. I told my son I couldn't make it and he'd have to go with a friend. Without him knowing I went down to the ground and paid for the tickets. It wasn't the money, you see. It's just you expect some thanks when you've played 700 games for a club. It was a matter of pride. It was like that down there for a couple of years. The atmosphere was bad and our attitude was bollocks to you. It wasn't Howard's fault. He was always very pleasant to us, but someone didn't want us there. I got upset and disillusioned with it, but it's great now. Now they appreciate us going down there.'

So they should. Lorimer is steeped in Elland Road, like many of the other players of the Revie era, but it is typical of the pace of change in football and its mercenary values that those who have paid their dues are condemned to history. Don Revie revolutionised the club, but only when he had motor neurone disease did the club see fit to honour him with a benefit game. Similarly, nobody saw fit to commission the magnificent, evocative statue of Billy Bremner that now stands outside Elland Road until the man himself had died.

To think Lorimer was deprived of a complimentary ticket is nothing short of scandalous. Even Lorimer's mishaps were part of Leeds folklore. Remember Jim Montgomery's wondersave from Hot Shot in the 1973 FA Cup final, a save so incredible it even overshadowed Ian Porterfield's winner. Montgomery had already parried Trevor Cherry's header, but as the keeper lay prostrate the ball broke kindly for Lorimer just eight yards out. 'As the ball was coming over I thought I don't have to blast this, just a nice little contact will do,' he recalls. 'I hit it exactly as I wanted to.' Montgomery somehow pushed the strike on to the bar and the ball rebounded to Cherry, who was lying flat on his chest. He flicked out a leg, but the ball bounced to safety and Sunderland completed the biggest FA Cup-final upset of them all. And then there was that penalty against non-league Wimbledon in the 1975 fourth round when Lorimer's strike was saved by Dickie Guy. Jimmy Armfield remembered: 'Peter Lorimer usually blasted his penalties and had a great record, but now he chose to sidefoot it to the goalkeeper's right just to make sure. Dickie Guy dropped on to it easily.' The game went to a replay, where Johnny Giles's deflected shot saw Leeds go through. If he was not terrifying keepers, Peter Lorimer was making their names.

'Football's like anything else,' he tells me. 'You get ups and downs in any walk of life. The sales rep can't win every contract he goes for and a footballer can't win every match, cup or title. It's exactly the same. The only difference is, football gets written about and is other people's lives. Part of the job is training, part is looking after yourself, part of it is winning and part of it is losing.' Lorimer looks thoughtful and pauses. 'We were just glad we didn't lose as much as most people. Leeds United is still part of my life and, because of my past association, I still want them to win every game.'

Times have changed. The megastars of the '90s now have a fleet of BMWs, villas on the Algarve and are so elusive that would-be interviewers have to indulge in a tacky brand of computer dating with faceless French cyberchicks. Sit in a dull Yorkshire pub and the megastars of yesteryear will come to you.

If Sabine has not come up with the goods I decide what my next message will be.

'Get a life.'

JOHN CHARLES — The Italian Job

These days he'd be worth £20 million.
JOHNNY GILES

Vittorio Fioravanti is one of Juventus's oldest and most knowledgeable fans. He has an encyclopaedic memory for the minutiae of the club's history and he leaves me in no doubt as to how good William John Charles was. 'He was a great man,' he says. 'Not only was he a great player, but he was a great person, a man who left an extraordinary mark on Italy, which was a country with a certain anti-British character. To be called *Il Gigante Buono* (the Good Giant) by both friends and opponents is clear evidence of his human quality and a passionate proof of the Italian people's admiration. I met him once when I was studying in Padua, just before the Serie A game in the Stadio Appiani. It was a great moment for me.'

Now the 69-year-old Welshman is suffering with his health and sits largely unrecognised in the back bar at Peter Lorimer's pub. His hair is snow white and his face is a red mask which shows the strain of the hard times which befell him after his playing days were over. Yet Charles still has a presence. He is a big man, a pumped-up pensioner, and if no longer the dashing hunk of post-war football, he is still smartly turned out. Without doubt he is also the most modest of the players I have met to date. Perhaps this is a result of him playing in an era which few now remember; or perhaps it is an inbred self-deprecation which came from his working-class roots. However, despite his habit of belittling his achievements, some believe Charles to be the greatest ever Leeds player, and in 1997 he beat the likes of Michel Platini, Zbigniew Boniek and Zinedine Zidane to be crowned Juventus's best-ever foreign player. He was also a pioneering light, the first Briton to make it big in Italy. Versatile enough to be a star at both centre-half and centre-forward, he was never booked, sent off or even spoken to by a referee in a career spanning 17 years. Not for nothing was John Charles known as the Good Giant and revered everywhere he went.

It all started in 1946 when Charles got a job on the groundstaff at his home-town club Swansea. 'It was hard work,' he recalls. 'They didn't have any juniors and I didn't get a game for three years. You'd be cleaning boots, washing out the toilets and doing the weeding on the terraces. All the jobs nobody wanted to do. I was disappointed I never got a chance, but you just had your hope to keep you going. We used to train with the senior players on a Thursday and this fella called Alf Pickard from Leeds United would watch us. He saw something he liked and sent three of us – me, Bobby Hennings and Harry Griffiths – up to Leeds. He came to see my mother and father in our village just outside Swansea. My father was a steel fixer and my mother worked too. He told them what he wanted and my mother said, "John can't go to Leeds." Mr Pickard's face dropped and he asked why not. My mother said, "He hasn't got a passport!"'

Charles lets out a booming laugh. His voice is deep and smooth, like crushed velvet. Later Charles made several records, including the half-decent 'Sixteen Tons'. When in Italy he even played the nightclubs, travelling around the Mediterranean and Adriatic coasts with a pianist and an impresario. 'I was no Sinatra,' he says, but his baritone was at least genuine – and a million miles away from the helium-based Babycham champions Hoddle and Waddle, who looked like an accident between Man at C&A and a set of curling tongs when they appeared on *Top of the Pops* in the 1980s.

Charles now shakes his head as if in disbelief at his mother's parochialism. 'That's what she told him.' He pauses as the landlord provides him with another coffee. 'Thanks Peter,' he says and then he fixes me with his big, watery eyes. 'But I went. And I'm glad I did.'

The Leeds manager at the time was Major Frank Buckley, a former England international who was as eccentric and strong-willed as any of his successors. Buckley, who had fought in the First World War, had stunned football by suggesting his players should be given monkey-gland treatment to improve their reflexes and was in the habit of deliberately employing players out of position in an effort to develop their all-round game. 'Everyone had to be two-footed,' remembers Charles. 'If you could only play with one foot, you were only half a player. I don't know what he would have done with Ferenc Puskas, probably the greatest one-footed player in the world.'

For all his idiosyncrasies, it was Buckley and his convictions that made Charles into a legend. When Charles came to Elland Road he was a left-half. Using his curious branch of logic, Buckley immediately played him at right-back, before converting him to a centre-half and finally a striker. Some regarded Buckley, who was by now in his 60s, as a total idiot; others have said his methods were the antecedent of the total football peddled by the Dutch in the 1970s. Charles is adamant he was a 'great man'. He adds: 'He was desperate to win. If we were losing at half-time, he would run through the entire team and say what we were doing wrong. He had a quick tongue, too. One day he said to our centre-forward, "Frostie – Jesus Christ was a clever man, but if he'd played football he'd never have found you." He was like that. He had a sense of humour, but he was a very, very hard man.'

Charles first played as a striker in a 4–1 defeat by Manchester City in 1951. Buckley persevered, though, and tried him again in the West Riding Senior Cup final against Halifax Town. Charles scored twice, and when he added five goals in his next three games for the first team the debate about his best position was over. In the 1953–54 season Charles weighed in with 42 goals – still the club record – and he would be forever in debt to Buckley, whose madness appeared to involve a fair degree of method.

'I preferred playing as a striker,' he says. 'Everybody wanted to. If you scored goals you were in the papers, although I must admit I never paid much attention to them. The papers were personal. If they liked you, you were fine, but if they didn't, they would criticise you regardless of how you played. There were also times when they'd say I'd had a great game and I knew full well I'd been awful.'

Charles's view of the media was no doubt coloured by the press scandal which broke shortly after his move to Turin. A salacious magazine called *Guiren Sportivo* suggested this upstanding family man and father of three was hosting orgies at his apartment and was fraternising with prostitutes. They stopped short of suggesting Santa Claus was a serial killer. 'There were cartoons and articles of a most obscene nature,' he recalls. 'Nobody likes to read disgusting things about his wife and himself.'

Charles even sought the help of the British Consulate, which told him nobody paid any attention to such unfounded gossip and suggested he grin and bear it. He heeded the advice and soon realised all players, especially the overseas ones, were subjected to the same treatment. 'It was nothing to read that such and such a player was suffering from venereal disease,' he said. 'In Britain you'd sue them, but in Italy it would take years for the case to come to court.' Denis Law and Jimmy Greaves would also be savaged by *Guiren Sportivo* and Charles would regret the fact he had not been able to warn the latter of what to expect. 'Denis has a broad back, but Jimmy allowed it to get under his skin and life became hell for him.'

Such a streetwise nature had still to be cultivated when Charles was cementing his reputation with Leeds. In 1950 he helped Leeds undo their FA Cup hoodoo and they made the quarter-finals for the first time in the club's history before losing to Arsenal. They also managed to end Spurs' 22-game unbeaten run and ended up in a promising fifth place. However, the following years would be marinated in frustration, despite the heroic efforts of Charles, whose record-breaking goal tally in 1954 failed to prevent the side from finishing in a modest tenth place. The Major bit the dust. Raich Carter replaced him as manager and, in 1956, Leeds were finally promoted as runners-up to Sheffield Wednesday. Playing alongside the likes of Harold Brook, Albert Nightingale and a young defender named Jack Charlton, it was to be the highlight of Charles's career in West Yorkshire. 'It was a big thrill, winning promotion,' he says. 'I just went out and played. I was an out-and-out goalscorer and just loved playing football.'

In 1957 Charles caused a sensation by agreeing to move to Juventus for

£65,000. 'I was called into the manager's office and he said "Madrid are looking at you." I said "Madrid who?" He looked at me and said, "Real Madrid" and, of course, I'd heard of them. I'd seen them on television and they were one of the best teams in the world. But I didn't want to go. I was young and didn't have much experience of going abroad. Soon afterwards, he called me back in and told me Madrid weren't interested any more. I thought, fine. Then he said, "Lazio are after you." I said, "Where's Lazio?" He looked at me and said "It's in Rome." I asked him if he wanted to let me go and he said he'd have to if the money was right. So I said all right. But then two days later he called me into his office and said "Juventus want you." I said, "Who are Juventus?" and he looked at me once more and said, "They're one of the best teams in Italy." I'd never heard of them, but it was different then. You didn't have the television and press coverage you get now.

'Anyway, their officials came here and we had a meeting in the Queen's Hotel. I caught the bus down to the hotel and as I was walking along the street I saw Sam Bolton, the chairman, and Percy Woodward, the vice-chairman. They were both crying, so I asked them what was wrong. They said "Oh, you're leaving us." We went upstairs and we did the deal. Nobody said goodbye or good luck or anything like that. They just took the cheque and went to the bank as fast as they could. They were very upset to be losing me.'

So was the local businessman who offered him £10,000 cash to stay, but the deal was done and Charles was a man of his word.

Though his geographical knowledge may have been lacking, Charles was not as naïve as he portrays. That meeting in room 233 of the Queen's Hotel on 18 April 1957 would be the first at which a footballer was represented by his advisers. Teddy Sommerfield and Ken Wolstenholme (who would become famed for his commentary at the 1966 World Cup final) insisted Charles sign nothing until they arrived from London. He didn't and Juventus president, Umberto Agnelli, whose family owned the Fiat car empire, was made to wait as the Charles delegation went over the contract with a fine-tooth comb. Finally a deal was struck. On the day Charles's wife, Peggy, was expecting their third child, and with their house under siege from the media and horrified fans, a new Italian hero was born.

Italy would be a culture shock for Charles and Peggy. Turin was a different world and the football was unrecognisable from that which Charles had been used to in Yorkshire. 'Life for a forward in Italy was hell,' he recalls. 'It was very defensive football over there. If you scored it was a miracle. The popular formation was 1–8–2 and out-and-out attackers were luxuries nobody could afford.'

It was because of this dour philosophy that most British journalists predicted Charles would flop in Italy. They also questioned whether his reputation as an unflappable gentleman would survive the strict referees and the theatrical antics of the players. Charles admits it was difficult. Most referees were 'homers' and there was always an undercurrent of corruption, as shown when one Italian club president bought all the league referees lavish Christmas presents. The players, too, had some dubious habits. Though they were less physical – 'powder-puff tackling' as Charles calls it – and shocked by what they considered the barbarism of the English game, they were already honing their diving and shirt-pulling talents. Charles believes both styles have their merits. 'Don't, for goodness' sakes, make it a game for cissies, but don't let it become a dangerous game either.' In 1962 he summed up his feelings by saying: 'The continentals will have to accept that soccer is a man's game, but the British have to accept that soccer is an art.'

It is not difficult to see why Charles was such a success in Italy. He threw himself into Italian society, bought a stake in a restaurant in the centre of Turin, learned the language and always respected the fact he was the foreigner. 'The supporters were fanatical,' he says. 'I picked up the lingo, which you have to if you are living in a foreign country because it means you can go out and enjoy the new life you've got. The people there were fantastic to me. The Italians are lovely people, very warm, very much like the Welsh.

'I admit I didn't know where Turin was, originally, but I was determined to make it work. To start off with, I was lucky because I met a player who could speak English better than I could Italian. I got homesick, but I was determined to stick it out and I enjoyed it. It was a terrific era. Omar Sivori, a little Argentinian fella who was European Footballer of the Year in 1961, came at the same time as me and we mixed well. Then we had a big inside-right called Giampiero Boniperti as our captain and he was a fantastic player.'

Charles and Sivori would score 250 goals between them for Juventus, but the 'ugly little bugger', as Charles refers to his former strike partner, did present some problems. On one occasion Sivori was threatened with a Mafia bullet if he scored in the next game. In the bumbling manner of a Latino Mr Bean, Sivori did score when a ball ricocheted off the back of his head into the goal. Fearing a sniper's bullet, Charles and his team-mates formed a protective cortège around the little Argentinian and shuffled into the tunnel. Sivori flew back to Turin immediately. Meanwhile, the game went on and Charles scored the winner, only for the referee to disallow the strike. When Charles asked why the goal had been ruled out, the referee said: 'Like Mr Sivori, I want to get home safely.'

Such nuances of Italian sporting life were still to be discovered by Charles as he attended his first training session with his new club. He also made the mistake of buying a Citroën car, which was not the wisest of moves considering the Agnelli family owned the Fiat empire and provided free cars for every Juventus player.

Despite such *faux pas*, it took Charles just three weeks to conquer Italy. His début came on 8 September 1957 against Hellas Verona. Goals from Boniperti and Sivori had made the score 2–2 when up popped Charles to score the winner. The following week he scored the only goal in the victory over Udinese and he then hit the decisive strike in a 3–2 victory over Genoa. He had been the matchwinner in his first three games. Small wonder the likes of Vittorio Fioravanti were won over.

'It went from there and in the first year I was there we won the championship.

We were promoted from the Second Division with Leeds, but that was as far as it went. In Italy we won three championships and two cups.' In the stifling world of limpet-like defenders and the conservative style the Italians called *catanaccio*, Charles had also defied all the doubters by scoring an incredible 28 goals in 34 games, including a trio of hat-tricks, against Atalanta, Sampdoria and Lazio. It was enough for him to be voted Italian Footballer of the Year. As he prepared to lead Wales's World Cup campaign in 1958 he was firmly established as an idol in three countries and was reaping the financial rewards of his success.

At the time Britain's highest-paid player was Fulham's Johnny Haynes who was making £5,000 a year. That figure had caused the same sort of shockwaves as Roy Keane's demands would some 42 years later, but Charles suggested there would be a national strike if Italians were forced to play for such a pittance. In his final season in Turin, Charles's basic salary was £7,000 a year, but he made a small fortune from bonuses. 'Sometimes the supporters would get together after a game and themselves pay a bigger bonus to the players,' he recalls. 'On one occasion the Roma players were offered £300 each to beat Juventus. It varied all the time. Say the chairman had won a bet with the chairman of Inter Milan, it was not uncommon in those circumstances for each player to get a £500 bonus.' Unlike Britain, there was no maximum wage in Italy and individual salaries varied. There were also lucrative signing-on fees. 'When I first went to Italy I was getting £18 a week, which was less than I was getting at Leeds; but I got a £2,000 signing-on fee and a luxury apartment. I was lucky. Some of the other clubs were struggling to pay their players, and there were stories going around that people were having to wait two months to get their wages.'

There were plenty of other differences between Leeds and Turin and England and Italy. Whereas most British clubs were limited companies, Italian clubs were run by wealthy directors, who gained their position through money rather than votes. Charles believed that, despite the undemocratic approach, they were more effective. At the time he said: 'Don't think for a moment that I am subscribing to the popular image of an English director – a half-stupid slave-driver whose ever-increasing avoirdupois is covered by an antiquated gold watch-chain and whose knowledge of football, if it ever existed, deserted him years ago; but there are directors who try to run the whole show themselves and haven't the qualifications to do so.'

Training was also different. Fitness was viewed to be of paramount importance in Britain, but ball skills were valued more highly in Italy. The theory in Britain was that if you starved a player of a ball during the week, he would be chomping at the bit come Saturday afternoon. Again Charles sided with his new country. 'I have often found the British system makes a player, even if he is hungry for the ball, completely incapable of using it when he gets it.'

Social rules were another eye-opener for Charles. 'Young people are not allowed the same freedom as our young people are,' he wrote in 1962. 'If any young lovers are found necking in public, in the parks or cinema, they are hauled off by the police and fined. The girl can then get a reputation as being a loose young hussy.'

For those of us who believe Italians to be a bunch of oversexed lotharios, wearing leather jackets and Latin scowls as they drive around on their Lambrettas nicking old ladies' handbags, such a picture of moral rectitude sounds unlikely. But it was there, in Article Seven of the Football Clubs' Regulations, stating that the player should always 'conduct himself in a correct manner everywhere and live a decent moral and physical life'. Charles adds: 'They bought you lock, stock and barrel. The rewards were high, but you had to behave well. It was an education living over there.' Presumably, those rules had been waived by the time Paul Gascoigne arrived in the early 1990s.

Another difference was the sporting ethos of the country. On one occasion against arch rivals Torino, Charles was clean through on goal when he noticed a player who had foolishly tried to tackle him lying injured. Without a moment's hesitation, Charles immediately kicked the ball out of play to the consternation of the Juventus *tifosi*. 'That night there was a right racket outside our villa,' he said. 'I looked out and there were loads of cars, all full of Torino supporters. One of them came up to me and thanked me for what I'd done. I said, "No problem, anyone would have done it" and invited them all in. They stayed until the early hours of the morning and when they left they'd drunk all my wine.'

The World Cup in Sweden was Charles's chance to exhibit his talents to a wider audience still. He was already a seasoned international, having become the youngest-ever Welsh player when he made his début as an 18-year-old in a turgid 0–0 draw against Ireland. It was probably the least effective of his 38 appearances in the red shirt of Wales and Charles felt his dreadful performance at centre-half, albeit one that helped ensure a clean sheet, would derail his international career almost as soon as it had begun. Championed as the great new hope of Welsh football beforehand, he was slaughtered by an unsympathetic press. Leeds boss Major Buckley convinced the depressed Charles that he would get another chance, but another nervous display the following season saw him exiled to the international wilderness for two seasons. Such a myopic decision was typical of an era in which international officals were figures of fun. On one occasion Charles said he and his Welsh team-mates were sitting in the foyer of a hotel after a defeat by Scotland when in walked a Welsh official. 'You were too good for us today lads,' he said. Charles had to explain that they were the *Welsh* team.

When he returned in 1953 for a game against Ireland, Charles was now regarded as a centre-forward. It was the turning point. He scored twice and created the third for Trevor Ford in a 3–2 victory and was never left out of a Welsh side again while a Leeds player. However, it was while playing for Wales that Charles came the closest to losing his icy cool and sullying his impeccable disciplinary record. Playing against Austria at Wrexham, Charles's brother Mel, who earned 31 caps himself during his time with Swansea, Arsenal and Cardiff, was floored by a brutal tackle which would sideline him for weeks. John admitted:

'For the first and only time in my career I was near to losing my temper and my first inclination was to go up to the Austrian concerned and lay him out cold.'

Needless to say, Charles resisted the temptation and the brothers were back in tandem for Wales's World Cup campaign in 1958. 'It was a great feeling to be playing in the same side as Mel,' he says. England and Scotland both failed to win a single game in the tournament and were eliminated at the first hurdle. However, the British minnows were biting and Northern Ireland and Wales went through to the quarter-finals. The Irish were thrashed 4–0 by France, while Wales faced the might of Brazil following a 2–1 play-off victory over Hungary. That victory had taken a lot out of the Welsh and no one more so than Charles, who was battered and bruised by his Magyar mauling. Nevertheless, they gave everything against Brazil, only to lose 1–0 to Pelé's first World Cup goal. Pelé would finish the World Cup with six goals and the first of his three winners' medals, but he always referred to that strike against Wales as 'the luckiest and most unforgettable goal I ever scored'. Charles's chance had gone, however, and when Wales failed to qualify for the 1962 Finals in Chile his World Cup dream was over.

Back in Italy life continued to be an unqualified success for *Il Gigante Buono*. In 1960 he scored 23 goals in 34 games as Juventus clinched the League and Cup Double. The following season he scored 15 goals in 32 appearances as the title was successfully defended. By the time he left to return to Elland Road, Charles had scored a staggering 93 goals in 150 games in Serie A. He was a genuine hero, idolised by the fans he loved and, by his own admission, living the life of a film star. He was wallowing in *la dolce vita*. Sophia Loren, Italian glamourpuss and international movie star, was counted as a friend. So why leave?

Initially he looks momentarily upset and says, bluntly, 'I'm not going to talk about that.' My mind starts to throw out suggestions. Maybe the *Guiren Sportivo* had been right after all. Charles finally relents and tells me the truth. 'My wife wanted to come back and I bowed to her wishes,' he says. At the time Charles elaborated more freely on his reasons. He cited his sons' education, the fact his wife was from Leeds, and their shared homesickness as the causes for his request to leave Turin. However, it is an old footballing adage that you should never go back and Charles struggled to rekindle the fires of the '50s when he stepped back out on the Elland Road turf. 'It just didn't work out,' he says. 'When I came back to Leeds it wasn't the same any more. Don Revie was in charge then and he was a lovely man, but I just didn't hit it off.'

Some pundits suggested Charles was a shadow of his former self, but the truth was that after five years away he had become fully integrated into the Italian footballing philosophy. He decried the English game with its focus on the long ball and 'hurrying and scurrying as if stamina was the main requirement for a footballer'. Charles admitted that he had become 'Italian by association'. He added: 'My football was Italian football. No longer could I settle in Britain.'

Any suggestion that Charles had become an advocate of football for cissies should be dismissed, however. Jack Charlton recalled: 'When he went on a surge he would leave a terrible trail of human devastation behind him. Bloody gentle giant indeed! I once questioned an instruction he gave me and he pinned me against the wall and told me he'd give me a bloody hammering next time.'

Nevertheless, after just 11 games and three goals, with season-ticket prices hiked to exploit the return of the prodigal son, the second coming was over. At the time Charles was only 30. Leeds were still in the Second Division, but two years later they would be promoted and the Revie era would begin in earnest. Who knows what might have happened had Charles stuck around and played a part in that halcyon age? As it was, he opted to go back to the warmer climes of Italy, but the Juve bridge had been burnt and replaced by a bridge of sighs. Although Juventus had offered him an incredible £14,000 signing-on fee at the end of his previous contract in an attempt to convince him to stay, they washed their hands of him once he walked out of the door. 'When you leave Juventus you leave Juventus for good,' he says with palpable regret. 'I remember an old Juventus fan breaking down and crying like a baby on hearing the news, but I'd made up my mind.' When he quickly realised he had made 'a ghastly mistake', there was no point in crawling back to Juventus and Umberto Agnelli. 'There was no chance of going back. If Juventus sold you they might buy you back, but if it was you who had asked to move then that was that. The Italians don't take kindly to players asking to leave. It's almost an insult.'

After just 91 days in his unhappy second spell at Leeds and with his marriage crumbling, Charles moved to AS Roma for £70,000 – netting the Elland Road club a tidy £17,000 profit in the space of a few months. However, Rome was another bad experience for Charles. In the 1962–63 season he played only ten games and scored four goals. 'Rome is a great city, but I just didn't get on, either playing-wise or socially,' he says. 'The people in the north are different from the people in the south. It's the same in England, the same in Wales and definitely the same in Italy.'

Less than a year later, Charles quit Italy for good. He returned to Wales and joined up with his brother Mel at Cardiff City. Three years later he joined non-league Hereford United as player-manager and then had spells with Swansea and Merthyr before moving back to Yorkshire to run a pub. In the late 1980s he tried his hand in the Canadian Soccer League before coming home and struggling to eke out a living. As he sits here, the racing still babbling away to the accompaniment of the bleeps of the fruit machine and Lorimer's pinging cash till, I realise there is nothing that reflects the brevity of fame – and life itself – more starkly than the image of an ageing footballer. It's like a variation on *The Picture of Dorian Gray*. The last time I saw images of Charles, Lorimer, Currie and co., they were gleaming stars, imbued with energy, athleticism, skill and style. Now I've found my way into the attic and the picture is of a normal everyday figure – wrinkled, blubbery and weathered with regret, alcohol and gambling debts.

It is easy to forget that this man has locked horns with some of the greatest players the world has ever seen. Who was the best? 'Alfredo Di Stefano was one of the all-time greats,' says Charles. 'Luis Suarez, the Spaniard who played for

Inter, was very good too. Sivori would tell me that he, himself, was the best inside-forward in the world, but when Suarez signed from Barcelona and his wages were printed in the paper he blew a fuse. Sivori went to see Agnelli and demanded his contract. He tore it up but Agnelli just smiled at him and handed him another. "Here's your new contract," he said. And then there was Jose Altafini. He was Brazilian, but he played like an English style centre-forward. Fantasic.

'I played with a lot of great footballers and I loved my time in Italy. I wasn't the first to go out there. There'd been a few English players before me, but they'd all come back. I suppose I paved the way and after me there were a lot. Denis Law, Jimmy Greaves, Gerry Hitchens, they all came over after I'd gone. In life most people start at the bottom and work their way to the top. I did it the other way round. I started at Leeds and ended up at Merthyr. They didn't pay me much, but I just wanted to keep on playing for as long as I could. After football I did a few things. I took a sports shop in Cardiff for a bit and had a job in a steel works. You miss your Saturday afternoons. I never thought of myself as a superstar, although you were to the ordinary people who respected you and what you did. But they were never in awe. They'd always come up and say, "How are you, John?"'

Now Charles lives locally and is a regular at Elland Road. 'I go to every game,' he says. 'They're a good, young side and they have two good men in charge in Davy and Eddie. I think in two years' time we will have a great side and it will be like the Revie era again.'

It is typical of Charles's generosity of spirit that, in spite of the problems he has encountered, he does not look at today's stars with envious eyes. 'When we were playing we'd get crowds of 50,000,' he says. 'Where did all that money go? Not to the players, that's for sure. Now the players are getting huge rewards and I say good luck to them. They deserve it. They're entertaining thousands of people. Singers get big money so why not footballers? Anyway, it's better that the players get the money rather than the directors. I mean the directors don't entertain anyone, do they?'

Charles is not one to wallow in the past, but he does admit he believes his era had one advantage on the modern game. 'I don't think there are enough characters around these days,' he says. 'We had some great personalities back in the '40s and '50s, people like Tommy Lawton, Joe Mercer and Stanley Matthews. There aren't those types around any more. Mind you, there are a lot of things which are better now. You only have to look at the pitches. These days they are perfect all year round, but when I was playing for Leeds you would be up to your knees in mud. It was hard work. Then there was the ball. Crikey, it was heavy. When it was wet and muddy it would weigh a ton. I've seen people knocked out just from heading the ball. The Major would say to me sometimes, "Head the ball, Jack." I'd say "You head it!"' He laughs another hearty Welsh roar. 'Yes, there are a lot of things which are better now.'

With that, I leave Charles to ponder his forthcoming return to the eternal city to watch Leeds play Roma. 'I rang them up and they said they'd get me two tickets,' he says. 'That's nice, because tickets are expensive over there. It's about £50 a throw. I don't know why, but it's always been dearer. I'm looking forward to it. I've still got friends out there and it will be good to go back to Italy. They still remember me, even now.'

I thank Lorimer, who gives me phone numbers for Bobby Collins and Allan Clarke, and leave the Commerical. I drive home feeling incredibly lucky. Things are falling into place. I have already crossed five legends off my list. And so, blessed with this feeling of providence, I tap into my PC to see what Sabine has come up with. There is a message. Excitedly, I click on to it and read what the new Brigitte Bardot has sent me.

> Dear Rick,
> I have some badges and an Eric Cantona doll. I don't know now
> where lives. I LOVE ERIC. He is best. I help. Please mail me quickly.
> Sabine.

My luck appears to have departed. I had been hoping Sabine would be able to put me in touch with someone who might know Cantona's whereabouts or, at least, know some old colleagues or friends. As it turns out, she will only be able to help me if I want to add to my Barbie collection.

Rather than being a source of priceless information, the Internet seems to be the domain of anal-retentive anoraks, a sort of poor man's *Multi-Coloured Swap Shop*. The Eric Cantona Mailing List is like a themed lonely hearts club, and I realise that the people on it are probably dangerous. Their affection for Cantona is probably the *Fatal Attraction* sort. I decide that if I ever get to meet Cantona, I'll warn him to lock up his rabbit or risk the wrath of these puddled pot-boilers. I unsubscribe from the list and leave Sabine to e-mail the other 749 members on the list with details of her love for Cantona and her protestations of aid. If there's one thing worse than a do-gooder, it's a do-gooder with an Eric Cantona fetish.

BOBBY COLLINS — Short Story

He would kill his mother for a result.
JACK CHARLTON

It may be some 35 years since Bobby Collins last played for Leeds United, but he is taking an early shower. I should not be surprised by this, as this diminutive 69-year-old was as responsible as anyone for giving Leeds their reputation for toughness and cynicism. If John Charles was the Good Giant, Bobby Collins was the direct opposite. Standing five foot six inches short, he made up for his lack of height with a huge heart and an irascible streak. When I put it to him that his size must have made it harder for him to make it in the professional game, he is obviously amused. 'Me struggle?' he asks. 'I've never struggled in my life.'

Collins has forgotten about our arranged meeting. When he opens the front door of his home in the Alwoodley area of Leeds he is clad only in a bath towel and is dripping on the shagpile. He says he is happy to talk and rushes upstairs to get changed. Meanwhile I entertain myself in the lounge by looking at the framed picture of Collins leading out the Leeds team in the 1965 FA Cup final, and studying his Footballer of the Year trophy which sits on the hearth next to a discarded U2 video.

Soon he is back with me. He is a sprightly figure, with lively eyes and a rasping Glaswegian laugh. It soon becomes clear that this pocket battleship is no shrinking violet. In fact, as he looks even smaller than the height given in the old stats book, shrinking violent would be a better epithet with which to describe Collins.

It is the morning after Leeds' 1–0 victory over AS Roma in the fourth round of the UEFA Cup at Elland Road (the first leg in Italy, attended by both John Charles and Peter Lorimer, ended 0–0). It was an intoxicating night in front of a packed house. Harry Kewell scored the solitary goal and both Collins and I were there to witness it. We also witnessed two Roma players being sent off for headbutts in the dying moments after substitute Alan Smith successfully riled the Latin defence. 'I like Smithy,' says Collins with a devilish flicker. 'He's got a lot of aggression and he puts himself about, which some of the others don't. I like to see that. You've got to be able to play as well, but a bit of both is ideal. I like this Leeds team a lot. The only thing they don't do is pick up. Take last night. They knew Totti was the danger-man for Roma, but he had 30 yards of space in the middle of the bloody field. Luckily, his shooting was awful. The thing you could always say about the side I played in was that if we went a goal up then that was that. Game over. We'd shut up shop. Some people didn't like it, but we were good at it and successful.

'The good thing about the side they've got down there now is they have a great attitude. They are all in it together. It's all for one and one for all. That's the way to be, although Big Jack was never like that with me. Why? Ah, there's just some people don't like it when you make suggestions. Mind you, he's changed his mind a bit lately and has been quite complimentary.'

Jack Charlton conceded Collins made Leeds more professional, but frowned upon some of his win-at-all-costs antics. One particular game at Everton ended in a mass brawl, after a series of personal vendettas and tackles high enough to cause haircut fractures, and Charlton admitted the uncompromising style of Leeds' play then disturbed him. He also recalled how, the day before the 1965 Cup final against Liverpool, Collins had a full-on fight with Norman Hunter, because the latter had accidentally kicked the ball in his face and bloodied his nose. The red mist descended and there was no thought given to whether either player might be injured on the eve of the biggest day in Leeds United's history. Hunter may have been bites-yer-legs, but the smaller and stockier Collins was mauls-yer-ankles.

Both Collins and Charlton were stubborn and independent players, which is probably why they periodically clashed with each other. Nevertheless, there is a mutual respect between the two and Charlton accepts that it was Collins who dragged Leeds United up from the verge of the Third Division and set them on the road to becoming the most feared side in the country. Bobby Collins was simply *the difference*.

'I was 31 when I came to Leeds in 1962,' he says. 'My manager at Everton was Harry Catterick and he'd just bought Denis Stevens from Bolton, so I had an idea my days were numbered. I still knew I could play and I wasn't the type to drop down the divisions for the hell of it. I wasn't coming to Leeds to take life easy and I wanted more success. In the game before I left, I only scored the first goal and the third goal.' He lets out one of those Glaswegian guffaws and mimics Catterick: '"You're not the same player any more, son!"' He adds: 'I just thought, fine, there's something wrong here. If they don't want me I'll leave. The funny thing was, the same thing happened when I was at Celtic. It was sad because I'd been there nigh on ten years. The manager was a funny fella named Jimmy McGrory. In my entire time at the club he only gave one team-talk and that was, "Boys, the turnstiles aren't clicking." That was it. Incredible. He wanted to get rid of me, too. I was playing golf at Tower Glen and when I came off, the secretary said there'd been a call from Mr McGrory and I was to phone him back. So I did and he said, "Everton are interested in you, will you go?" It wasn't "Do you want to go?" and I was never one to stay anywhere if I was not wanted.'

Though they were entirely different types of players, the similarities between Collins and Gordon Strachan are manifold. Both were fiery Scots, small in stature but big in presence, and they joined Leeds in similar circumstances. Both were past 30 and considered over the hill by many; and both were quitting glamour clubs to join a side struggling in the Second Division. However, both would be the pivotal figures in revamping the club's fortunes, regaining their Scottish international places in the process, and would end up being named Footballer of the Year. 'I suppose there were similarities,' says Collins. 'Gordon was a good player and some people thought he might be past it when he came, but he was one of the best players in the side, a clever player.'

Initially, Collins was called in to do a salvage job. 'Don Revie was a lovely fella and was a good talker,' he says. 'He outlined his plans and he offered me the same money as I was on at Everton. Considering Leeds were in the Second Division, I thought that was something. It showed a bit of faith. I knew they had some good players, too. What I didn't know was they were second bottom of the Second Division at the time. It was like that when I went to Everton too. I knew they were a big club, but I had no idea they'd played six games and lost six.'

Though Revie impressed Collins, the Leeds boss was yet to make a name for himself in the managerial world, and Collins reveals he came very close to joining up with the most respected gaffer in the game. 'I'd been to see Don and was happy with things, but when I got home my brother-in-law told me some fella had been on the phone a few times asking for me. He said he was Scottish, but he wouldn't leave a name. I thought, fine, and left it at that. I didn't think any more of it. The next day the phone went again and this voice growled, "Son, is it true ye've signed for Leeds?" I could only say, "Yes, Mr Shankly" and to his credit he said, "Ah well, orra best anyway, son." Who knows what might have happened if he'd rung a day earlier?'

As it was, Collins became a Leeds player. 'I arrived at Leeds in March and there were only 11 games left,' he recalls. 'You could call it a rescue mission. My first game, we had a crowd of 11,000 there, but the following week we had 19,000. The turnstiles were clicking. Jimmy McGrory would have been happy.'

Leeds survived by the skin of their teeth. 'We got out of jail with a 3–0 win over Newcastle United on the last day of the season,' continues Collins. 'That was a great day and the start of the glory days. The next season we got promotion and the year after that we almost did the Double. Don knew what he was getting when he signed me. He wanted good pros with good habits and he had a knack of building up a comradeship. We loved him and respected him, though I admit I'm glad I left before he introduced the team bingo sessions. I don't think many of the players liked all that stuff. A lot is said about the spirit and how he liked us all to go out together, but I didn't socialise too much with the rest of the lads. It's just the way you are. I had a pal or two, but you meet a lot of nice people, not just inside football. Things are different now. We could go anywhere we wanted and not be bothered, but players now earn more in a week than I'd earn in a lifetime.

That's just the way things go. Nothing stands still. It's the same with this city. It's so busy these days. When I got here in the 1960s there were hardly any cars in this area, but now, Jesus, it's like Piccadilly Circus.'

After Raich Carter's reign, Leeds had appointed Bill Lambton as manager. His major contribution to the development of the club was his signing of Billy Bremner and Don Revie. At the time Bremner was a precocious teenager while Revie was an England veteran with a handful of caps to his name. He was also famed for what became known as the Revie plan. At the time it was considered revolutionary, though it has often been employed since. Revie would operate as a centre-forward and wear the number nine shirt in an era when your number was an indicator of position, but he would play just in front of the midfield. It had worked and was the first sign that Revie was a deep thinker about tactics. However, those two signings could not save Lambton and he was replaced by Jack Taylor. But this change did not stem the decline and Leeds were relegated in 1960. With Leeds hurtling lemming-like towards the Third Division, Taylor jumped ship and resigned. Revie, who had joined Leeds from Sunderland in 1958, was named Leeds manager. It was the start of the revival.

'Don Revie knew how to build a team,' says Collins. 'In the early days he had me and big John Charles to provide the experience and then some of the younger lads started to come through the ranks. Billy Bremner was already there and in the team and you could tell he was a good player. Norman Hunter was coming through too. He was a great player, was Norman. People remember him as a hard case, but he had a lot of ability. I would just put my hand up and the ball would be there on a plate for me. When Johnny Giles came from Manchester United things began moving; but the thing was, Leeds already had the players but they didn't know it, because a lot of them were in the reserves or in the juniors. When I got here the trainer was Les Cocker: after about two weeks, he said to me, "Come and watch the youth team play. We've got this terrific centre-half. He's quick and he can play, but the only trouble is, he's a little bit small." I went along to watch and could see what Les meant, so I said, "Why don't you make him into a full-back?"' The man in question was Paul Reaney, who would become the most celebrated right-back in the club's history, an England international, and a virtual ever-present through the great days of the late '60s and '70s.

Having won promotion, Collins would enjoy his greatest ever season in the 1964–65 campaign. The season would become a head-to-head duel between Leeds and Manchester United and any current fans who wonder where the mutual disdain between the rival sets of supporters originated need only look to that year. Leeds went 25 games unbeaten until they lost to Manchester United at Elland Road. Nevertheless, they were still the league leaders by the time the final day of the season arrived. It all came down to one game. If Leeds won at Birmingham they would be the champions. Collins takes up the story. 'They scored very early on and by half-time we were 3–0 down. We couldn't believe it. We knew we had to win, but we were throwing it away. I don't know what happened. Maybe it was nerves. In the second half we went out and gave it a real go. With a few minutes left Big Jack made it 3–3, but we couldn't get that final goal. We got beat on bloody goal average. We had the same points as Manchester United, but they'd scored more goals. We were one goal away from winning the League in our first season up. Then there was the FA Cup final and it was the same thing there.'

That game in May 1965 was the first time Leeds had made it to Wembley. Having gained some sort of revenge for the championship by beating Manchester United 1–0 in the semi-final replay, they found themselves up against the mighty Liverpool and their maverick manager, Shankly. It was a chance for Collins to show the Anfield legend just what he had missed out on three years earlier. But it was not to be. 'It was something special getting to the FA Cup final, but unfortunately it was probably one of the worst games I'd had all season,' recalls Collins. 'We also had two forwards who went amiss that day. There was a big Scots lad called Jimmy Storrie, who was injured but never told anybody because he was desperate to play and get a medal. Then there was Albert Johanneson, poor lad. Albert was South African. He was a smashing player who could really fly, but I think he lost confidence in himself. At the start of the season Albert had run this guy ragged, but he never got a kick at Wembley. He just froze and we couldn't hope to get away with playing with nine men against a side like Liverpool.'

Collins, who has a habit of rocking back and forth in his large armchair, clapping his hands and guffawing in a manner that resembles Ronnie Corbett in storytelling mode, is suddenly less animated as he ponders the fate of Johanneson. 'Poor Albert. A lovely lad, but he just lost touch with everyone and I think he was drinking too much. They found him dead in his flat a few years ago. It was very sad. He could play, though. Oh yes, he was great, was Albert.' On that day at Wembley, Johanneson did not do himself justice, but the match was still goalless after 90 minutes – the much-maligned Gary Sprake, later famed for throwing the ball into his own net, making two outstanding saves to keep Leeds in it. In extra-time Roger Hunt finally broke the deadlock for Liverpool, before Billy Bremner fired home a sweet volley to equalise. 'With Jimmy Storrie and Albert gone amiss, it was very hard for the midfield,' says Collins. 'Our back guys played very well, but Liverpool were slightly better on the day and Ian St John scored the winner with a header. We were disappointed. But to think I'd joined in 1962 and we were bottom of the Second Division and, within three years, we'd got beaten on goal difference for the League and were in the FA Cup final. Well, it was incredible.

'I also got this thing here that season.' He points to his Footballer of the Year award. 'I was the first Scottish player to get it and in all my years in football it remains my fondest memory. It was excellent getting that. The second season I was at Everton I had a great time and scored something like 18 goals from midfield. We had a marvellous forward line, people like Bingham and Young, all internationals, but we never won a sausage. We never won the League and never even got close. But at Leeds things happened.'

It all went sour for Collins the following season. Leeds were by now established as a force and they would again finish runners-up in the championship race, this time to Liverpool. Collins was now pushing 35 but was still a key member of the Leeds side. However, when Leeds travelled to Turin to face Torino in their first European tie in the Inter-City Fairs Cup, Collins's career was about to reach a crossroads. 'I can still remember what happened very clearly,' he says. 'I'd had a great first half and I got the ball and went out wide. I saw the right-back coming and I had an idea what he was thinking, so I knocked the ball past him and started running. The ball must have been 20 yards away, but it made no difference to him. He wasn't interested in the ball. He went for me instead and he made a bloody good job of it, too. He never got booked, but it was different then. These things happened. Today's game is different. You can't look at a player without getting booked or sent off.'

The Torino full-back had broken Collins's femur, which shows just how high and dangerous the tackle had been. Though Collins can be philosophical and suggest these things happened, his team-mates, who were not opposed to a bit of the rough stuff themselves, were shocked. Billy Bremner admitted the injury reduced him to tears. In the book *Bremner!* he recalled:

> I snarled at the player who'd done it: 'I'll kill you for this.' Believe me, I meant it too. That player probably didn't understand what I had said, but he certainly got the message and stayed well away from me for the rest of the match. When they carried Bobby Collins off to hospital that day, I was convinced that it was the last time we would ever see him on a football pitch. If anyone had said to me that he would be back, and not only walking but playing for the first team at Leeds United again, I would have snarled in his face 'Who do you think you're kidding?'

Meanwhile, Jack Charlton was also in the midst of the action, as he described in *Jack Charlton: The Autobiography*. 'I knew that if Bobby Collins wouldn't get up, he must have broken something,' he said. 'I stood over him, whacking one Italian and punching another.'

Collins was taken to hospital. His team-mates visited him after the game and winced as he proudly revealed the extent of his injuries. 'He smiled when he saw us,' recalled Charlton. 'And then he said, "Take a look at this." He threw back the tent thing and there was a bolt through his leg – not a shiny silver bolt, but something that looked like it came out of a scrapyard.' Charlton recalled that Collins thought their reaction was funny. 'He was a hard man, Bobby, very hard. Great player, but tough as nails.' If anything summed up the steel of Bobby Collins it was his reaction to the dodgy alloy sticking out of his leg in that Turin hospital. 'Bobby was one of the toughest players ever,' Norman Hunter told me. 'He didn't see danger. He just went in hard but fair.'

At the time Collins refused to condemn the Italian player, Poletti, who was responsible for maiming him. 'I'm not finished,' he vowed. 'I'll be back. It's a pity this should happen, but it was a good sporting game and I do not blame him.'

Revie was quick to pay tribute to his linchpin. 'In three and a half years with this club he has been my teacher,' he told reporters. 'His skill, his enthusiasm, it has all rubbed off on the younger players. Nobody knows what he has done for Leeds United and myself. I would rather we'd lost against Torino and Bobby not been injured.'

Though Leeds were winning few friends at home, the Italian press were quite taken with Torino's conquerors. The *Gazetta del Popolo* said:

> Torino have not made it and perhaps they were not even in a condition
> to make it. They crashed desperately into the white wall of Leeds
> United. Leeds are a complete team and can splendidly adapt
> themselves to circumstances, attacking and defending with a perfect
> timing.

Having lived by the sword, Collins died by the wayward studs of an Italian hatchet-man. 'It was a bit naughty,' he says now, with characteristic understatement and without a trace of bitterness. 'But there were some hard men around then. Men like Sammy Cox. When you played against a team, you always knew who the hard men were and they would know who yours were. Even so, there wasn't that much that went on. A foul was a foul and that was that. Today's player must practise diving and winning fouls. It irritates me. I think we were harder but more honest. It was just a case of having to suss out which players were the ones who were going to kick you into the stands. Leeds were solid and hard, but that's better than getting beat. You've got to win, the game's all about winning, and we played real hard. And no, I can't say that I was an angel, but I don't apologise for that.'

It is strange to see this old, grey-haired man sitting in suburbia in his slippers as he tells me how the players of today are a bunch of jessies. A few weeks earlier, Leeds and Spurs were charged with misconduct by the FA after what was fancifully described as a 22-man brawl by the tabloid Press. The clubs would end up being fined £150,000 apiece. The trouble started when Lee Bowyer made an awful challenge on Stephen Clemence, whereupon players charged in and started wielding their handbags as if it was the opening day of the Harrods sale. No punches were thrown, but several players hit the deck in the sort of melodramatic fashion that would have shamed the hammiest of actors in a cowboy matinée. Suffice to say David Ginola, D'Artagnan on ice, has probably suffered more pain when he has misplaced his lip gloss, but the media ravaged Leeds. The game was in anarchy, we were told. Standards had slipped and this half-hearted contretemps was held up as a symptom of the systematic moral decline in Britain. Of course, it was just an excuse for a lot of pompous journalists masquerading as pacifists to give Leeds a good kicking, and I consider that Collins would be staggered to think people seriously think the game is more physical now than it once was.

However, despite Collins's broken femur, Jack Charlton's little black book and rabid pitbulls like Chopper Harris and Tommy Smith, Collins insists: 'It wasn't that bad in my day and everyone accepted it. I was never much involved with rugby before I came here, but with Leeds being a rugby city I got to know big Arthur Clues, a player who was a nice chap and, God bless him, is no longer with us. He used to call us Leeds Urinals because we took away all the rugby team's crowds. But if people say football is hard, they should have watched some rugby league games. In rugby league there's two guys pulling you down and another one punching you. Now football's not like that. Yes, someone might take a dislike to you and, when that happens, it's amazing what they'll do. But that's football. When I started out I used to be a ball. Do you know what I mean by that? I mean they used to kick the shit out of me. The thing is, if you were playing well and making a name then you knew there were going to be people who wanted to nail you. That's the way it worked. It's a compliment, really.'

For someone with such a resilient nature and iron will, it was fitting that Collins made his Celtic début as an 18-year-old in the Old Firm derby against Rangers. 'I remember going through the middle and Willie Wood fouled me and we got a penalty. He moaned like hell, but he clipped me. Fortunately, we won 3–2 and I was never out of the team thereafter. When Celtic played Rangers you simply had to win and it didn't matter how. If you didn't win then you knew you wouldn't be able to go out for a while!'

Collins won a championship, a Scottish Cup and two League Cups during his time at Parkhead, but was sold to Everton for £23,500 in 1958. He joined Leeds for £25,000 in 1962, but as he lay in his Italian hospital bed three years later it seemed that his career was finally over. 'I thought I was finished,' he admits. 'But I had this wonderful orthopedic surgeon in Italy who was the top specialist in the world at the time. He did a marvellous job for me and I asked him, "Will I ever play again?" He said, "Of course you will" and he was right. But it took quite a while for it to heal, around six months, and quite a lot of things changed in that time. Johnny Giles had been playing on the wing before, but quite rightly he moved infield to his normal position of inside-forward. That sort of thing often happened. Wingers usually went to inside-forward, while the inside-forwards went to the wing or out of the club. They expected me to be back to my old self straight away, whereas sometimes you have to give a bit of leeway and accept it takes a while.

'I did get back into the first team that season and played a few games, but they said to me, "You're not the player you were." I thought that was debatable and I didn't like the way it was all done. As far as I was concerned, I was playing reasonably well and I'd signed a contract before the accident for another two years. But Leeds had a lot of good, young players coming through and somebody had to go. As chance would have it, that was me. I wasn't enthusiastic about going, but it's like I said before, if they don't want you there's no point staying.'

Life after Leeds saw Collins call in at some of the less salubrious locations on the footballing map. He joined Bury on a free transfer and had a couple of years there before going back north of the border to Morton. His peripatetic existence then saw him join Ringwood City in Melbourne as player-coach, followed by spells at Shamrock Rovers, Oldham Athletic (whom he led to the Third Division title as player-coach), Huddersfield Town, Hull City, Blackpool and Barnsley. He also had a brief spell as youth team coach at Leeds in 1976.

His coaching job at Barnsley reunited him with Norman Hunter, who was then the manager. 'He became youth team coach under me at Oakwell,' recalls Hunter. 'I knew he'd been a marvellous player, and good with the kids, and I wanted to use his experience to help bring them along. As it happened, I got sacked and he took over as manager.'

Collins would soon follow suit, in 1985. 'I took over from Norman and we finished sixth in the Second Division and had a decent cup run,' he says. 'I was so pleased I took the lads away to Majorca for a break. I'd just got home when the phone went and it was the chairman telling me I'd got the bullet.'

In 1988 Collins shared a joint testimonial with John Charles and he has a wealth of memories from the days when he dragged Leeds United, kicking and screaming, into the higher echelons of the football hierarchy. 'I always think about the big games when I look back,' he says. 'The games against Manchester United and Liverpool were always special. There were so many great characters around, people like Dave Mackay.' Another Glasgow growl fills the room. 'Dave was a superb player. There was that time when he had Billy [Bremner] by the throat. Ha ha. I was playing that day. It was after I'd broken my leg. We were down at Sprus and Billy had fouled Dave. He didn't like it, so he just grabbed Billy by the scruff of his neck and nearly lifted him off the floor. Billy could get under your skin, no two ways about that.'

If the comparison with Strachan is obvious, Collins and Bremner seem cut from the same cloth, pint-sized assassins with sublime gifts and tempestuous natures. Collins fails to see the link, though. 'We weren't similar players, me and Billy,' he insists. 'Billy was more a half-back whereas I'd be up the field, down the field, all over the ruddy field. I always thought Billy was a good player, though. He did it his way and I admired him for that. Nobody told me how to play and nobody could tell Billy how to play either. What were my strengths? Well, let me put it this way, there weren't many things I couldn't do on a football field.'

Collins and Bremner were just two members of the Scottish invasion and Leeds' success over the years would have a healthy input from north of the border. As well as Collins and Bremner, there were Peter Lorimer, Eddie and Frankie Gray, Joe Jordan, David Harvey, Gordon McQueen, Gordon Strachan and Gary McAllister. Elsewhere it was the same story, with Scots regularly playing leading roles for the great teams. Think Graeme Souness, Kenny Dalglish, Frank McLintock, John Wark. The great managers were often Scots too, from Shankly and Stein through to Alex Ferguson and George Graham. Now the tide is changing. The Leeds side that played the previous night against Roma did not include a solitary Scot; and even Liverpool recently fielded a side containing nine non-British players and no Scots.

'Things have definitely changed a lot,' says Collins. 'There used to be lots of great Scottish players. All the great sides seemed to have a hardcore of Scots in their side, but that is not happening now. The trouble was, the best Scots would come south to England, but they were not replaced at the other end. Now I can't understand for the life of me why the Scottish FA has four leagues when there are only two cities with a decent fan base. There used to be eighteen teams in the top flight and now there's ten. It's ridiculous. The other problem is the foreigners. They are going the English way now in Scotland. Even Celtic and Rangers are bringing in lots of foreign players instead of looking for Scottish talent. That was never the case in my day, but the game was still popular. I remember Celtic playing Motherwell in the cup and there were 132,000 people at Hampden, and Celtic would regularly get 80,000 for League games. Great club, Celtic. I went there with Leeds for a pre-season game, but the Leeds fans upset the Celtic supporters. They started singing 'God Save The Queen', which is not the best thing to do up there!'

Nowadays Collins is a regular at Elland Road and excited by the new side being built under David O'Leary. 'Leeds haven't done too badly over the years,' he reflects. 'OK, they got relegated in the 1980s, but I don't think things will go wrong now with the manager and assistant manager they've got. The trouble is, they've got a lot of games and a lot of internationals. Look at someone like Harry Kewell. I know from experience what it's like having to fly to Australia. It's a hell of a trek being cooped up for 26 hours in a seat. That's not going to help him or Leeds. If they stick together then there's every chance they could win something, though. There's a buzz about the place again.'

I take a snap of Collins holding his Footballer of the Year trophy, thank him and leave. Later that day I am leafing through the latest copy of the *Leeds, Leeds, Leeds* magazine when I come across a double-page spread of pictures from the 80th birthday gala dinner at Elland Road. A whole host of greats were there and an expert panel voted for what they considered to be the greatest-ever line-up. They plumped for Martyn, Reaney, Charlton, Hunter, Cooper, Lorimer, Giles, Bremner, Kewell, Clarke and Charles. The bench comprised Currie, Madeley and Harvey. Collins does not feature and I cannot help thinking this is harsh, as he was the launching pad from which the Revie era took off. However, I know from my own experience how hard it is to draw up a list of legends and the black-tie panellists had an even harder job as they were picking the best team rather than the best 11 players. When I drew up my own list, I also wanted to include players that had made a big impact and had a story to tell. It's an impossible job and my list includes personal favourites too. They are a taste of history, rather than the full five-course meal.

Nevertheless, there are inevitable absentees and the magazine spread did make me think that I should give honourable mentions to those who could justifiably have merited places on my hit list. From the Revie era Terry Cooper, Paul Reaney, Paul Madeley and Mick Jones could easily have made it. Later there was the bewitching Duncan McKenzie, who famously hurdled a mini at pitchside prior to a game in the '70s; while Joe Jordan, with his toothless grin and scoring prowess, was the watershed between Clarke and a series of duff strikers who had us all choking on our rancid Bovril in years to come. Alex Sabella, the Argentinian from Sheffield, showed fleeting glimpses of talent, while Arthur Graham and Carl Harris were rare spirit lifters in the tedium of the early '80s. After that, Leeds fans were treated to an array of journeymen and hapless hopefuls who were not fit to lace the drinks of their predecessors.

There was the odd exception. John Sheridan was a silky stylist and an oddity in Eddie Gray's Leeds team; he briefly forged a fine partnership with Ian Snodin, a multi-talented mullet-head complete with a moustache borrowed from a spaghetti western. Briefly, there was the Elvis Presley fanatic Frank Worthington. He was past it when he arrived at Leeds, but was still coolness personified, a long-haired layabout who could easily have played understudy to Dennis Hopper in *Easy Rider*. Mel Sterland was more 'Deflated Spacehopper', but the rider was, he was surprisingly effective and a real crowd favourite. In fact, come the Howard Wilkinson era, Leeds actually began signing quality rather than unqualified rubbish. Tony Dorigo, Rod Wallace and especially Gary McAllister had ability in spades; Lee Chapman looked like a carthorse in search of a glue factory, but paradoxically scored goals for fun.

There were others, too, and everyone has his or her personal heroes and villains. I was always exasperated by Terry Connor, a lively centre-forward who would leave his centre of gravity on the team bus each week. My antipathy was sealed when I read an article in the matchday programme quoting him as saying, 'I just can't stop scoring goals.' Unless I was watching a different game, it seemed like Connor had refrained from such a practice on the very day he got into the first team. But at least he was a trier, unlike some of the pampered stars who signed in the '90s, the worst case in question being Tomas Brolin. It was the first time Leeds had signed a Cabbage Patch Doll, and he flopped spectacularly like a wilting lettuce. Tony Yeboah set the home fires burning again with a series of stunning strikes, notably the volley against Liverpool which won the goal-of-the-season award, but he soon burned himself out. Then there was Jimmy Floyd Hasselbaink, the best striker Leeds had had since Jordan. Sadly, he was also the greediest.

All of these have contributed in different ways and to varying extents in making the history of Leeds United such a colourful one. However, not one of them played such a monumental role as the vertically-challenged midfield ace from Glasgow. If Bobby Collins had sold his mother to get a result, you can bet your life he would have got a good price for a 5–0 victory.

ALLAN CLARKE — Sniffer

One of the best ever.
TONY CURRIE

It's not what you do, it's the way that you do it.' So said Bananarama, the 1980s pop trio who covered all options by singing dreadful songs very badly. Their maxim may have had a ring of truth about it, but it is nevertheless an incontestable fact that the most stylish of centre-halfs is rarely as idolised as the most average of strikers. For many of us, football begins and ends with the finishers. The middle is a muddle populated by creators and destroyers. During the 1970s every Leeds Coronation Street was populated by snotty-faced artful dodgers kicking a ball beneath washing-line garlands and pretending to be Allan Clarke. Those imitating Jack Charlton and Trevor Cherry were few and far between, while a pre-pubescent penchant for Norman Hunter's terrible challenges would have you labelled as cerebrally challenged and carted off to the nearest child psychologist.

Football is first and foremost a question of scoring goals. Careers, fortunes, livelihoods and legends are made and broken on the altar of the three-yard tap-in: had England hit the onion bag more frequently, Graham Taylor would not have ended up in the vegetable patch and Geoff Thomas might be remembered for more than one pathetic shot against France in 1992. However, few of us have ever been any good at scoring goals. It is an art and a science. At school the social pecking order would be decreed by your position on the football pitch. The strikers were the confident, extrovert girl-magnets, sporting neat haircuts, olive glows and an impressive playground entourage. Centre-halfs were brusque and prosaic, taller, spottier and with squarer haircuts than the rest. Wingers were quick-witted nancy boys who wore gloves and played under sufferance; and full-backs were black holes of talent. I was a sweeper. Too clumsy to be a midfielder and too soft to be a genuine centre-half. I was an apology for a footballer. Neither fish nor flesh, I constituted the offal of the team. They might as well have hung me in a gibbet from the crossbar and used me for target practice. As time moves on, this order is subject to change, but the one immutable element is the status of the goalscorer. He is king. And Allan Clarke was the king of all goalscorers.

I feel like mentioning this to the Frenchwoman on the other end of the phone. I presume she must be the secretary of Jean-Jacques Bertrand, Eric's lawyer. My friend, who is a sports journalist, has given me his number and suggested I try it. Perhaps the lawyer would know of Eric's movements and even arrange a quick meeting.

I wade in with my carefully constructed plan of attack. It is the 'parlez-vous anglais?' pincer movement. Unfortunately, she is wise to this and responds with her 'ne pas du tout' rearguard attack. There follows a flawed conversation in pidgin Esperanto and I can appreciate how Captain Hook felt when asked to play paper, scissors, stone. She says something about 'semaine', which I recall from my Longman Audio-visual French lessons and lustful longings for Marie-France Lafayette to mean 'week'. At least that's what I think she said. I conclude that Monsieur Bertrand will either be back next *semaine* or has been carted off to a seminary in the Marseilles hills. Unfazed, I try to make up for my lack of technical wizardry by gabbling away in the manner of a Gallic Jimmy Adamson, but this merely means I confuse myself as well as her. So I try the patient approach. This is the beauty of the phone, I suppose. Pick it up and you never know who's on the other end – friends, lovers, lost ones and dimwitted British folk who believe speaking English very slowly in an accent that makes Charles Aznavour sound like a pearly queen will endear themselves to you. I feel like telling Monsieur Bertrand's secretary that this is an awful lot of effort to have to go to in order to speak to a man who only scored 11 goals for Leeds. I can tell she feels like nipping up to Calais to congratulate the French lorry drivers. Maybe I'm paranoid. I hang up with my hang-ups.

Life's ironic. Cantona scored 11 goals for Leeds and is as accessible as the works of James Joyce. Allan Clarke scored some 151 goals in 364 appearances and answers my phone call by arranging to meet up the following afternoon at the Post House in Derby. Clarke says he is in Derby on business, but will be happy to meet me afterwards. It is only later that evening that I learn there are two Post Houses in Derby and I fret about which one he meant. This is one interview I want to get to on time. For some totally unfounded reason I have imagined that Clarke will be one of the more difficult interviewees. Maybe it was the fact he had a reputation for being something of a rebel. Or maybe it was the fact he could mix it with the best of them and someone as apparently mild-mannered as Kevin Keegan said he 'couldn't stand him as a player'.

It might also have something to do with his close resemblance to Big Daddy, not the big-breasted wrestler who donned a leotard and whose real name was Shirley Crabtree, but the hardest bloke in town when I was growing up. A gaunt tower of tattoos, Big Daddy was said to be involved with the Service Crew, Leeds United's band of football terrorists who wrought havoc in the '70s and '80s. I am therefore relieved and slightly anxious when Clarke arrives at the same Post House

I plumped for. Maybe my luck is in. He is very smartly turned out in a deep blue suit and tie. He has weathered well. His face still has that chiselled angular look and his eyes have retained that slightly haunted sallowness. It is an image I somehow consider to be intrinsically Yorkshire. Give him 20 years and he'll look like an elongated Michael Parkinson. Clarke, though, is only an honorary Yorkshireman. He tells me, 'I'm a Black Country boy,' and occasionally a Noddy Holderesque sound replaces his clipped Yorkshire vowels. 'Yowl', he says, when he means 'you'll'.

I order us some coffee and we sit down. 'I make my mind up the first time I meet someone,' he says rather unsettlingly. 'I either like you or I don't.' However, any fears are soon banished and Clarke is brilliant company. As he regales me with some of the stories from yesteryear he becomes increasingly animated, tapping my arm and standing up on several occasions to explain his point. I remind myself that, despite his fearsome reputation, Big Daddy was also always very nice to me when I played for the same local football club he belonged to. If not quite a father figure, he at least refrained from covering me in tar and feathers while beating me over the head with a rusty scythe. Maybe Clarke is the same. A softie with a mean streak.

Think Leeds United and you come up with a million images. The team trotting out with their names on the back of their tracksuits, lining up in the centre of the pitch and saluting the crowd. The tallest floodlights in Europe (was I the only one inordinately proud of that statistic and suitably devastated when they pulled them down?). The little numbered tabs with their frilly borders which the players wore on their socks. They used to sell those in the shop. I had number four, Billy Bremner. Even in the park I could never pretend to aspire to be Allan Clarke. Players, managers, fans, championships, riots, red cards, they are all there in the memory bank. The pitch invasion against West Brom, the win at Bramall Lane, defeat in Paris and Salonika. However, the majority of Leeds fans would surely choose five past four on Saturday, 6 May 1972 as their desert-island memory. It was the moment Clarke scored the goal which won the FA Cup for the only time in Leeds United's history.

He is out of his chair as he recalls the strike in vivid detail. It may be 28 years ago, but you do not tire of telling how you wrote your name in folklore. 'Arsenal were attacking and I was Royal Box side, 15 yards in, tussling with Frank McLintock. Frank and Peter Simpson were the two centre-halfs for Arsenal that day. Frank nudged me, I fell to the ground and he trod on my fingers with his studs. The ball breaks to Alan Ball and Bally tries to play a pass to John Radford, but Paul Madeley intercepts it and plays it to Peter Lorimer on the edge of the centre-circle. He plays it out to the right to Mick Jones. At that point I'm shaking me hand and Billy [Bremner] is well in advance of me, so I thought I'd better leg it. I remember Mick taking on Bob McNab and Pat Rice, the full-back, coming across to cover. As the ball's coming over I'm thinking right-foot volley, and I fancy my chances; but when it was about ten yards from me it started to lose pace and

I'm thinking it ain't going to get to me. Now you've only got a split second to make up your mind, so I think I'd better take off. So I did. You know the rest.'

That diving header was a tremendous goal and won Leeds the cup at the third time of asking. However, no Leeds triumph seemed possible without some degree of ill fortune and Jones, Clarke's tireless foil, dislocated his shoulder in the very last minute after a clash with keeper Geoff Barnett. Leeds' trainer, Les Cocker, attended the distraught number nine and put his arm in a sling. As Leeds celebrated, the poignant sight of Jones being helped up Wembley's famous steps by Norman Hunter to receive his medal from the Queen became one of the FA Cup's most touching images.

'It was a marvellous feeling to have won the cup,' says Clarke. 'We were disappointed that Mick had done his shoulder in, but it was still tremendous. I played in four FA Cup finals, three for Leeds and one for Leicester, but I only won one. I always say I won the important one because it was the Centenary Cup final and the Queen was there. When I was leaving the house to go and play in the semi-final for Leicester I said to my wife, "I don't care if we lose the final as long as we get there." I meant it, but it's a killer losing at Wembley. In the three games with Leeds we were the best team on each occasion, but the best team doesn't always win the FA Cup.'

Although Leeds had won the most prestigious domestic cup competition in world football, there was no time to celebrate. As Clarke explains: 'The thing about it was, we were due to play at Wolves on the Monday and we only needed a point to do the Double. We didn't attend our banquet in London that night. The wives, girlfriends, directors and everyone who worked for the club all attended this big function at a posh hotel, but we left Wembley on our coach and drove to Wolverhampton with the FA Cup. We had a couple of beers, but that was it. We went to bed. On Sunday morning Eddie Gray, Johnny Giles and myself were at West Bromwich Albion's ground having treatment. If it had been a normal, nothing-at-stake League match then the three of us wouldn't have played, but its importance meant we had to. We were missing Jonah, so Billy played up front alongside me in attack. We lost 2–1 so we didn't do the Double. If you'd been in our dressing-room you'd have thought you were at a funeral. It was like a morgue. We went from total elation to being utterly dejected within 48 hours. I suppose we were the only team that won the FA Cup and never got to celebrate.

'Now I look back and wonder what would have happened if the FA had given us another couple of days, because it's true what they say about Wembley – it really takes it out of your legs. Our gaffer didn't miss a trick and I'm sure he asked for the game to be moved, but they said no. That's why it makes me laugh when Arsène Wenger and Alex Ferguson go on about games now. One year we played 76 games and we were playing Saturday, Wednesday, Saturday all year round. We had a squad of 19 players and the gaffer would always want his best 11 on the pitch. It meant we were always playing through injuries. That was hard. We became victims of our success. In 1970 we were going for the Treble but we won nothing. We were second in the League, lost the FA Cup final replay to Chelsea and lost to Celtic in the European Cup semi-final.'

Unlike many of his team-mates at Elland Road, Clarke was an outsider. While Billy Bremner, Norman Hunter, Gary Sprake and Paul Madeley had all come up through the ranks and had been in at the start of the Revie revival, Clarke was a big-money import. He made his name at Fulham, where he scored 45 goals in 85 appearances. Tommy Trinder was the chairman and took great delight in mimicking Clarke at their first meeting. 'He said, "Yow all roit son" to me and I remember thinking, "Is he taking the mick out of me?" It was strange. He was a big showbusiness personality then and I'd seen him on TV at the London Palladium. I was only a kid. But I signed and I got to play with Johnny Haynes, the first £100-a-week footballer, and some player he was.'

The 21-year-old's form for Fulham did not go unnoticed and even attracted the envious eyes of Matt Busby at Manchester United. 'Bobby Robson was my manager and he said Man United wanted to meet me, so I said OK. I met Matt Busby and his assistant, Jimmy Murphy, at King's Cross Station. Matt Busby pointed to a taxi so I got in and he told the driver to just drive around London. He said, "We're going to win the championship this season and next year we'll win the European Cup. I'd like you to join us." I was a bit in awe and just said "Thank you Mr Busby, I'd like to join you," and I went home to Chessington. But then Bobby told me Leicester were also keen, so I arranged to meet their manager Matt Gillies in the reception at Highbury after I'd played for England Under-23s against the full England side. We won that game and I scored a couple of goals. I waited for half an hour, but he didn't show up, so I went home. Later that night I got a call from him saying he was coming to my house by taxi. It was the early hours, but I liked him so I signed. I rang Matt Busby and he just said "fair enough". There's not many 21-year-olds turn down the chance to play for Matt Busby and Manchester United, but I did and I'm glad. I'm a great believer in fate and if I hadn't signed for Leicester I might never have gone to Leeds. And looking back, Man United were already in decline by then, while Leeds were on the up.'

Clarke signed for a British transfer record of £150,000 and spent a year at Filbert Street, the highlight of which was getting to the FA Cup final in 1969. Leicester lost 1–0 and by that point Frank O'Farrell had replaced Gillies. 'I never got on with him,' says Clarke. 'He played me in midfield in the Cup final. Now only an Irishman could do that, even if I did get the Man of the Match award. If Gillies had stayed I probably would have too, but that's fate taking a hand again.'

And so in 1969 Don Revie signed Clarke for another British transfer record of £165,000. However, Leeds were very much a family by then and there was a good deal of wariness among the seasoned stars when the precocious youngster with the troublesome reputation turned up for training on his first day. Foremost among the dissenters was the man who would become Clarke's closest friend, Billy Bremner.

'I became great pals with Billy and he was like a brother to me,' said Clarke. 'I still miss him now and there's not a day goes by when I don't think about him. But the funny thing is, and I've never told this story before, when he'd heard I'd signed he told his wife Vicky. "I'm not playing with that bastard Clarke." She told my wife Margaret when we went out one night. I mentioned it to him later when we were room-mates and he tried to get out of it. I think he remembered when I'd played against Leeds and I'd been kicking him and Gilesey. I think the gaffer remembered that, too. I was hard. I could give it out. We all could at Leeds. I think they'd got a reputation when they were trying to get out of the Second Division and it stuck. But I'd been on the other side of the fence. I'd been in opposition changing-rooms with the manager's saying, "Try and outfootball this side and they'll destroy you, so rough them up a bit." The trouble was, we could play it any way you liked at Leeds. We'd outplay you or outfight you. If one of our lads got in a bit of bother there'd be ten white shirts around him in an instant. We looked after each other.'

After quickly dispelling any of Bremner and co.'s preconceptions, Clarke became an instant hit at Leeds and struck up a legendary partnership with Mick Jones. The pair were chalk and cheese, but were christened fish and chips by one commentator because of the way they gelled. Signed from Sheffield United for £100,000 in 1967, Jones was the perfect counterpoint to the more stylish Clarke – a point he was quick to acknowledge. 'I was a bustling, hard-working type of player, whereas Allan had more flair,' he remembered. 'Our characters were very different as well. I've always been a placid person, but he could be quite volatile.'

It is not unfair to Jones to suggest most of the would-be strikers in the schoolyard opted to be Clarke. He had the arrogant swagger, whereas Jones was the honest hustler. Nice guys even finished last in the third form. These two were different sides of the same coin. Clarke was the blond-haired, lean pipe-cleaner, his shirtcuffs pulled down over his hands, elbows held out wide like an anorexic Eddie Gray. His celebration, the single hand held aloft, became his trademark. You can keep Jimmy Floyd Hasselbaink's gouty somersault or Peter Beagrie's Olga Korbutisms: Clarke's celebration was pure and simple class, just like the player himself. He scored all manner of goals, but I will always remember Clarke charging in on goal, outfoxing the keeper with a sleight of foot and bodyswerve, and walking the ball in. 'The best player I've ever seen running in on goal,' said Revie. Jones was crucial to Leeds' success, but will forever be remembered as the redhead who did his shoulder in during the 1972 FA Cup final. Somehow it was significant that Jones got injured while Clarke was underlining his legendary status. I suppose it is the role of some players to be loved and others to be idolised. That's just the way it goes.

'Striker and goalkeeper are the two hardest positions on a football pitch,' says Clarke with utter conviction. I am not about to argue. 'If you're a goalkeeper and you mess up, then you pick the ball out of the back of the net. If you're a striker and you miss, you're the worst player in the world. I'm lucky. I was born with a gift. I can score goals. That's my business. No coach or manager can ever teach you that.

It's a God-given talent. Normally, I would say it takes a full season for a strike partnership to build up any sort of understanding, but Mick and I clicked straight away. He was the target man and I used to drop off and roam around midfield. We had great balance. It was telepathic. My first game was in the Charity Shield against Man City, who I'd lost to in the previous year's FA Cup final with Leicester. We hit it off straight away and the following week I scored on my League début in a 2–1 win over Spurs.'

Clarke still sees the man he calls Jonah and accepts that the older man did much of the donkey work in the partnership. 'I bumped into Frank McLintock a few years ago,' he recalls. 'I'd been to a Leeds game with Billy. Frank says, "How's your mate these days?" I look at Billy and say, "He's here," but Frank says, "No not him, your strike partner." I tell him Jonah's fine and Frank says, "Was he mad or what?" I looked a bit blank and he says, "There were so many times a ball was running out of play and he'd chase it. It was obvious nobody could catch it, but he kept running all the same, and because he was running I had to track him just in case. He'd never catch it, but he never gave up. I used to think 'I could do without this, I could save me energy'. He was daft as a bat." I laughed. That was Jonah. When he retired, Joe Jordan took over and it was never the same. The only thing that disappoints me is that we never played for England together. When I got in the England side I played with them all – Jimmy Greaves, Peter Osgood, Geoff Hurst, but never Jonah. And make no mistake about it, we were the most feared partnership in Europe. No question.'

One year on from their FA Cup-winning combination and Clarke and Jones were back at Wembley. This time their opponents were Sunderland. I was four. On the evening news they flashed up a picture of a red, white and hairy team and my dad swore at the television. I would like to say I was interested, but I was four. These days it is fashionable for thirtysomethings to tell you they have been lifelong fans of this team or that. It's rubbish. As far as I'm aware you cannot buy rosettes in the fallopian tubes and there are no concessions for embryos anywhere in the Premiership. At the age of four I presumed my dad had a downer on the newsreader. I was more concerned with Captain Pugwash and the Wombles, whom most people would have given more chance of beating the mighty Leeds than little, lowly, unfashionable (in every sense: just cop a load of Bobby Kerr who, even for the follically-frenzied days of 1973, looked as if he was metamorphosing into a werewolf) Sunderland.

'It was one of the biggest upsets of all time,' admits Clarke. 'They got an early goal and defended magnificently, but if we'd got one goal we'd have got ten. [Jim] Montgomery had one of those days that keepers have from time to time. It just wasn't to be. At least that year we got to go to the banquet. I remember us getting the coach to the Café Royal and going through London. I was sitting next to Billy and we're sick as you like. I can still vividly remember looking out of the window and seeing grown men with Leeds United scarves crying. Then the gaffer got up at the front of the coach and he said, "Look lads, I know you're disappointed, but you've had a half-decent season." Now in those days every team did four weeks' pre-season training, but the gaffer said, "When we come back in the summer, instead of having four weeks' training, we'll have five. Let's sweat blood."'

Sweat blood they did, and by the time of the first game they were in the peak of health and ready to make amends for all the mickey-taking and amusement their FA Cup final defeat had caused. 'The first match of the season was against Everton,' recalls Clarke. 'Now, they had some players and they'd won the League in 1970. They had Bally, Colin Harvey, Howard Kendall, Gordon West and Brian Labone. Our routine on matchday would be to sit in the players' lounge watching *Football Focus* from 12.30 and then have the team talk. So at 1 p.m. in comes the gaffer. He says, "Right lads, I've been having a little think during the close season. I'd like you to go through the entire season unbeaten." Now we know we're the best, but blimey, to ask that! We look at each other and start asking is it possible, and decide well, yeah it is. But you have to remember that at that time there were eight or nine teams who all fancied their chances of winning the championship. Anyway, we stuffed Everton 5–0 and then went 29 games unbeaten.

'I remember the great Shankly, who had a half-decent side at Liverpool, saying "If someone does not beat Leeds United soon, they'll have the championship wrapped up by Christmas". We were unbeaten in 29 games when we went to Stoke at the end of February and lost 3–2. It had been an incredible run. The following week Don came in and said, "Last week I was very disappointed and I'm going to tell you lads something – if you can't do the business I'm going to get the chequebook out!" He didn't need to say that, because we'd have run through a brick wall for him. He loved us and we loved him. We went out and hammered Spurs, Greavsie and the lot of them.'

In the days of two points for a win, Leeds were nine points clear of second-placed Liverpool, but the fingernails and lead were whittled away simultaneously. Defeats at Liverpool and West Ham straddled an awful 4–1 home defeat by Burnley. Liverpool were suddenly just four points adrift with three games in hand, but they too began to falter and, when Arsenal's Ray Kennedy scored the winner at Anfield, Leeds were guaranteed their second title.

It was perhaps fitting that in the summer of 1974 both Don Revie and Bill Shankly retired from club football. The two great patriarchs of their generation had enjoyed numerous tussles throughout their careers. Their departures within a week of each other meant the League and Cup winners would start the new season with fresh faces. However, while Shankly has been deified ever since, Revie has often been portrayed as a traitorous neurotic. His tactics have repeatedly been maligned by a jaundiced Press, while his decision to quit England for a lucrative overseas coaching job ended up with a High Court judge declaring his conduct a 'sensational, outrageous example of disloyalty, breach of duty, discourtesy and selfishness'.

'There's no doubt he was the right man for the England job,' insists Clarke as he pours another coffee. 'Billy and I often used to talk about it. He was a man who took Leeds from the depths of the Second Division and built one of the greatest sides this country has ever seen, or is ever likely to. Now, Sir Matt Busby and Bill Shankly were great managers and did great things for Manchester United and Liverpool, but Don Revie was just as good and he has never received the recognition he deserved. I don't know why that is, but it's a fact. People can say what they want, but we know. The players know.

'He built an incredible spirit. I used to love the bingo sessions and the carpet bowls. It brought us all closer together. People ask me what is my greatest memory from my days at Leeds and they expect me to say scoring in the FA Cup final, or winning the championship, or the European trophies. The truth is, my best memory was just turning up in the morning for training and having a crack with the lads. We had some characters and there was lots of leg-pulling. One day I remember we were all in for our salt massages. Big Jack takes a towel and goes into the bog with *The Sun*. Now the toilets don't have a roof on, so me and Gilesey got a bucket of ice-cold water and followed him. So we're there, looking down at Jack, and it's not a pretty sight, he's naked and there's that big bald head with a strand of hair swept across like he did. Anyway, Gilesy chucks the water on him and we rush back to the dressing-rooms, which are across the corridor. Everyone's pissing themselves, but there's no sign of Jack. About five minutes later he comes in. "Anyone who goes to the toilet is a dead man," he says. Then there's a pause before he says, "And anyway, you missed me." Like hell we did. He was soaked. We all just cracked up.

'People say they can see a similarity between the current Leeds side and our team. The one thing I can see that's the same is this spirit of togetherness and that's a good start. We were a family. The other year I was on that *Fantasy Football* show with Frank Skinner. Peter Bonetti, the Chelsea keeper, was on with me and Brian Labone, the old Everton captain. Brian asked me if I ever saw any of the old lads and I told him we had about four reunions a year. He said, "Christ, I knew you were close on the pitch, but I didn't know you were all mates." He couldn't believe it. He didn't see anyone from Everton, which I thought was a bit sad. That's the way we were, though. I'd never seen a spirit like it. You couldn't have fallen out with a team-mate if you'd tried.

'Don was responsible for creating that atmosphere. His attention to detail was incredible. He always liked us to be smart and made us wear a collar and tie. His attitude was, if you look smart you play smart. Some teams would just turn up in their tracksuits and the like, but we were different. Don wanted us to be the best in every way and that rubbed off on us. I wanted to be the best striker in the business and every time I walked on to a football pitch I believed I would score.'

It is a curious twist of fate that, in the season after Revie's departure, Leeds made it to their only European Cup final. The nearest Revie had got had been the semi-final defeat by Celtic in 1970, but mild-mannered Jimmy Armfield – 'a lovely man but a bit too nice', according to Clarke – took Leeds all the way in 1975. This was the year my dad introduced me to Leeds United. He did so in the semi-final against

Barcelona. I wondered what the fuss was all about. Dad tried to reason with me, telling me about all the great players I was watching. But to the initiated youth, Cruyff was a dog show and I was distinctly unimpressed. This was probably why we ended up in that Cornish cottage with no television on the day of the final. In Dad's despair at his son's ignorance, we were all made to suffer. But then, every Leeds fan suffered on that night. And how.

'The one thing we all wanted was the European Cup,' says Clarke. 'I remember watching the great Real Madrid side on the box when I was a kid. It was brilliant. When Don took over he changed the Leeds kit from blue to all-white, because he wanted us to be viewed in the same way people looked at Real Madrid. I think he did a half-decent job of doing that.

'The final against Bayern Munich was another game where we were done. Franz Beckenbauer brought me down for a definite penalty, but the ref didn't give it. Then he handled it in the area, but the ref didn't give that either. We were all over them. Gerd Muller, a great goalscorer, must have made it over the half-way line twice, which shows the amount of pressure we had. After the break the bell sounds and we go back out on to the pitch. Now it's traditional for both sides to come out together, but we have to wait for what seems like a lifetime before Beckenbauer brings his side out. Over the years I got into the habit of looking at players' faces at the start of the second half to gauge their feelings. You can tell if players are scared or if they're confident. Well, I looked into Beckenbauer's eyes and then into Muller's and I could tell they knew they were getting murdered. And then Peter Lorimer scores a perfectly good goal, which the ref chalks off for offside. It was incredible. They ended up winning 2–0 and it was the worst feeling I've ever had in football – that and the time we lost at Wolves and missed out on the Double. We couldn't believe it.'

Those strikes from Franz Roth and Muller sealed Leeds' fate and the night ended in shame when rioting fans ripped up seats and fought with the Parisian police. In the aftermath Leeds were banned from Europe for four years. 'To be fair, it wasn't our fans who started it,' says Clarke. 'The French police were the ones to blame. The things we heard afterwards from normal, lovely people, middle-aged women and familes – it was just awful.'

Maybe Clarke's partisanship is understandable, but there is no doubt some Leeds fans disgraced themselves and the club. Prior to the game, the *Yorkshire Post*'s Terry Brindle wrote: 'The French police are ruthlessly efficient in dealing with crowd disturbances, but I fear they could have their work cut out tonight.' He then described the Leeds fans as 'noisy, chanting and drunk, all unkempt and boisterous. There is one corner of a foreign city which may well be forever sorry that the Leeds United lunatic fringe paid a visit.'

There were more than 200 tracksuited judo experts from the Paris Police Sports Club in the stadium as a precautionary measure. When Bayern's lap of honour arrived at the Leeds section, the players were pelted with bottles and cans, while seats were ripped up and used as weapons in the running battles with the police. Bobby Collins, an interested onlooker, was punched in the face. Sepp Maier, the Bayern and West Germany goalkeeper, said: 'The Leeds crowd were more of a danger to me than the Leeds forwards.'

Nevertheless, many in the Leeds contingent put the blame on the police. 'They enjoyed getting into a fight,' claimed one fan. 'I was beaten over the head and back, my clothes were torn from me, and I was thrown into the moat around the pitch.' Another said the trouble started when a single fan tried to get to the pitch. 'About six policemen beat him with truncheons and then others tried to get to him to help.'

However, Leeds' goose was well and truly cooked. A 13-year-old fan admitted: 'On the way back to the coach I smashed a few windows. I was so mad at being cheated out of the goal.' Billy Bremner and Jimmy Armfield insisted the majority of fans had been superb, but UEFA were outraged – not least by the way the Leeds players rushed to their fans at the end and applauded them. UEFA secretary Hans Bangerter said: 'That was totally inexcusable and has been taken into consideration.' Leeds, who had already been fined £500 following a pitch invasion in Brussels when they faced Anderlecht in an earlier round, were quickly punished. Their reputation was sealed. Leeds' immense achievements would now always carry riders about their gamesmanship and their violent fans.

As a footnote to the Paris riots, it is worth remembering that when Leeds fans went on the rampage it was Leeds who got banned; but when Liverpool fans rioted at Heysel every club in England were excluded. It is facts such as this which have added to the Leeds fans' paranoia. Whether it be the FA refusing to shift matches, dodgy referees or the vilification of Don Revie, your average Leeds fan seems to have reasonable proof that the world and his rabid dog are against him.

'I've often wondered about that referee in Paris,' says Clarke. 'It was his last game before he retired and if I'd been Jimmy Armfield I think I'd have objected to that. There were some bad things happening in Europe. I remember playing for England against Italy in Turin and we lost 2–0. Both Italian goals had been a good ten yards offside, and after the game Alf Ramsey found out that the referee and both linesmen have been given brand new Fiat cars. I'll say no more.'

With Leeds banned from Europe, Don Revie departed and Mick Jones forced into premature retirement (through a knee injury which had cruelly forced him to miss the European Cup final), the end of an era was fast approaching. According to Clarke, it finally arrived in September 1976 when Billy Bremner played his last game for the club. 'When Billy left to go to Hull it affected me more than when the gaffer left,' he says. 'When Billy left it was never the same. The heart had been ripped out of the club. He was my mate and he was gone. It hit me really hard.'

Clarke uses a striking example, pardon the pun, to highlight what Bremner brought to Leeds. 'In those days we had the Home Internationals and you had to make sure you beat Scotland because there were quite a few Scottish lads at Leeds. In 1973 we beat them 5–0 at Hampden Park. Near the end I'd just knocked the ball off and I was exposed with Billy charging towards me. I thought, "Oh no, I'm going to get clattered here." But suddenly, when he's about three yards away from me, he stops. I couldn't believe it. Afterwards I asked him how he was and he said he was glad to be going back to play for a decent team at Leeds. Then I mentioned what had happened near the end and I asked why he'd backed off. He said, "Allan, the game was lost by then and I need you in my team for Leeds United on Saturday." I thought, fair enough; but then he added, "Mind you, if it'd been 0–0 I'd have killed you."'

A couple of years after Bremner walked out of Elland Road, Clarke followed him. The injuries had been piling up and the countless games when he played with injections to cancel out the pain had taken their toll. 'I came back from an operation and scored and the Kop were singing "Clarkie's back", but I knew I was finished. I lost my speed over ten yards and that's fatal for a striker. Peter Lorimer said I should hang on for a testimonial because I had two years left on my contract and I was due one, but that would have been cheap money and that's never been my way. So I took over at Barnsley as player-manager. I must have been daft.'

Certainly, having won 19 England caps, a title, an FA Cup and a Fairs Cup, it was something of a culture shock to drop down into the Fourth Division. However, Clarke proved a success, got Barnsley promoted and then returned to Elland Road as manager in September 1980. 'Leeds were second bottom and I'd sent someone to do a report on them,' he recalls. 'They'd come back and said a major rebuilding job was needed, but I was promised £2 million to spend, so I took the job. I brought on some good players, people like David Seaman, Denis Irwin, John Sheridan and Scott Sellars. Youth has always been my way, although I did put a couple of years on Eddie Gray's career by moving him to full-back. He didn't have the legs any more, but he could still play.'

He did buy some players, however. Gray's younger brother, Frankie, came back from Nottingham Forest for £300,000, while the mercurial Peter Barnes arrived for £900,000. 'I fancied Frankie, so I rang Cloughie, but I didn't want to let on who I was after. So I asked him if John Robertson was available. He said, "Not a chance." I mentioned a couple of others and then said, "Well what about Frank Gray?" and he said "Maybe". I knew I'd got him then and we arranged to meet. Peter Taylor did most of the talking, while Cloughie just sat there watching me. I deliberately got there late and I refused a glass of sherry, which was my drink then, and that impressed him. I'd done my homework and knew they had no money and I ended up getting Frank for £150,000 less than we'd sold him for three years earlier. Not a bad bit of business, but I never had the £2 million I was promised.'

It all ended sourly when Leeds were relegated and Clarke was sacked to be replaced by Eddie Gray and then Bremner. 'I'm not bitter about it, but it does rankle,' he says. 'Why weren't we given the same backing that Howard Wilkinson was? I mean, he was given millions of pounds to spend, whereas we'd had to do it on a shoestring. I had the nucleus of a decent side and if I'd got the backing I could have done something. When Billy got the job the first thing he did was to go to the directors and say, "You should have stuck with Allan. He'd have got you promoted if you'd had the patience."

'Billy and I fancied working together in management, but it just never happened. I think we'd have been a good team. I was like Cloughie, whereas Billy was more like Taylor. I had no time for directors and I'd be the one with my arms round someone's throat, while Billy would be saying "Now, now, Mr Chairman, he's not really a bad lad."'

Bremner and Clarke as good cop, bad cop? It's an interesting idea. A sort of Danny Glover and Mel Gibson for the football classes. With that thought we conclude our chat. Clarke has been unnecessarily generous with his time and after a couple of hours we shake hands. He is off to see his 90-year-old dad on the way back to Scunthorpe. I watch him walk through reception with that familiar loping gait. The businessmen with their cloned suits, spreadsheets and mobile phones are oblivious to the living legend winding his way through them. There is even a workman wearing a Leeds away shirt and a pair of decaying jeans, who does not raise an eyebrow as the King exits. 'Allan Clarke has left the building,' I am tempted to shout, but of course I don't. Instead I ask the woman behind the bar for the bill. Nevertheless, I cannot help feeling this is another example of the injustice that has plagued Leeds over the years. Clarke's company has underlined how unlucky Leeds were in the '70s. A point here and a goal there and they would have been Double winners, European champions, and had multiple FA Cups. Fixture congestion, the FA, referees from hell and a raft of backhanders conspired to ensure they never gained such rewards. And the media have relished rubbishing those achievements, along with the memory of Revie, Bremner and Clarke ever since. We wuz robbed.

The woman hands me the bill. It's £5.90 for coffee for two. I suddenly know how Sniffer feels.

LUCAS RADEBE & ALBERT JOHANNESON
– Nailing Colour to the Mast

The moment to bridge the chasms that divide us has come.

NELSON MANDELA

On Tuesday, 15 March 2000, Jonathan Woodgate and Lee Bowyer were charged with grievous bodily harm and affray in connection with an assault on an Asian student, Sarfraz Najeib, outside the Majestyk nightclub in Leeds city centre. The FA immediately suspended the pair from England duties, while David O'Leary insisted he would still pick them unless there came a point when they were found guilty. The police had already revealed that they were treating the incident – which left Najeib hospitalised with a broken nose, broken leg and scarred face – as racially motivated. Two other Leeds players, Michael Duberry and Tony Hackworth, were bailed pending further inquiries. Curtains twitched in the House of Football as a black cloud descended on Elland Road.

Two days earlier Leeds had played at Bradford, a city with some 97,000 black and Asian residents. Prior to that game the clubs' chairmen appealed for calm, knowing an already volatile meeting could become a powderkeg with the spectre of race hatred looming. 'It's important for football in general – not just Bradford and Leeds – that we include racial minorities at our clubs,' said Bradford's Geoffrey Richmond. His Leeds counterpart, Peter Ridsdale, added: 'The police announcement that it was definitely a racist attack would have been better left unsaid. Those statements have increased tensions in what has been a vacuum between the incident itself and the eventual outcome.' At the game a group of Bradford fans vented their feelings by hoisting a banner proclaiming 'RACISM – ALIVE AND KICKING!'

In a quieter part of West Yorkshire is Lawnswood Cemetery. It is a vast, sprawling ocean of death. A riot of marble headstones. Wind chimes sound as passing bells. I feel strange as I walk across dead-man's land. The place is chock full of the dear and departed. It's a tenement tower of silence. I get a grip of myself. 'What's wrong with you?' I say. 'Are you man or mausoleum mouse?'

The man in the office is incongruously cheerful and wears a bright orange tie. Prozac's answer to undertaking. 'You want to see Albert,' he says and I nod, somewhat disconcerted by his phraseology. He leads me to plot 926 and I note graves spread out from us in all directions like petrified ripples. 'We get quite a few people wanting to see him. It was an unmarked grave for a while, but then the club paid for a headstone.' He leaves me in peace and I kneel before the mottled grey monument to Albert Johanneson (1942–95). There is part of a poem by the writer, actress and civil rights activist Maya Angelou inscribed in black on the stone. It is a poignant and apt epitaph:

> Out of the huts of history's shame
>   I rise
> Up from a past that's rooted in pain
>   I rise
> I am a black ocean leaping and wide
> Welling and swelling I bear in the tide
> Bringing the gifts that my ancestors gave
> I am the dream and the hope of the slave
>   I rise
>   I rise
>   I rise

A couple of lines have been omitted: 'Leaving behind nights of terror and fear, I rise into a daybreak that's wondrously clear.' Maybe they would have hurt too much, as the nights of terror and fear ultimately proved too numerous for Johanneson to bear. The first black player to appear in an FA Cup final died in an alcoholic haze in an indifferent Leeds tower block in September 1995. The body lay undetected for several days until neighbours were alerted by the smell. It is part of history's shame that Johanneson, the flying winger for Leeds in the 1960s, a South African who brought numerous gifts to the British game, ended up a slave to his depression. The black ocean had drowned himself in booze and drugs.

One hour earlier I was watching Lucas Radebe and Lee Bowyer messing around on a motorised scooter at Leeds' Thorp Arch training ground. I had just finished interviewing Radebe and he told me how he had read all about Albert Johanneson. 'It was sad that he died before I got the chance to meet him,' said Radebe. 'It's one of my regrets.'

The similarities between Johanneson and Radebe are as evident as the differences. They were both black South Africans, who escaped the poverty of their homeland to become heroes in West Yorkshire. They were reared on institutionalised violence and prejudice, but managed to strike out into a clear daybreak and find a better life. Yet while Radebe is reaping great financial rewards and, at the time of our meeting, is being mooted as a possible Footballer of the Year, Johanneson's story is among the saddest in sport.

> Albert Johanneson was frightening on the wing and used to turn defenders inside out. He was fast, clever with the footwork, very accurate with crosses, and had a terrific shot. I always thought that he did not get a fair deal from the media because he was black. They were forever on about him being the first black player to do this, or the first black player to do that. They completely overlooked the fact that he was a terrific player and deserved recognition as a human being and a professional footballer.

That obituary from Billy Bremner, quoted in *Bremner!*, shows the affection in which Johanneson was held by his peers. But it oversimplifies the race issue. In 1960s Britain neither Albert Johanneson nor the media could forget that he was black. This was the Britain which spawned Alf Garnett, a national treasure and racist bigot. Signs proclaiming the blunt message 'No blacks, No Irish, No dogs' could be seen in parts of the country. The 'fuzzy wuzzy' was seen as an imposter, a lazy infiltrator with a habit of stealing the white man's jobs and women. For Johanneson, a sometimes timorous man who found himself thousands of miles from home, his blackness was a barrier to acceptance.

When he signed from Germiston Colliers in 1961 it caused a major stir in Leeds. At the time my mother was working for Wimpey just across from Elland Road. 'I wasn't really into football then, but I remember Albert Johanneson,' she told me. 'It was the talk of the town.' One can only presume that that was largely due to Johanneson's skin colour, as he arrived in Leeds as an unknown, just a few weeks after Don Revie took over as manager. He was a left-winger and was blessed with blinding pace and a bag of tricks which would astound both fans and his colleagues. Johnny Giles would later claim Johanneson had the raw natural talent to put him up there with the likes of George Best but, like the Irish maverick, the diminutive African found the pressure of fame too great.

However, between 1961 and the 1965 FA Cup final, when Bobby Collins claims Johanneson froze, he was the exotic magician in an essentially dour side. His freakish ball skills were an anomaly in a team of artisans toiling at the wrong end of the Second Division. In 1964 Johanneson was Leeds' top scorer, netting a memorable strike against Newcastle when he killed a long ball with his peerless control, waltzed past a trio of flailing defenders and slid the ball past the keeper. That was Johanneson at his best. Dazzling, enchanting and brilliant, the swish of the svelte striker descending on goal was a sound to be feared.

However, Johanesson's time in England in the early '60s was not easy. When an Everton player called him a 'black bastard' during a game, Johanneson complained to Revie. His manager's response was, 'Well, call him a white bastard back.' For a personality plagued by self-doubt, such a ready dismissal of the racism that was common in the game at the time was hardly helpful.

Leeds teacher Paul Eubanks has tried to preserve the memory of Johanneson. As part of the Euro 96 celebrations he decided to put on an exhibition about his hero at his Leeds school. He asked each Premiership club to donate a shirt signed by their black players and wrote to scores of black players. It was hard work. Sheffield Wednesday even accused him of being racist. Mark Bright was the only player to write back. 'Nobody seemed to want to remember this man who paved the way for black players,' says Eubanks. Eventually he did get some support. Sheffield Wednesday, Manchester City, Middlesbrough, Southampton, Liverpool and Leeds provided shirts. Viv Anderson, assistant manager at Middlesbrough, invited Eubanks and his class up to The Riverside. 'I just wanted to make sure he was remembered,' he says. 'I'm a 42-year-old black guy and in the 1960s black footballers were non-existent. I never wanted to be Denis Law or George Best in the playground, I wanted to be Albert. I was besotted with him. I'd never seen such skills. He was a genius, but people just think of him now as being an alcoholic.'

On his début against Swansea, Johanneson produced the perfect cross from which Jack Charlton scored. As his team-mates ran towards him to congratulate him, he froze. 'Albert came from South Africa where it only meant one thing when white men chased after a black man,' says Eubanks. 'I've spoken to people who knew him in the '60s and they say he had a mental block at that point. He went through incredible mental torment.'

The confused Johanneson also refused to have a white apprentice clean his boots until Don Revie insisted. On another occasion he carefully avoided jumping into the communal bath with the rest of the team until they grew impatient, grabbed him and threw him in. 'It must have been terrible for him,' says Eubanks. 'He'd play at grounds and there'd be the monkey noises and the bananas, but he was suddenly allowed to go places he hadn't been and talk to people he couldn't even look at before.'

After the FA Cup final, Johanesson's career hit a hiatus from which it never fully recovered. He was all too aware that he had been the first black player to appear in a final and he knew he had failed. Leeds had lost and Johanneson knew he was partly to blame. He would find his first team chances became rarer and rarer as the prodigious talent of Eddie Gray and the arrival of Mike O'Grady knocked him down the pecking order. The Black Flash, as he had become known, dimmed.

Johanneson undoubtedly had the talent to match the best of them, but he lacked the confidence and iron will of his contemporaries. When I met Gray, he told me he had no doubts whatsoever about his own ability and that nobody was going to prevent him from getting into the first team. Such self-belief was alien to Johanneson, who was raised in a divided country whose whole political ethos revolved around the fact that he was an inferior. Gray's faith was nurtured, Johanneson's was neutered. 'On his day Albert could do any defender anywhere, but he lacked consistency,' said another team-mate, Norman Hunter. 'It was unfortunate that he was around at the same time as Eddie Gray. Albert was one of Don Revie's most promising signings, but when Eddie got a grip of his place on the wing, something had to give and that was Albert.'

Though Billy Bremner and Jack Charlton acted as his on-field minders, Johanneson literally had his faith battered out of him by caustic hitmen. Some people began to question his heart for the fight. History's shame is that it has marked him down as the forerunner of a stereotype – the silky-skilled but soft-spirited, glove-wearing black footballer. The doubters added to his insecurity, though Hunter again dismissed such talk: 'Albert was a brave player and took a lot of punishment,' he said. Nevertheless, Johanneson's name will always be synonymous with underachievement and Peter Lorimer was another to suggest that he never fulfilled his potential. 'Albert could be the scourge of defences and was a joy to watch, but he never quite achieved what he could have,' he said.

Lorimer would be one of those who tried hard to help Johanneson when he ended up a poverty-stricken drunk, but he prefers to remember him as a multi-talented footballer. 'We tried to help him,' he says. 'We wanted to get him to join the association, but it was no good. Albert would just go missing.' Bobby Collins, never one to suffer fools, also has fond memories of his former team-mate. 'Albert could fly,' he told me. 'I would put the ball on the spot for him and when he was in full stride, there wasn't anyone was going to catch him.'

Johanneson was not the first black South African to play for Leeds. That honour belongs to Gerry Francis, a former cobbler from Johannesburg who saved all his wages to pay for his passage to England and freedom. Few people now remember Francis, but he was a pioneering light. He arrived in 1956 when Raich Carter's Leeds were back in First Division football at the tenth time of asking and later played a key role in helping to abolish the wage restrictions which the Football League imposed at the time. 'We were prepared to go on strike,' he said. 'Jack Charlton and myself went to Manchester along with Jimmy Hill, Stanley Matthews, Tom Finney and Bobby Charlton to see Alan Hardaker, the League secretary. He told us we had no chance, but less than a year later Johnny Haynes became the first £100-a-week footballer in the country.'

Francis only stayed at Elland Road for four years, but his legacy was more enduring as he was largely responsible in bringing Johanneson to England. 'Albert and I were good friends,' he recalled. 'He was the best man at my wedding. In 1961 we helped Leeds United create a bit of history when we played in the same side against Stoke City. I was on the right wing and Albert was on the left and it was the first time an English First Division side had played with two black players in the same side. It caused quite a stir in the Press at the time.'

Johanneson was an instant hit at Elland Road. One reporter said his uncanny ball control suggested he had been signed from the Harlem Globetrotters, while in the *Yorkshire Post* Eric Stanger described his début as follows: 'The 19-year-old coloured South African got off to a most promising start. He has a good left foot, a great bodyswerve and looked very good when he came infield.'

Howard Wilkinson later claimed he was 'our first glimpse of that kind of silky, soccer player', but the physical nature of football in the '60s only served to undermine his brittle self-belief. Leeds general manager Alan Roberts recalled: 'I remember what happened to him against Tottenham at Elland Road. Cyril Knowles was marking him. Albert was very quick and very skilful but he was a timid sort of a man. Quiet, meek, unassuming. Well, Cyril gave him a hell of a whack in the first five minutes and it put him right off his game.'

Francis left Leeds to join York later in 1961, while Johanneson approached hero status. However, his FA Cup final performance became a weight around his neck and, with his first-team opportunities becoming limited, he began the slippery descent into a gaping chasm whence he would never return. In the late 1960s Johanneson was drinking heavily and smoking marijuana. Later pictures of him show a blubbery, bulbous face place atop a squat, stocky frame. The dashing winger of yesteryear, sweating chocolate balm and exuding exotic vitality, racing around on taut, polished legs, was gone forever. Having followed Francis to Leeds, he also followed him to York in 1970. That fall from the First to Fourth Divisions was a microcosm of his life. He had scored 67 goals in 197 appearances for Leeds, but his playing days were almost over.

Johanneson's marriage broke up and he lived in a tiny council flat. His daughters moved to America. One of them, Alicia, is now researching a book about his life. His later years would see him playing out time as a cadaverous relic. He was a tragedy waiting to happen. Despite Leeds' strong old boys' network, Johanneson somehow slipped through the net and lost touch with most of the people he had known. He died alone.

For a while he lay in an unmarked grave. As part of his exhibition, Eubanks had arranged for an official from the South African High Commission to lay a wreath on his grave. 'I went to see it and was disgusted that there was nothing but a plot number marking the spot,' he said. 'I got in touch with Leeds United and they said they'd pay for a wooden cross while a tombstone was made.'

In the Portakabin where I am interviewing Lucas Radebe, the walls are plastered with photographs of Leeds players. There is Harry Kewell, hair flailing in his wake like an antipodean Bay City Roller; Nigel Martyn, leaping across his goal in a green-and-black blur; and many, many more. There is little room for the walls to breathe under the glossy covering of white and yellow and blue. On a cupboard is a tiny mugshot. It has faded to sepia with time. 'That's Albert Johanneson,' says Dick (the press officer) to Radebe, who studies him. 'My favourite player. He was absolutely brilliant, he was.'

Radebe nods dutifully. Perhaps he realises that in some small way he is indebted to the man in the fading photo. Of course, things are different now. If Radebe is sensible, which he certainly appears to be, he will be able to retire a rich man. To set up this interview I have had to make several calls to the London offices of his South African lawyer. He drives a top-of-the-range Jeep. As captain of a multi-racial South Africa, he is a national hero. There is little chance of this man ending up in squalid poverty in a monolithic rabbit hutch. Radebe has an easy manner, a panoramic smile and a relaxed, carefree attitude. I can't help thinking such characteristics might have saved Johanneson. Yet nobody should suggest Radebe has had it easy.

It was a decade ago when the terrors of Soweto paid a personal visit to Radebe. 'I was driving along with my niece and younger brother, Lazarus, in the car,' he recalls. 'In those days it was rough and there was always violence. You got used to the gunshots because they were constant, so they didn't bother you anymore. But when we heard that sound on that particular day it was different. Nobody saw anything. We just heard an almighty bang. My back was on fire and my leg went numb. I reached back and there was a lot of blood. That's when I knew I'd been shot. I thought "Jesus, this is it, I'm going to die." They shot through the back door of the car and the bullet went through my thigh. The two scars I've got are the best ones to have, because some people don't survive long enough to have scars. I was used to guns being everywhere, but I never expected to get shot while I was driving and I was only a few blocks from my mum's house. I stopped the car and my brother took me to hospital.'

The sniper was never caught and Radebe still does not know the motive behind the attack. 'In those days there was a lot of rivalry between the different clubs,' he says. 'If a player went from one team to another then he would get threatened. I know of a couple of players who were shot because they moved to new clubs. My being shot was not because of that, though. It just came out of the blue. Looking back I think I was very lucky, because the bullet could easily have hit Lazarus, who was only two at the time.'

At the hospital Radebe felt his escape route from this life of civil warfare, fear and discrimination, had been shut off. 'I thought that was me finished,' he recalls with one of those disarming smiles. Even when recounting his brush with death, Radebe is a jolly raconteur and has a tusky white grin that reminds me of a fully extended harpsichord. 'My football was my first concern. When I realised my leg was numb and I had no feeling, I was very worried. I couldn't do anything. I got shot in the hip and the bullet went through my upper thigh. My first question was, "Will my leg be all right?" The doctors had a look and told me how lucky I'd been. The bullet had gone through a bad position where it could have damaged a lot of organs, but luckily it just went through flesh and didn't touch any bones. They said "Your career is secure" and I breathed a sigh of relief.'

After that it may be no surprise that Radebe is now so good-natured. 'I was out for about three months. That made me realise how important life is and makes me appreciate how lucky I am. I savour every day. I was playing for Kaiser Chiefs and everybody wanted to know who was responsible. It was rough then. If *they* got their hands on you then you would not survive.'

Maybe it was incidents such as that which helped Radebe forge an unbreakable resolve and imbue him with a determination to succeed. 'Our parents had high hopes for us all,' he says. 'They wanted us to be doctors or lawyers and earn good money. Life was hard for footballers, because we didn't have any facilities. We grew up treating it as a hobby, not a career, and we'd go for a kickabout in the streets of Soweto after school. In the apartheid days it was very difficult, especially for the blacks. There were no resources and no money. Only violence. There were a few teams, but the people were playing for the love of football, then. There were always a lot of talented players, though. My family all liked sports. My mum was very keen and my dad was a supporter of Kaiser Chiefs, who I later went to play for.'

It was when Radebe had to give up teacher-training studies because of his football that he realised his hobby might develop into something more. 'It was then I knew I would have to make the best of it,' he says. 'I started setting goals and once you reach a certain target you want to go further and further. Going abroad was always going to happen once I went professional. There were a few offers for me, but the owner of Kaiser didn't let me know anything about any of them. Eventually they told me about Leeds and, to be honest, I didn't know anything about them. We had no exposure to English football and the only teams we knew were Man U, Arsenal and Liverpool. I played against Man U and Arsenal for Kaiser Chiefs, so I knew a bit more about them. But when I realised the opportunity to come over was there I knew I could not refuse it. It was great to think that I could make the grade as a footballer, that I could maybe earn a living from something I'd always treated as fun.'

However, the move to Leeds was not a *fait accompli*. Leeds scout Geoff Sleight arranged to fly out to Sydney to watch Radebe play for South Africa against Australia in a couple of friendlies. Radebe knew this was his big chance. 'Two days before we were due to leave for Australia I suffered a very bad ankle injury, so I didn't make the trip,' he says. 'I couldn't believe it. To make it worse, Geoff Sleight had already flown to Australia. He went all that way to watch me play, but I wasn't even in the country. I thought that was it and they didn't come back to look at me. But then they discovered Phil [Masinga] and they took him. Maybe they asked Phil about me, because they decided to take me without ever having seen me play. They took a chance on me and for that I will always respect Howard Wilkinson.'

In the grand scheme of things Leeds had little to lose. Radebe cost a desultory £250,000, which is the equivalent of you or I staking fifty pence each way on Desert Orchid. Radebe was 25 and had plenty of potential, but Leeds were in a state of flux. The memory of the title had been quickly erased by a series of wacky Wilkinsonisms. The magnificent midfield quartet of Batty, Strachan, Speed and McAllister was systematically broken up when Batty got offloaded to Blackburn for £2.75 million and Strachan decamped to Coventry. Wilkinson signed the loose-limbed, loosely-termed footballer Carlton Palmer for the same fee Batty had fetched. Palmer was the Stretch Armstrong of Elland Road. He would gambol around Elland Road like a runaway giraffe. His fans said he covered lots of ground and made some great tackles, but to me these were desperate lunges made when the ball had ricocheted off his spindly, breadstick shins. Palmer was deceptively ineffective, I insisted, while up front we had the oft-maligned Brian Deane. He had his moments and was as lugubrious and graceless as Lee Chapman – but he lacked the latter's finishing skills.

This was the Leeds Radebe joined. It was not the happiest of ships and it took Radebe some time to settle. 'It was a culture shock at first,' he recalls. 'Everything was different. Everything was opposite. The weather, the lifestyle, the attitude, the food. When I first came I was not a full-time pro. I knew it was a great opportunity, but it was very hard for those first few months. I wasn't getting into the first team and I ended up getting very depressed. That first Christmas I nearly went home for good. I was miserable. Imagine training very hard when you haven't any games and the weather is so black. You miss home so much. It was the first time I'd been away from home for a long time and it was not like I was a few hours away. I couldn't just nip back. Me and Phil were in digs in Beeston with Mrs Jones, but we found it hard to cope.'

Just as Johanneson had been fatally undone by a lack of assertiveness, so too Radebe and Masinga kept a low profile in their early days. 'There was a guy at the club at the time called Rob Bowman, who we were very friendly with, but you'd look at the first team and it was full of people like Gordon Strachan and Gary McAllister – big-name players with reputations and lots of experience. We'd just stay back and keep our distance. We didn't want to interfere. I think if England was not so far away I'd have gone home to South Africa and not come back. People don't truly understand how hard it can be. But once I got past Christmas I realised, no, I had to try. I decided to give it until the end of the season and see what happened.'

Ironically, it was Masinga who initially looked the more likely of Leeds' South Africans to make it in the cut and thrust of the Premiership. After Christmas he scored a hat-trick within nine minutes to rescue Leeds from further embarrassment against Walsall in the FA Cup third round at Elland Road. 'Phil did brilliantly for the club,' says Radebe. 'If it hadn't been for the work-permit thing then I think he'd still be playing for us and doing well. He was a quality player.' In the summer of '96 Wilkinson continued to dismantle his title-winning side. Gary Speed was sold to Everton for £3 million and Gary McAllister soon severed the final link with the magical midfield of 1992 when he went to Coventry for £3.5 million. Almost unnoticed, Masinga also exited Elland Road, moving to St Gallen of Switzerland for £500,000. His Leeds career had promised much, delivered a little and left Leeds fans with good memories of the striker. Meanwhile, his compatriot's career was a slow-burning affair as he found himself vying with the likes of John Pemberton and Richard Jobson for a place in the first team. It was a struggle. He fell out of favour with Wilkinson and then a serious knee injury ruled him out for almost an entire season.

'It took a long time to establish myself,' he says. 'When I did get in the team I found it incredibly difficult. It was so fast and frenzied. God, it was terrible. Then I was played in all sorts of positions. My first game was against Sheffield

Wednesday and I played on the right wing.' He removes his baseball cap and scratches his head as if still confused by that selection. 'Christ, right wing! I didn't have a clue. I just got lost in the game. It passed me by and I was drifting all over the park, but Jesus, the atmosphere was good. After that game, which had been terrible for me, I told myself I would give it a real go. I would rather fail, having tried, than not try my best. I started settling down then. I moved out of Mrs Jones's and into my own place with my girlfriend. We settled down and it made life a lot easier. I've never looked back since.'

Yet his early years at Leeds saw the club slumbering from crisis to crisis. The 1996 Coca-Cola Cup final was merely an intermission in the interminable decline of the Wilkinson dynasty. It ended with Aston Villa winning 3–0. Having struck out in my attempts to get a ticket in the Leeds end, I finally paid £60 for a £20 ticket after placing an ad in the classifieds in the *Birmingham Post*. My answerphone was inundated by dodgy Brummies seeking a clandestine rendezvous at M6 service stations. I took a fancy Swiss corkscrew with me to the arranged meeting place as protection. I don't know why I did this. If I came under attack, I suppose I was planning to clip Mr Big's nails while uncorking a bottle of Chardonnay. Luckily, the deal went off without me having to resort to such methods.

The game itself was appalling from a Leeds perspective. The only plus point was the form of Andy Gray, son of Frankie. Needless to say, he would end up sold too. Wilkinson was booed off the Wembley turf by the disgruntled fans. The Brummie next to me kept trying to kiss me. It was a bad day. 'I couldn't believe the way our players performed,' said Wilkinson afterwards. 'I almost wished one of them would take a swing at the referee or they would start fighting among themselves. Anything to show they were actually interested. What should have been a marvellous experience, win or lose, turned into a nightmare. I was emotionally disembowelled, close to walking away from it all.'

The numbers of those wishing to physically disembowel Wilkinson grew as Leeds lost six of their remaining seven games. In one of those, Radebe ended up playing in goal at Old Trafford after an injury to Mark Beeney. To his credit, Leeds only lost 1–0.

'Playing in goal was not a problem for me,' he says. 'When I started off playing football I was so happy just to be involved that I'd go anywhere. So I ended up in goal and won quite a few trophies as a keeper. I played in Inter-State games, but when I went to Kaiser Chiefs it all changed. I played a few games in midfield and then went into the defence. That's when my career began to take off.'

Wilkinson, whose signings had become increasingly eccentric (Ian Rush, Mark Hateley . . .), was inevitably forced to walk away after a 4–0 home defeat by Manchester United the following season. The fact that Eric scored the fourth from the penalty spot and then celebrated as only he could, in front of a manically frustrated Kop, made Wilkinson's position untenable. 'The fans were really hurt to see Cantona, a fantastic player who they'd let go, rubbing it in,' said former favourite Frank Worthington. Wilkinson was understandably upset. He had breathed new life into Leeds, won the First and Second Division Championships, and restored some pride to a club that had been in cold storage for a decade. But he had to go. Having rewritten the script, he had lost the plot.

Under George Graham, a man with a fetish for defenders, Radebe would flourish and become established as one of the mainstays of the team. When Graham left and David O'Leary took over, Radebe continued to improve. Whereas a few years earlier we had Ian Rush, a greying scouser as skipper, we now had the captain, hero, role model and idol of the new South Africa.

Radebe relishes captaining a free South Africa. 'It was 1992 when we were readmitted to international football and I have enjoyed every second of it,' he says. 'Growing up in Soweto, I could never imagine that I would ever play in a multi-racial side. The difference those years of struggle have made cannot be counted. The change in attitudes has been incredible. You start to enjoy life more. At first it was strange, realising you could go where you wanted, that people did not look at you in the same way.'

He is even bosom buddies with Nelson Mandela. In 1996, as he prepared to captain the South African team, Bafana Bafana, to victory in the African Nations Cup finals, Radebe received a letter:

> Dear Lucas,
> I have been observing with interest the preparations of Bafana Bafana for the defence of the trophy and your preparations for the 1998 World Cup. As is the case with all transitions and moments of change, a turbulence will always occur, and it's how we conduct ourselves in such situations that our true character shows.
>   I charge you to go to Burkina Faso to represent your country and your people and of course to pursue the cause of African Unity. On behalf of the millions of South Africans, I wish you success and good luck. We shall be with you through the finals.
> Nelson Mandela.

'I have met the former President and he is a great, great man,' he says. 'I count him as a friend. We have lunch together sometimes. When we played in the national team he would always come to our camp and say a few words. We called it *Madiba*, which is his nickname, Magic, because every time he talked to us we would go out and win. In the African Nations Cup we got to the semi-final against Nigeria but he did not come. We lost. There was no magic. As a boy, I'd sung his name like the other black children. Everyone would cry for him to be freed from prison. It was incredible when I then met him. In normal life you do not get the chance to meet great icons like that, someone who made enormous difference to the lives of so many people. It was a unique opportunity and it came to me through football.'

The demasking of apartheid has not solved South Africa's problems overnight. There is still racism, poverty, violence and a crumbling infrastructure. 'I love Soweto and am proud of my country, but I am glad I play in England,' says Radebe. 'By being a success over here I provide hope for other Africans. They look to the players in Europe and they can see that if you work hard and are determined, there is a way out. It is the Africans playing in Europe who are held up as symbols for the people back home.'

After a difficult initiation, Radebe is now settled in West Yorkshire. He has a family in Linton and his six sisters and five brothers have all visted from South Africa. 'It's such a breakthrough to be able to see the world,' he says. However, I wonder whether he has ever experienced the racism that still lingers like a malevolent cancer. I recall those dim, dark days in the 1980s when the National Front merrily plied their wares outside the ground, when fans would make monkey noises at black players and when John Barnes was pelted with bananas. In the foreword to Phil Vasili's book *Colouring Over The White Line*, Shaka Hislop told how, when he was at Newcastle, a team-mate confessed to chanting racist slogans when he was a young boy. Hislop reasoned that his team-mate had been ignorant rather than overtly racist. A passive fascist, if you like. He is probably right, too. The prevalence of racism in pre-1990s Britain meant people became inured to it, just as television images of corpses and killings no longer inspire the revulsion they once did. The racists are Pavlovian dogs, salivating at the sight of the black man.

Much has been done to stamp out racism and Leeds United have been at the forefront of such efforts. Prior to that Bradford game, Geoffrey Richmond said: 'Leeds and Bradford are leading the way in the fight against racism. In fact, it's ironic that racism is playing a part in the potential tensions linked to this game.' Ridsdale did his best to dismiss allegations of racism at Elland Road. 'In the 1960s we were one of the first clubs to employ a black player in Albert Johanneson. We now have a very good young Asian player called Harpal Singh in our reserve team.'

Nevertheless, there is still an unthinking minority in search of a morality. I attend the game at Leicester, which effectively ends Leeds' title hopes. It is their ninth game in a month, just three days since they ensured their passage to the semi-finals of the UEFA Cup. At Filbert Street, Bowyer is injured and Leeds are awful. They lose 2–1. Manchester United are suddenly seven points clear at the top of the table. 'You've got a town full of Pakis,' chant some of the visiting fans, as they do each year. As John Barnes said: 'While there is racism in society, there will always be racism in football.' As if to prove the point, the day after I meet Radebe, the black Liverpool striker Emile Heskey is racially abused and spat at during an England Under-21s game against Yugoslavia. The previous year Heskey turned down a £10 million move to Leeds. One of the reasons he cited was the racial abuse he received from so-called supporters at Elland Road. The FA demands an inquiry into the Yugoslav incident, but what is there to say? The fact of the matter is, more than 100 years since Arthur Wharton became the first black player in Britain, racism is still alive. Those Bradford fans were right.

'I have never really encountered much prejudice in England,' says Radebe, though I suspect there are some memories lurking behind those crystal-clear eyes and the words 'really' and 'much'. He then backs up my suspicions by adding a rider: 'But I made up my mind when I came here that nothing would destroy me. I have a God-given talent, so use it. This club has a great future and I want to be part of it.'

And so he shall. When he does finally hang up his boots he should be a wealthy man. He plans to give himself back to his people. 'After football I would like to share my experiences with young players at home. When I started out I had role models and I know many people look to me in that way now. I would like to go back to South Africa and pass on my knowledge to the kids. I want to tell them that they, too, have an opportunity to reach their dream.'

Radebe is the 'dream and the hope of the slave'; Johanneson the warning that Britain can be just as pitiless and brutal a place as Soweto. I re-read the inscription on Albert's tombstone and leave. An overlong hearse worms its way along the adjoining road. The next day I am still thinking about Albert Johanneson. I pop into Waterstone's and pluck a book of poems from a shelf. *The Complete Works of Maya Angelou*. I flick to 'Still I Rise' and recognise the words there. I also read a verse which I feel could have come from the mouth of Johanneson himself:

> Do you want to see me broken?
> Bowed head and lowered eyes?
> Shoulders falling down like teardrops
> Weakened by my soulful cries.

So the next time you abuse a player, black or white, take a step back and remember Albert Johanneson. They may be megastars these days, but money cannot buy the skin of a rhino. The next time you verbally bully some player, remember The Black Flash and think of what Billy Bremner said. Black or white, great or small, rich or poor, they are still human beings.

BILLY BREMNER – Statuesque

You can't put into words what Billy Bremner meant to football.

SIR ALEX FERGUSON

ric once said that the public don't forget those that make them dream. It was typical of Eric to say something like that. Most players are a mess of vaporous cliches. Terrified of providing a headline to alchemic reporters, they submerge themselves in tedious twaddle and uniform irrelevance. I watch *Match of the Day* every week in the vain hope of hearing David Beckham tell John Motson: 'Liverpool? Bunch of tossers. Titi Camara sounds like a dodgy nightclub act, Robbie Fowler's got a face like burnt scrubland and, as for Michael Owen, he smokes fifty tabs a day, is cruel to animals and that goal against the Argies was a fluke.' Of course, it will never happen. Footballers have media training these days, which is a laugh in itself. In fact, I might try and get a job as a media trainer for footballers. Talk about an easy job. 'Right lads, repeat after me: "Very much so, Brian". That'll be £5,000 each, please. Thanks Harry. Haven't you got anything smaller?'

However, these monosyllabic miserablists do share Eric's ability to make us dream. They would no doubt be lost by Eric's statement that Pelé's pass to Carlos Alberto, to set up Brazil's fourth goal in the 1970 World Cup final, was exactly the same as the poetry of the young Arthur Rimbaud. And while Eric had artistic airs and graces, the modern footballer would probably be bemused by the poetry of Pam Ayres. Nevertheless, by their feats and feet, their skill, goals and capacity for drama, footballers still transport us from the ordinary world.

The first player to make me dream in such a way was Billy Bremner. He knew what it was all about. 'Days when you can cry your eyes out and walk on air,' he said. 'There is nothing to compare.' It was the same for the fans as for the players, although in the days of Billy Bremner the line between the two was distinctly muddier. Bremner lived for Leeds United and would have died for the cause. He played for 17 years and then came back to manage them in the 1980s. Gary

McAllister recalled meeting Bremner during his time at Elland Road. 'He was a real supporter,' said McAllister. 'He was Leeds United,' corrected Don Revie.

When I first started going to Leeds games, Bremner was still there. In those days Saturdays were swathed in rose-tinted romance. I would play for my school team in the morning and then go home, the drying mud coagulating on my legs. I would read *Roy of the Rovers* in the bath and then leave the black shroud of the footballer forming mystic patterns in the plastic tub. Having been steadily marinated in earth, I'd have fish and chips. (As an exiled Yorkshireman, that is one of the things I miss most about the place. It's the batter, you see. Beef dripping reacts with the vinegar to produce northern nectar.) And then it was off to town. We'd drop my mother off on the Headrow so she could go shopping in Schofield's and we'd wind our secret way through the backstreets to the hill above Elland Road.

You'd start to see the odd scarf hanging from a window and you would begin to get excited. The radio would chatter away with its predictions and previews. My dad, my brother and I would then join the yellow, white and blue human python which snaked down the hill towards those four pylons which stretched like beneficent beanstalks into the grey skies. Our seats were in the North-East stand. As season-ticket holders it meant we were unfortunate enough to sit next to the same people each week. One of these would be mute for long periods, occasionally punctuating his silence with the catchphrase, 'You black enamel get'. This was directed at the referee and, even now, I don't quite understand it. Then there was the woman with the blue rinse and the blue mouth. She was one of life's great complainers, a moaning moth who would unfailingly be drawn to 'the flaming hell'. She would gripe about everything under the sun – the buses, her pension, Kevin Hird's haircut. She was the sort of person who could win the top prize on *Who Wants To Be A Millionaire?* and then moan about Chris Tarrant's dress sense.

I always remember the volume, too. In those days the Kop was vibrant and strident. Ear-splitting thunderclaps would resonate around the stadium and it was true that Elland Road was the most intimidating ground in the land for away teams and fans. Sadly, that has all changed now. With more seats, fur coats and expense, the atmosphere at Leeds has changed from those mesmerising days in the '70s. Now the fans say 'Go on, then, entertain me.' In those days the fans wanted to play too.

However, the thing I remember most about Leeds United in my early days, the one thing that stands out above all others, is Billy Bremner. He just looked so out of place. In what was a land of giants to a six-year-old, Billy Bremner was reassuringly short. He just didn't look like a footballer, either. Science teacher, maybe, but footballer? His ginger hair was receding on top and thick and curly on the sides. He looked prematurely middle-aged, and he was a fragile figure as he lined up alongside the likes of Gordon McQueen and Joe Jordan. I was surprised he didn't have leather patches on the elbows of his tracksuit. But then he started to play and you realised Billy Bremner was the footballing equivalent of the Tardis. He was a giant trapped in a dwarf's body. He was aggressive and skilful, fast and fiery, he could shoot like Lorimer, pass like Giles and tackle like Hunter. And he just oozed spirit. Quite simply, Bremner was stunning. The six-year-old sitting in the North-East Stand was dreaming.

Almost a quarter of a century later, I am standing outside a deserted Elland Road, dreaming that my friend the journalist will come up trumps. He is in Spain to cover Manchester United's Champions League quarter-final clash with Real Madrid. He called me the night before to say there was a rumour going around that Eric would be at the match. I had already gleaned the intelligence that Cantona was now living in Barcelona, which I felt was fitting. Barcelona was swamped with art galleries, fine architecture and bohemian Basques, invigorated by gently bubbling Latino temperaments. Eric would be at home. And of course Barcelona was also home to the famous albino gorilla, Snowflake. If you wanted to be different then surely this was the place. Now I suddenly felt there was a chance. Eric would be in Madrid to watch his Manchester United chums in action. The British press would surely be granted an interview. My friend the journalist promised to ask him about Leeds and whether he would be willing to meet me at a time and place to suit him. OK, it was a long shot. But if you had told me I would one day see a gorilla with an orange face and peroxide hair I'd have laughed at that too.

That is in the future. For now I am happy to wallow in the past. Billy Bremner died two years earlier. He had been feeling ill at his home in Conisborough, near Rotherham. He went to hospital in Doncaster, where he was diagnosed as having pneumonia. He died on 7 December 1997. His funeral was a who's who of football. Alex Ferguson was there, even though Manchester United had been playing against Juventus in Turin the previous night. David Batty, his protégé, arrived from Newcastle. John Sheridan and Ian Snodin were there, as were most of his former colleagues from the Revie era. The tributes poured in. In *The Mirror*, Mike Walters wrote: 'His death did more damage than leaving growing men crying in the streets of Yorkshire. It was as if the lights had been turned out on a famous chapter in soccer history.' *The Sun's* Peter Fitton hailed him as 'football's ultimate warrior'. At the funeral in Edlington, near Doncaster, Gordon Strachan and Gary McAllister summed it up when they provided a floral arrangement with the message: 'To Leeds United's greatest captain. It was an honour to follow in your footsteps.'

Outside the South-East stand at Elland Road there now stands a magnificent statue of Bremner, arms held aloft, unabashed grin enlivening his bronzed face. It is a touching tribute, but someone has put a traffic cone on one of his fists. Although it was probably just a drunk, or a student, or both, it irks me. I stand on the statue's plinth and remove it. Billy is restored to his statuesque glory and any visitors are again freed to dream their dreams.

Typically for someone who epitomises Leeds United, Bremner's career was not without its controversies. His sending-off in the 1974 Charity Shield after a punch-up with Kevin Keegan was an infamous incident, as was the controversial life-ban he received from Scotland after a row in a Danish restaurant. However, he would be remembered primarily as an unparalleled competitor and a great player. John Wray of *The Telegraph and Argus* pinpointed his will to win when he wrote: 'To sit in on a card session with the little fellow losing his cash is to experience something akin to the eruption of Mount Vesuvius and the explosion of an atomic bomb. He is an extraordinary competitor.'

Bremner, himself, explained why he was such a fighter when he reflected on his career in 1974. 'Everybody seems better off in this day and age. No one seems to have a grievance to fight about. Everyone seems content. It was so different when I was a boy – born during the war and born into the social problems of the times. We played football in the streets not only because there was nothing else for us to do, but because we saw the game as a way to break out of the depression of our surroundings.

'We grew up the hard way. We learned that if you wanted anything in life you had to fight for it. Our upbringing made us determined to hang on to success if it ever came our way. To me, if a thing is worth doing it's worth doing well. In football that means fighting for everything. It means driving yourself to the limits to be more successful than the next man.'

Bremner was born on 9 December 1942 in the Raploch area of Stirling. He lived in a council house and soon realised that his diminutive stature would mean he had to try more than the rest. 'I made up for my lack of height by getting stuck in that little bit harder,' he said. It worked. Though he never weighed much more than ten stone during his playing days, the additional steel Bremner cultivated to compensate proved his most potent weapon. As the teenage Bremner began to earn a reputation it was clear that if he was to miss out on his dream, it would not be by a matter of inches.

Rangers were one of the first clubs to come calling, only to miss out through their religious bigotry. Bremner was a Catholic and that put paid to any deal. On the other side of the sectarian divide, Celtic were interested, but they would be gazumped by Leeds, who were then managed by Bill Lambton.

Bremner later admitted he had really wanted to join Celtic, for whom his boyhood hero, Bobby Collins, had played before moving to Everton. However, his father was adamant that he would not become a pawn in the religious bickering between Rangers and Celtic and so he went to Leeds – despite further English interest, from Arsenal, Aston Villa and Chelsea. As a 15-year-old, Bremner was far from enamoured with his new surroundings and he decided he would quit and return to Scotland if he failed to make it into the reserves by the end of the season. Luckily, for Leeds and Bremner he did, but he was still disillusioned and again came close to leaving the following season.

Lambton, whom Jack Charlton damningly described as not being a player, a coach or anything, deserves a place in Leeds folklore for the fact he signed both

Bremner and Don Revie during his short time in charge. Bremner was a 15-year-old upstart with terminal homesickness, while Revie was a 31-year-old veteran who had six England caps and a Footballer of the Year award on his mantelpiece. The former Leicester and Manchester City player immediately took Bremner under his paternal wing and they began to room together. And then on 23 January 1960, Bremner made his first team début in a 3–1 win over Chelsea at Stamford Bridge. 'He plays with my full confidence,' said manager Jack Taylor, who had by now succeeded Lambton. 'I am not going to make him big-headed but he is a natural footballer and well able to take care of himself.'

Jack Charlton was initially less convinced. 'He didn't have much to say for himself when he first came here,' he said. 'I remember his first game against Chelsea and there was a gasp when he came out because he was so small. But we all knew he had something special under the bonnet. He might not have said much, but he always had skill and he was pretty crafty.'

At 17 years and 47 days, Bremner was then Leeds' second-youngest player and he went on to make another ten appearances that season alongside Revie. However, despite having made the breakthrough, that was an unhappy season for all at Leeds. It ended in relegation and Taylor being sacked. Revie took over, but for Bremner even the fact that his friend and surrogate father was now his boss did not exorcise his doubting demons. Deeply depressed, he put in a transfer request and Hibernian quickly offered £25,000. 'Leeds are a great club and they couldn't have done more for me,' said Bremner. 'Mr Revie . . . Well, he's my idol, but I've been down here for nearly four years and I'm longing to get back to Scotland for good.'

However, Revie had no intention of letting Bremner get away and priced the Scottish side out of the market by slapping a £30,000 figure on the youngster's head. The deal fell through and, like it or not, Bremner was forced to stay put while Revie kept a careful watch on his charge – sometimes driving all the way to Stirling to meet Bremner's girlfriend Vicky, who worked in a factory, to discuss ways to deal with the disillusioned firebrand.

It was an arduous process, but Revie knew it was worth it. Nevertheless Bremner, who was becoming renowned for his temper and indiscipline, was persistent and again asked for a move in 1963 – despite the fact his hero, Collins, was now at the club. Again nothing happened and when Johnny Giles arrived from Manchester United for £33,000 in August 1963, the seeds of the greatest midfield partnership in the club's history were sown. Billy Bremner finally stopped his bleating and began to take his anger out on the opposition.

Revie was famed for his man-management skills, but he soon showed his tactical nous by converting Bremner from an inside-right-cum-centre-forward to midfield general. For the opening game of the 1963–64 campaign, Bremner was handed the number four shirt and three weeks later he walked into Revie's office and said: 'Please take me off the transfer list.' He missed just three games that season, as Leeds were crowned Second Division champions ahead of Sunderland.

Leeds were on their way and Bremner had made up his mind that he would be a part of the great adventure.

Revie would never tire of championing the man who had been so intent on quitting Leeds and England. 'It is one thing to have that star quality which makes you stand out from the crowd,' he said. 'It is quite another thing to have star personal quality and leadership qualities so strong that others would follow you to the ends of the earth. That is Billy Bremner. No manager could wish for a greater leader or a greater player. If I was in the trenches on the front line then the man I would want on my right-hand side would be Billy Bremner.'

Bremner and Revie were a mutual admiration society. 'I've been lucky that my manager is the best in the world,' he said in 1974. 'The Busby Babes couldn't have thought more of Matt Busby and all he did for them than we think of our boss. He is unique – one of the best managers in the history of the game. He never says a wrong word about any of us in public and he never lets anyone else say it either. He has our total respect and if you have the respect of a footballer, your battle as a manager is half over. I want to be a manager myself one day and if I am a fraction as good as our boss, I will be satisfied.

'I make no apology for saying I'm a Don Revie fan. What this fellow has done for Leeds United, since he took over, is little short of miraculous. My father was the biggest influence on my career, but Don Revie comes a very close second. He's a new, modern breed of manager, always accessible to his players. In the old days football managers could be remote figures, but not the gaffer.'

Certainly, it can be no coincidence that so many of Revie's players went into management. Inspired by their former boss, Jack Charlton, Norman Hunter, Terry Cooper, Johnny Giles, Eddie Gray, Allan Clarke, Terry Yorath, Bobby Collins and Bremner would all become managers when their playing days finished.

However, that was in the future. For the time being Leeds were cementing their reputation, which was not a glowing one in all quarters. In the first season back in the top flight, Leeds played out a game that did much to make them the most unpopular side in the country. It was 7 November 1964 when Leeds travelled to Goodison to play Everton. They won 1–0 but the result paled into insignificance as both sets of players flew at each other in a manner Eric would later perfect at Selhurst Park. Attacking moves which owed more to Jackie Chan than Jackie Milburn were the order of the day. A bad challenge on Jack Charlton started the carnage and then every player seemed intent on finishing it. Bremner admitted the ball 'got in the way of revenge missions'. Referee Roger Stokes took the players off for ten minutes in an effort to restore some sanity and get the sabre-toothed players at least temporarily declawed. Leeds were branded the dirtiest team in the League, although Everton had been equally to blame. 'There were some shocking tackles from them,' said Bobby Collins. 'Turn the other cheek and they'd try and kill you. It was bloody tough out there.'

That image would stick with Leeds, but Bremner often tried to defend his side. 'We thought a lot about our game and picked up traits from the continentals,' he revealed. 'What we called cynical in this country was called professional when the Italians did it. We picked it up from them: how they would just walk out to take a corner, or feign injury if the game was getting heated. Things like that. We earned a reputation for being dirty and defensive, but that was never true. We were a hard side, but we didn't go around kicking people as some like to think.'

Later Bremner would admit that Leeds had sometimes gone too far. 'I never thought the rather unfortunate image we had of backchatting referees and refusing to accept decisions had any effect on my game, but it must have done. Once you start to show dissatisfaction and start to argue you're obviously not concentrating your whole attention on the game. You may as well be back in the dressing-room.

'Looking back, I was fiery because if I saw someone kick one of my own players I got a bit upset about it. Some teams had vendettas against us. They disliked us intensely because we were the team to beat in that era. I've taken stick from opponents and their supporters, but there's one thing I'd like to get clear. I do not go out looking for trouble. The way some folk describe me you would think I was a regular fire-eater, but the plain fact is, I set out to do my job as a footballer.'

Leeds finally clinched the championship for the first time in 1969. They had earned a record number of points, lost just twice and conceded a miserly 26 goals. Johnny Giles's goal five minutes from time at Nottingham Forest secured the points record, but the championship was sealed on that exhilarating night in Liverpool.

There were 53,750 people packed into Anfield, with thousands more locked outside, and the atmosphere was electric. The game was played at an agitated pace to the backbeat of the Kop, which swayed like a field of red rape in the wind. Bremner was on top of his game, fighting his corner in defence and prompting Leeds' attacks. Geoffrey Green in *The Times* described it as 'a total entanglement of heart and body', which could well have summed up both Bremner and Leeds throughout the entire Revie era. By the end Leeds had a 0–0 draw and the point they craved. Bremner labelled it one of the greatest experiences of his football life. 'We even went on a lap of honour,' he is quoted as saying in *Bremner!*, 'and they cheered us as if we were their own team. It was a fantastic moment and one of the greatest gestures that I have ever experienced. The Liverpool players were also sporting and generous in their congratulations and even Bill Shankly came into our dressing-room and said, "You're worthy champions – a great side. Well done boys."'

According to Allan Clarke, Revie and Shankly enjoyed a mutual respect. 'They used to ring each other three or four times every week,' said Clarke. 'And Shankly even used to pay for the call to Revie on a Sunday! He called when Don used to go to bed at tea-time to read all the papers. Shankly used to phone him for a friendly chat. They were great friends.' Revie was deeply touched by the reception his team had been given by the Liverpool fans on clinching the championship. The following day he sent a telegram to the club, addressed simply to The Kop, Anfield: 'Thank you for your warm-hearted gesture. We nominate you as sportsmen of the century. Your great team and wonderful manager deserve each other.'

The following year saw Leeds play in the European Cup for the first time. Their first tie was against a team of part-timers from Norway called Lyn Oslo. Leeds won 13–0 on aggregate and then put out Ferencvaros and Standard Liege before they met Celtic – the club Bremner had wanted to join as a teenager. Leeds trailed 1–0 after the first leg at Elland Road, but in front of a record 136,505 crowd in Glasgow they took the lead when Bremner cracked a thunderous shot into the top corner. It was a magnificent return for Bremner, who had been carried off with concussion in the first leg, but more bad luck was to follow when Gary Sprake and Mick Jones were both forced to go off in the return game. Then there was Jimmy Johnstone, the Celtic winger who was in marvellous form that night, inspiring the Glasgow comeback which saw them win to go through and face Feyenoord in the final where they surprisingly lost.

By the time Leeds were banned by UEFA in 1975, they had played in Europe for ten successive seasons. Of 88 ties they had won 48 and lost 14, scoring 159 goals and conceding 65. Bremner had been at the forefront of it all. The point-blank save Sepp Maier made from him in the 1975 European Cup final and Bremner's crestfallen reaction are unforgettable. Then there is the picture of Bremner, clad in blue, leading the celebrations after the 1971 Fairs Cup triumph over Juventus. Leeds drew 2–2 in Turin after the first attempt to play the game had been abandoned after 53 minutes (because of a waterlogged pitch). The game was hastily rearranged for three days later and the team stayed on in Italy, Revie threatening to resign when several players insisted their wives come and stay in the hotel. As usual, Revie got his way. Leeds drew 2–2; then the second leg also finished all square at 1–1, Allan Clarke scoring the opener, and Leeds won on the away goals rule.

However, for Revie the abiding memory of Bremner in Europe came on a cold night in Edinburgh when Leeds faced Hibernian in the second round of the 1974 UEFA Cup. 'His performance that night was the finest I have ever seen from any individual in all my years in the game,' he said. 'It was a classic exhibition of reading the game, controlling the game – of passing, of incredible confidence. Billy, playing in a new role at sweeper, was a revelation. Even the furiously partisan Edinburgh crowd had to rise to their feet to cheer this miniature gladiator off the field at the end. When Billy stopped the ball on the goal-line, and stood with one foot on it and his hands on his hips, the crowd froze. Two on-rushing Hibernian forwards slithered to a halt in amazement. It was the cheekiest thing I have ever seen in football.'

He was not the only one impressed by Bremner that night. The game eventually went to penalties and as Pat Stanton, the Hibs captain, stepped up to take the first kick, Bremner shouted: 'Don't worry Pat, there's only the whole of Edinburgh watching you.' Stanton missed and Leeds won the shootout 5–4. Bremner – who else? – took the decisive last kick. Derek Wallis of the *Daily Mirror* wrote: 'Gamesmanship? Maybe, but I prefer to think of it as part of the humour in Billy, who for all his troubles with referees in the past, has enriched the game with his skill, knowledge and leadership.'

After the 1969 championship win, Leeds would be runners-up to Everton, Arsenal and Derby in successive seasons. They were third in 1973 and then finally claimed that second title in 1974 when Arsenal won at Liverpool. Three days later Leeds celebrated in style when they played at QPR in front of a packed house. Allan Clarke scored the solitary goal as West London was besieged by Yorkshiremen. Referee Jack Taylor would pay a glowing tribute to that side when he said: 'If they played in another country, you put different shirts on them and blacked their faces, I'd still know it was Leeds United.'

However, that game also marked a watershed. Revie had been linked with Everton the previous summer, but now he really was going. England manager Sir Alf Ramsey was unceremoniously sacked by the FA, who even denied the man who had won the World Cup the dignity of resigning. Joe Mercer took over as caretaker boss, but on 4 July 1974 Revie was named as his successor. After their shoddy treatment of Ramsey, the manner in which Revie would desert the FA three years later was perhaps a case of divine retribution.

New manager Brian Clough would at least have the honour of leading Leeds out at Wembley in the Charity Shield against Liverpool. The game is supposed to be a pre-season jaunt in the sun, a gentle curtain-raiser to the season proper. Usually the games are about as memorable as Marcel Marceau's after-dinner speeches. They are friendly, half-hearted affairs as football fans shed their interim inertia and re-acquaint themselves with their lost love. That's the idea, anyway. For some reason Leeds and Liverpool never follow that plan. In 1992 Eric would score a hat-trick in an absolute classic against Liverpool. Eighteen years earlier, Bremner and Kevin Keegan became the first British players to be sent off at Wembley. Allan Clarke and Johnny Giles lit Keegan's fuse and then Bremner tried to put it out with paraffin. 'Bremner took a dig at me,' said Keegan. 'I got hold of him and aimed a blow and he aimed one back. I was provoked.' Bremner just called it one of those things. 'I'm blessed, or maybe cursed, with a temperament which matches my red thatch,' he said. 'Despite my size I'm a robust player. It's something born and bred in me. I hate to see an opponent get the ball and it's my job to see this doesn't happen. I go in hard, but fair, but the temperament sometimes erupts.'

It sure did at Wembley. To compound matters, Keegan and Bremner both took off their shirts as they departed the game. Keegan later said he was distraught because he had ruined Shankly's last game in charge. Bremner was equally upset and came into the Liverpool dressing-room to apologise. 'He was almost in tears,' recalled Keegan, who was being comforted by his father. 'He said he was sorry and I said, "It's all right." Then my dad told him to bugger off.'

They were both fined £500 and banned until the end of September. 'Undoubtedly we will miss Billy,' said Clough. 'What team wouldn't miss Billy Bremner? – a living legend and a player who will go down in the annals of the game as one of the greatest ever. If I had to pick any member of the first-team squad at Leeds to miss games through suspension, the last name on the list – and even then it would be way behind the rest – is Billy Bremner's.'

Bremner would again be at the centre of a storm the following year. Scotland had played Denmark in Copenhagen in a European Championship qualifier and a group of Scottish players ended up in a nightclub. Details of what actually happened that night have remained sketchy, but suffice to say there was some trouble when the players felt they were being overcharged for a meal. The SFA banned the guilty players for life. Bremner, Arthur Graham, Willie Young, Pat McCluskey and Joe Harper could scarcely believe it. Neither could the Danish FA, whose spokesman said the SFA had been 'unduly harsh on the players involved'. Gordon Dunwoodie of the Scottish PFA said: 'All five players should be acquitted. From the facts that I have gathered, the meeting that decided on the bans was a shambles.'

Bremner never said much about the incident, but did admit there had been a contretemps because the players felt they were being ripped off. However, the punishment imposed by the SFA, who refused to let the players state their case, was a draconian knee-jerk. The irony was, no player has probably ever been more patriotic than Bremner, who had won 54 caps and skippered his country in the 1974 World Cup finals. He later claimed that anyone who thought he would bring his country into disrepute needed to see a psychiatrist – a statement which probably had the pin-striped pinheads at the SFA booking in for group therapy. In Germany at the World Cup, Bremner skippered Scotland to draws against Yugoslavia and Brazil and a win against Zaire. He came inches away from scoring a dramatic winner against Brazil, but it was not to be. Scotland went out of the tournament on goal difference.

That Bremner should be banished to the wilderness by Scotland was a travesty. In this age when players are multi-millionaires and we have had assaults on referees, attacks on fans and brawls in bars, it scarcely seems possible that the SFA would act in such a manner. 'I can't ever remember him having a bad game for Scotland,' said Denis Law. 'He played with such passion and enthusiasm that it was great to be on his side.'

The *Daily Mirror*'s Frank McGhee summed up the farce better than most: 'His ability as a player, his performances for his country and his passionate belief in Scotland's football should have ended one day with a pat on his back. Not a kick up the backside.'

Bremner was understandably hurt by his banishment. If he was Leeds through and through, he would have bled blue blood for Scotland. You couldn't have got a more archetypal Scot. Flame-haired and with the pale complexion of an anaemic snowman – you could have daubed his face in woad and you would have had Billy Braveheart. If the SFA didn't appreciate him, and they had no representative at his funeral, his peers most certainly did. Take Dave Mackay, who was famously pictured grabbing Bremner by the neck and threatening him during his Spurs days. 'The truth is, I was scared and was bluffing my way out of the situation,' said Mackay who was just coming back from a broken leg. 'When Billy kicked me it was like a warning that there were other reprisals to come. We had a drink afterwards in the bar and were pals.' When Bremner died, Mackay said: 'Billy's memory will live forever.'

Bremner left Leeds in 1976 to join Hull City. As a player who defined hyperaction it was inevitable that there would come a time when he began to slow down. I had only watched him play for little more than a year, but I remember the sadness that flowed around Leeds like flat beer when he went. After 770 appearances and 115 goals, Bremner's Leeds career was at an end.

Two years later Bremner retired from playing and became manager at Fourth Division Doncaster Rovers. He was soon joined by Les Cocker, who had been his trainer at Leeds during the great days. Cocker had quit Elland Road to join Revie on the England throne, but his prospects went west when Revie went to the Middle East. Without a job, Cocker was delighted to team up with Bremner, but he tragically collapsed and died after a training session in October 1979.

There would be other links with Leeds at Doncaster. Terry Cooper joined as a player, but by then he was a falling star. Aidan Butterworth, a striker with the physique of Toulouse Lautrec (and the only semi-famous person to have gone to my school), joined from Elland Road, while Ian Snodin went the other way. His brother Glynn, later to be carried around Dean Court on my shoulders in May 1990, was sold to Sheffield Wednesday.

In 1985, after getting Doncaster promoted twice and relegated once, Bremner returned to Leeds. I was 17 and, like all teenagers, an authority on everything. This, I was sure, was a good move. I detested the board for their treatment of Eddie Gray, but was glad to be reunited with Bremner. A decade after I had first seen him play, he was home. In the '70s I'd always thought Bremner looked older than his years. He seemed frozen in the future. Now he really was old and it seemed sad watching players tumble around in their ham-fisted efforts to emulate the suddenly still figure on the sideline in the oversized overcoat. Just as Bremner's Leeds had so often been runners-up, so Bremner the manager would come within a whisker of being regarded as a huge success. In 1987 Leeds made the FA Cup semi-final. David Rennie headed the opener and Leeds led 1–0 at half-time. Then Brendan Ormsby tried to shepherd the ball out and got caught. The ball was squared across the goal and Micky Gynn equalised. Keith Houchen, who would score one of Wembley's greatest-ever goals in the final against Spurs, made it 2–1, but Keith Edwards equalised for Leeds. Then, just as paramedics had dragged your hope from the mire and given it the kiss of life, the ambulance crashed. Dave Bennett hit a pretty pathetic winner in extra-time as Merv 'The Swerve' Day swerved out of the way.

Bloody hell.

And so to the play-offs. In those days the final was a two-legged affair, played home and away between the dregs of the First Division and the nearly-men of the

Second. Leeds faced Charlton and both games ended 1–0 to the home side. The return at Leeds was the first game I took my future wife to. To my eternal embarrassment, she and my younger brother started singing songs with the Kop. I could only frown with the authority of a pukka fan going through hell. My face was a study in seriousness: I knew full well that it is a brave and foolish man that puts his faith in Bob Taylor and co. The game went to a third match at Birmingham City's ground. John Sheridan scored a peach to open the scoring, but Peter Shirtcliff bagged a brace to put Charlton up.

Bloody, bloody hell.

The following year Bremner was sacked. Like Gray, he had just led his team to a victory in the League Cup when the board took their decision. If getting rid of Clarke and Gray had been bad enough, sacking Bremner seemed sacrilegious. It was like the Vatican deciding the Pope was a bit past it. 'Sorry John, I don't care if your last mass was a blinder.' Bremner's wife Vicky admitted how much it had hurt her husband: 'When they sacked him it was like chopping his legs away from him.'

Leeds was too much a part of Bremner for him to turn his back on the club in bitterness. You could boot the man out of Elland Road, but you could not take Elland Road out of the man. Bremner would have a second spell as manager of Doncaster, but would be a regular visitor at Leeds for the remainder of his life and he was overjoyed when Wilkinson's side won the title again. 'The fans here are the best in the world and they deserve this day as much as the players,' he said.

There have been great players at Leeds since Bremner, but there has never been as indefatigable a spirit. When Bremner was in hospital just prior to his death, Allan Clarke told Vicky that he wanted to visit him. 'He sent a message back saying he didn't want me or any of the lads to see him like he was,' said Clarke. In some ways you can understand that. Bremner was the unbreakable ethos of Leeds United and wanted to be remembered that way. He was the copper-haired heartbeat of the club, buzzing around the ground like a belligerent firefly.

When he died his team-mate Johnny Giles, by then a respected journalist for the *Daily Express*, wrote:

> It is shocking to think I will never again hear him break into his favourite song 'I Left My Heart In San Francisco'. After a few pints he would always sing that he left his heart high on a hill. Billy left much of his heart at Elland Road, not so much when he lost his job there as manager, but when he stopped playing, when his life was no longer filled with the challenge of producing the hair-trigger reflexes which made him such a unique force in the game.

It is entirely fitting that this bundle of manic energy is now paused in bronze outside the ground. If you witness a bore-draw or a game which makes you consider the merits of being dropped off on the Headrow to go shopping on a

Saturday afternoon, pay a visit to Billy Bremner's statue. Read the caption and study the picture of unbridled delight. Dream your dreams and don't ever forget.

* * *

Two days after I write those words, the statue of Billy Bremner is draped in the Yorkshire tricolour of yellow, white and blue. He has a black armband on one of his biceps and a woolly scarf around his neck. A BBC reporter is standing in the foreground addressing the camera. He holds one of those oversized furry things, a microphone with an Afro. 'The statue of Billy Bremner, one of the club's greatest ever players, has become a focal point for the mourners,' he says. Flowers rise up from the stony ground and scarves are tied to the blue railings that surround the stadium. The grim northern weather shrouds a kaleidoscope of colour on this, the blackest of days. There is a Liverpool shirt and a Sheffield Wednesday shirt, tributes from two clubs who know all about suffering above and beyond the normal course of fandom.

Leeds have just lost 2–0 to Galatasaray in the first leg of the UEFA Cup semi-final. The most important game in the club's history since Paris 1975 was a sideshow. The night before, two Leeds fans were brutally murdered in Istanbul. Kevin Speight and Chris Loftus were stabbed to death. The Turkish club helped to heighten tensions by not holding a minute's silence before the game or making their players wear black armbands. Emotion is running high.

The week that follows is traumatic. Leeds say Turkish fans should be banned from the return leg, while Galatasaray, showing an almost inhuman insensitivity, claim the game should be switched to a neutral venue to guarantee the safety of their own fans. The Turkish sports minister says that he hopes Galatasaray win the return leg to 'show' the British people. Show them what? – he fails to elaborate. That they can play football better than Leeds? Frankly, few in Yorkshire care about such trivialities with the dead still waiting to be buried. An official of the Turkish FA denies the people involved were Galatasaray fans. He then proves to be just as crass as his sports minister by claiming Leeds fans provoked the violence by abusing the Turkish flag and making obscene gestures. So that's that, a public order offence warrants 17 stabs in the chest. Welcome to Hell and all its Styx and stones. I consider that only a daft man would wash his hands and then start mud-slinging.

Of course, the official from the Turkish FA does not mention the fact the authorities do nothing to stop Galatasaray fans being ferried to the airport to abuse incoming teams. Nor does he mention the terrible treatment meted out to Manchester United fans on their visit in 1993, nor the cut-throat gestures of their supporters and the death threats received by the Leeds players prior to the match.

This is football. The beautiful game. Ignorance is blistering.

JOHNNY GILES — Mr Nice?

Players like him come along once in a lifetime.
DON REVIE

A week after that game in Turkey, I am sitting in the front room of Johnny Giles's house in the smart Harbone area of Birmingham. His wife wants to make me some supper, but after my assurances that I am not hungry she restricts herself to providing a couple of rounds of toast and a cup of tea. Giles works as a pundit for Irish television these days, providing co-commentary for Champions League games and taking the Alan Hansen role on the Gaelic version of *Match of the Day*. His commitments mean he does not get to watch Leeds more than any other team these days, but he says he wants to go to the second leg of the semi-final. However, when we meet UEFA have still not decided where the game will be played, or whether Turkish fans will be allowed to attend.

Giles slumps into a comfortable armchair and tucks into his jam and toast. He pauses to give me his view on the Turkish affair. 'I think the whole thing has been a total disgrace,' he says. 'Everyone seems to have forgotten that two men have been murdered. That's all that matters. Full stop. The Turkish FA say they want the game played at a neutral venue if their fans can't travel. To me that is disgusting. They are using this tragedy to try to improve their chances of getting to the final. If they had any decency at all they would have told their fans not to travel. Two people have been killed, but that seems to have become secondary to the matter of where this game is going to be played. Does it really matter? It's only football. We should be talking about lives.'

They are eminently sensible sentiments, but typical of a man whose views are regularly printed in a *Daily Express* column under the slogan, THE MAN THE PLAYERS READ. Humble, articulate and affable, the softly-spoken Giles is as nice a man as I have met on my travels so far. I can readily understand why some people, Billy Bremner included, once wondered whether he would be too placid to make the grade as a First Division footballer.

However, lest we forget, this is Johnny Giles we are talking about. George Best recalled how Giles almost broke his leg in one game with a vindictive challenge, and then had the temerity to tell the maverick Irishman that he should behave more like Bobby Charlton because *he* was a real gentleman. Now Best's antipathy to Leeds is well known. He has often stated how Leeds players would abuse opponents during games by saying appalling things about their mothers and children, and Best says he only ever wore shinpads when he played against Leeds. However, even Giles's own team-mates sometimes questioned his mean streak. In his autobiography, Jack Charlton said:

> John Giles used to do some awful things to players. We would have rows about it in the dressing-room. I once said to him, 'What do you do it for, John?' And he said, 'Well, I once got my leg broken, and I'm gonna make sure nobody ever does it again.' I said, 'Sure, every bugger in the League is going to get punished because you once got your leg broke.'

Lest we forget, this is also Johnny Giles, football genius we are talking about: probably the greatest midfielder to ever play for Leeds United. His passing was unparalleled, his shooting magnificent, his skill unquestioned. He scored 115 goals in 526 games between 1963 and 1975 and Don Revie called him one of the most 'complete players' he'd known. 'His partnership with Billy Bremner was the most effective ever in football,' said Revie. 'Both were quick, with fantastic brains. Both helped each other. Both had guts, drive and knowledge. These two must take a lot of the credit for what happened to Leeds United. At Leeds Johnny Giles was one of 14 world class players, which is why he probably never got the credit he deserved.' He had it all. And of course, he could mix it with the worst of them.

'When people talk about Leeds United we always have to defend ourselves,' says Giles defensively. 'It's always "you were a great team, but . . . " That's fair comment. The legacy we left was a negative one. However, it's not always accurate. I saw an article in one of the national papers the other day talking about David O'Leary's side and it said, "I hope we're not in for an unfortunate repeat of the Leeds team of the '70s." That's ridiculous. People made too much of one facet of our play. Of course we did things that weren't right and we are the first to admit it. But we did an awful lot more that was right. Look at the players we had. Eddie Gray, Paul Madeley, Peter Lorimer, Mick Jones. They were beautiful players who wouldn't kick anyone.'

Leeds' reputation for the seedier side of the game was developed when they were still in the Second Division, but Giles denies the suggestion that the side kicked their way to promotion. 'You still have to play football and your opponents are not from Mars,' he says. 'It's still football, the same pitch, goalposts at either end. Don wanted us to be aggressive, though, and he instilled that in us. Looking back, we did things which weren't necessary and it didn't help us win matches. I think if Don had his time all over again he would have done things differently. We were accused of gamesmanship and time-wasting, but none of those things helped us. They help you lose matches, if anything, and they don't win you any friends, that's for sure. As time went on, we became a great side and the image stuck long after we deserved it. We deserved a lot of the criticism, but we also played the sort of football which had nothing to do with bad behaviour. The football we played from 1969 to 1974 was unbelievable. Some of the matches we played, particularly at Leeds – well, I've never seen better football before or since. We were that good. People don't mention that.'

Giles and I finish our toast. Even though I am sitting in a legend's home with bready morsels pockmarking my shirt, asking questions about why he was so nasty, Mr Nice somehow makes me feel comfortable. He is interested to know who else I've spoken to. 'How was John?' he says with obvious concern when I mention John Charles. 'You know, he was a fantastic player. You've seen the size of him, but he was very skilful on the floor. One of the best ever. Blew all his money, but he's a bit simple like that. A very modest fella. When he came back from Italy he wasn't the same, though. He didn't get fit pre-season and had changed. In today's market he'd get £20 million.'

Giles would not be far off such a figure himself. As a young boy I knew he was a star because Ronnie Hilton made a record about him. 'The Ballad of Johnny Giles'. To be honest it was not as good as 'The Ballad of Billy Bremner' and may even have been a B-side if my memory serves, but getting the Hilton seal of approval meant you had arrived as far as I was concerned. Of course, Leeds have always been the bedrock of the 'quality football song'. This is generally regarded a contradiction in terms. Remember Gazza doing 'Fog on the Tyne' on *Top of the Pops*: a deranged Geordie leaping up and down and lip-synching like a badly-dubbed German porn star. It nearly scarred me for life. Then there was that Liverpool dance business where shellsuited scousers, led by an obviously typecast John Aldrige, tried a rap song. It was as if the Beastie Boys had left the door open on their Stanley Park nuclear shelter. But at Leeds, the tradition of singing is real. The players put 'Leeds, Leeds, Leeds (Marching on Together)' down on vinyl at a time when the only vinyl other sides were putting down was on the kitchen floor. Then there was Ronnie Hilton. With his Scottish accent, he made Billy Bremner sound like a be-studded Rob Roy in his song. When I left my Leeds collection in the back of the car and the tone-deaf sun melted them, I was devastated.

Johnny Giles's song was a bit poor, to be honest, but at least he had one, which is more than can be said for Sniffer, Big Jack, Hotshot or the rest. He was the midfield dynamo. General knowledge. However, had it not been for Bobby Collins's broken femur, who knows how long he would have had to wait on the wing before taking his rightful position in the centre?

'I was at Manchester United for seven years from the age of 15,' he tells me. 'I played against Leicester in the 1963 FA Cup final, but I'd had a bad year and I wasn't getting on with Matt Busby. I was playing on the right wing and I was never a right-winger. It all stemmed from the previous season's FA Cup semi-final when we got badly beaten by Spurs and I played very poorly. Things were never the same after that and Matt lost confidence in me. Whatever I did right was wrong. After we beat Leicester we played Everton in the Charity Shield at Goodison and lost 4–0. I wasn't in the team and I knew that was it.'

Giles's burgeoning career had reached a crisis point. But the man from Dublin, who had first attracted interest from across the Irish Channel while playing for Home Farm, knew what had to be done. 'I asked Matt for a transfer and he said OK. There was no great falling out, because you didn't fall out with Matt. He wasn't that sort of individual, he was too dignified. But he didn't try to talk me out of it either. He wanted me to go and I wanted to go. I was on the transfer list two days before Leeds came in. Don came up to see me, we agreed terms and I signed straight away. You always have some doubts when you move, but I was only 22 at the time and I was OK because I had time on my side. I knew that Leeds had come with a great run around Christmas-time the previous season and had just missed out on promotion. I knew they were making a move.

'What pleased me most was that Don never wasted any time. He wanted me, and being wanted is a big thing in a footballer's life. It hadn't been like that at Manchester United for the previous 12 months. Don wanted me and that made me feel good. And it was quick. I went on the transfer list on Tuesday, signed on Thursday and played on Saturday. I didn't have time to have any doubts about dropping down a division.'

There was another factor to convince Giles that moving from Old Trafford to Division Two was not a retrograde step. 'They had Bobby Collins,' he says. 'He'd been my idol for a long time. Bobby was the type of player who would drive a team on and I knew that he would not move to a club just to mess about. He was too much of a competitor to just go through the motions.'

The fact Collins was still pulling the strings for Leeds meant the famous midfield partnership of Giles and Bremner would have to wait. For the time being, Giles would stay on the right. 'I wasn't frustrated because it was more like a 4–3–3,' he says. 'It wasn't a case of me just sitting out wide on the touchline. I'd do a few bits and pieces on the right and then move infield. I knew my place then. Bobby was *the* midfield player and I respected him.'

He also garnered an admiration for the orange-haired Scot in the Leeds midfield. 'Billy Bremner was an outstanding talent,' he says. 'He was very bubbly and had this natural energy and drive. Even in training it was the same. If you stuck a ball in front of Billy he would happily stay there all day playing with it. He was not so clever on the cross-country runs, but he was never still. And of course he could play. He had a great confidence in his own ability and would try things that most players wouldn't even dare. Billy made things happen.

'When I got to Leeds he was already established and had played for the club in the First Division. But he was unsettled; Vicky was not happy and he wanted to get back to Scotland. But then the team just kept winning and winning, we played better and better and Billy had to come off the list because he could see that the club was going somewhere. He coudn't walk out on what we had. We lost three games out of forty-two that year.'

If Bremner made things happen, so too did Giles. Having made his début on 31 August 1963 in a 3–0 win over Bury, Giles was celebrating a title just nine months later. The revolution was nigh. The following season Leeds were runners-up in the First Division and the FA Cup. 'We did unbelievably well that year,' he says. 'I'd played in the top flight and a few of the others like Jack Charlton, Bobby Collins and Billy had too, but we were generally very inexperienced. When you go up to the First Division you never really know how you are going to cope. Most of us had built up these famous clubs in our own heads, too. There was a definite fear factor. Our first game was at Aston Villa, who were a middle-of-the-table side, and we won. It was incredible. Suddenly you think, maybe these lot are not as good as we thought they were. Our first home game was against Liverpool, who were a fantastic side with players like Ian St John, Roger Hunt, Tommy Smith and Ron Yates. We beat them 4–2. Our first thought that year was not to get relegated, but it soon became clear that we could do a lot better than that.'

The young Leeds team was surfing the crest of a wave, but some players fell by the wayside. One of those was Albert Johanneson, whom Giles thinks was guiltier than most of self-destructive mind games. 'In the Second Division Albert Johanneson was brilliant,' says Giles. 'He was quick, worked hard, scored goals. At a time when we didn't score a lot, he got 14 in one season. I honestly thought he would go on to be one of the very top players of the day, but I think the First Division got to him. He was South African and he was scared and intimidated by the big crowds and the big grounds. One year Albert was playing in front of 10–15,000 people at places like Rotherham, Grimsby, Cardiff and Swansea. The next he was at Old Trafford, Anfield and Goodison, and I think the very thought of those places intimidated him.'

If Johanneson was struggling with his frayed nerves, the rest of the team were proving to be precocious upstarts as they battled with the high and mighty. 'Bobby was our leader and his fighting spirit rubbed off on the rest of us. He was sure that he would win every game that he played in. Billy was a great fighter too, but he would be the first to admit the massive influence that Bobby Collins had on him and his career. Bobby was a scrapper and a model senior pro. In football, if you've got a great senior pro then there is nothing better, but if you've a bad one it's terrible.'

Manchester United eventually won their first championship in eight years on goal difference. 'Even though that was disappointing, I remember thinking we'd had a remarkable season,' says Giles. 'We chased Man United all the way to the title, which was incredible because, man for man, we were not in the same class as them. We stuck in there because of Bobby's influence, but most importantly because of Don Revie's organisation, his drive and his work. We were the first team to get more than 60 points, when it was two points for a win, and not win the title. It was an achievement to be proud of.'

So was making the first FA Cup final in the club's history. However, in 1965 Liverpool was the epicentre of a cultural revolution. Beatlemania was at its peak, mop tops were the fashion and the world was dancing to Merseybeat. It was perhaps inevitable that Leeds would lose that final and, although it went to extra-time, Giles had no complaints about the outcome. 'We didn't deserve to win it,' he says. 'Liverpool were a terrific side around then, they were very experienced and they were at their peak. But we were coming. We had Norman Hunter, Gary Sprake, Billy, Paul Reaney, all young lads, and we were nowhere near our peak. Liverpool won, but we'd sent out a message.'

According to Giles, Revie's Leeds would get better and better each season until the empire-builder quit in 1974. Like his siblings from that era whom I had already interviewed, Giles still regards Revie with an admiration bordering on obeisance. He says the superstitions and the dossiers have been exaggerated. He gives no credence to the stories of match-fixing and prefers to concentrate on his qualities as a manager. Maybe it is the case that in the land of the blindly loyal, the one-eyed fan is king. However, is that any worse than the expedience of the anti-Revie media who, on gaining their open goal via the match-fixing allegations, buried him in the sandy part of the penalty area?

For Giles, Revie could do no wrong. 'I think the thing that made Don such a great manager was the knowledge he brought to the game,' he says. 'His attention to detail was tremendous, but it was his knowledge of what was right and wrong and how to put it right which set him apart. Football is made up of a million little things and when something is wrong with a side, it is often not something major. It just needs a bit of fine-tuning and tweaking. Don had this brilliant ability to spot the tiny things, put them right and improve from one match to the next. We honestly learned something from every game we played.

'Why was he so good? Because he brought a knowledge to the game which I don't think anyone has ever come close to. I played under Matt Busby at Man United and he was a very different type. He was an older-fashioned type of manager, whose method was to get good players in, believe in them and let them go out and play. But Matt was never on the training ground, whereas Don was out there every day. If we lost a goal on Saturday, he'd be there, working out how, where, what happened and who was at fault, and he'd put it right.'

The following, 1965–66, season would define Giles's career. When Leeds played Torino in the first round of the Inter Cities Fairs Cup, Bobby Collins suffered the appalling injury which would see Giles moved infield to create a hard-faced hegemony with Bremner.

'I couldn't have planned it better,' he says. 'When I played in that FA Cup semi-final for Man United against Spurs I was only 21. I was playing in the middle of the park as the main schemer, as we called it then, but looking back I realise I wasn't ready for it. By the time Bobby got injured in Turin I was 25 and had had three years playing wide. I *was* ready. It was a nasty tackle which put Bobby in hospital. It was our first tie in Europe and in the first leg, which we won 2–1, Billy had a bit of a go at the guy who did Bobby. Now I don't know whether this guy mistook Bobby for Billy in the second game, but it was a terrible tackle which broke his thigh bone. Bobby actually played again before the end of that season – which shows what a fighter he was – and we played together, both as inside-forwards. But it got to the stage where Don had to make a decision. Bobby was about 35 then and I was ten years younger. He was still a great player, but Don obviously went for me and that was it.'

Despite the fact Collins was nursing his broken thigh, Leeds made it to the semi-finals of the Fairs Cup that season. Giles focuses on the positive side of that run, but the dichotomy that was Revie's Leeds meant the European campaign would have its darker side too. In the first round Collins ended up in hospital. In the third, against Valencia, two Spaniards and Jack Charlton were sent off and the Dutch referee took both sides off the pitch for 11 minutes in an attempt to restore order. In the fifth round more mayhem erupted as Giles was sent off for retaliating after being violently abused by Real Zaragoza's Violeta. Goals from Johanneson and Charlton in the return ensured the semi-final went to a play-off where the much-vaunted Magnificent Five of Zaragoza dazzled Leeds. They delivered the knockout blow with a three-goal combination early in the game. However, Leeds soon got another shot at the title.

'The Real Zaragoza game did get a bit rough,' Giles recalls. 'They were a fine side, but that was another great achievement by us. These days you hear people saying it takes a few years to get used to playing in Europe. That's what they were all saying about Man United a few years ago when they were struggling. Well, that was our first year and we got to the semi-final and were only beaten in a play-off. I think they make too much of the difference between home and abroad. It's like I said before. They might be from Spain, but they are not from Mars. There might be differences in style, but nothing too drastic, and good players should be able to play anywhere, against anyone.'

Leeds were fourth the following season, but made it to the Fairs Cup final, where their lack of attacking flair saw them lose to Dynamo Zagreb and prompted Revie's decision to pay £100,000 for Mick Jones. In 1968 they again finished fourth, but won both the Fairs Cup and the League Cup. And then in 1969 the title was finally clinched.

'We lost two matches all season,' says Giles proudly. 'Incredible. We were so consistent, which is what every manager dreams about. He wants a group of players who will go out and give the same effort every week, not a side who will get up for Man United and then go and lose to Coventry the following week. You also have to remember that it was a lot more open in those days, because there wasn't that imbalance which you get through money. There were around six or seven sides who would believe they could win the title any given year. Liverpool won it in '66, Man United in '67, Man City in '68, us in '69, Everton in '70, Arsenal in '71, Derby in '72, Liverpool in '73 and then us again in '74. No team was dominant like today and yet we lost just two games. We beat three records that season. We had a record number of points with 67; the fewest defeats with two; and conceded the lowest number of goals with 26. We had also scored the fewest goals of any championship-winning side and of course the headline said 'LEEDS WIN TITLE WITH LOWEST NUMBER OF GOALS SCORED'. No mention of our points tally, no mention of the fact we lost twice, or of our defence.

'The trouble was, we were judged by the London Press. Now they usually judged you from the games you played in London, they'd not be bothered to actually come up to Leeds. And of course you play very differently away from home. If you had Spurs or West Ham away then they were bloody hard games, but we'd give them a good hiding at Elland Road. There were two sides to the coin, but the London Press only judged us on the side they saw. Some of the football we played was stunning.'

In the summer of '69 Revie again moved to strengthen his squad and signed Allan Clarke. However, scarcely had Clarke been welcomed into the bosom of the family than popular winger Mike O'Grady joined Wolves. Having suffered from a carbuncle on his foot, the recovered O'Grady then found himself sidelined by a cold shoulder. As Leeds had won the title and O'Grady had widely been regarded as the side's most effective forward, Revie's decision caused no little consternation. Echoing the sentiments Tony Currie expressed to me at finding himself ostracised by Revie, O'Grady put Revie's disenchentment down to a dislike of his style. 'You'd be there thinking "God, just let us play,"' he said of Revie's almost paranoid diligence. O'Grady felt Revie preferred flare-ups to flair and that he, himself, was too much like a poor man's George Best to sit easily with his manager's authoritarian values. And so he was forced out. His departure did little to derail the bandwagon that was by now rolling, but who knows how Mike O'Grady would be remembered had he stayed at Elland Road? With his swashbuckling skills, Yorkshire roots and Fred Trueman-like arrogance, he might well have been on my tracking list all these years on. Ronnie Hilton might even have written a song about him. As it turned out, the '69 title was his swan-song. His career hit reverse gear and crashed into a black hole in the Black Country.

It was the season of discontent all round. In 1970 The Beatles split up. From the sharp-suited, sharp-witted comics of the early '60s they had developed into violently hairy, world-weary malcontents. At least they had won everything going. Leeds, meanwhile, were underlining their status as nearly men. By the time the Revie era was over Leeds won six trophies and finished as runner-up on 11 occasions. With more seconds than Seiko, Leeds would be forever remembered as the sort of unlucky team you wouldn't want to fly with. And the year that cemented that reputation was 1970, when Leeds finished runners-up in the League and FA Cup in addition to losing to Celtic in the European Cup semi-finals.

'The hardest part of that year was the FA Cup,' says Giles with a grimace. 'We should have beaten Chelsea and deserved to. It was 1–0 to us and then Gary Sprake made a dreadful mistake and let one go straight under him. It was infuriating, because when you work so hard to get ahead and then your keeper makes a howler, it's all for nothing. Gary was very talented, but he was the weak link in our side. He let us down on a lot of occasions. That's not being too hard, because it was there for all to see. He made a lot of howlers and he cost us some important games. I don't know if Don looked around for a replacement and my attitude was that you didn't question the manager. But Don stayed with Gary too long and the mistakes became more and more frequent. His nerves went. You looked around and all the other top sides never had a goalkeeper who made mistakes, because it's bloody hard when you give soft goals away.

'The Chelsea final was hard for everybody, but we had no complaints in the League. To be fair we were never really in the running, even though we came second. At the start of the season Don had said we would concentrate on the European Cup that season and we really fancied ourselves against Celtic, but they beat us and beat us well. We had no complaints apart from the fact we had so many games to play that year. We had three semi-finals against Manchester United, two finals against Chelsea and Celtic in between. Say what you like, but it does make a difference when you don't have those extra few days' break.

'People often talk about how we were always finishing second, but you can only do your best. In 1971 we were second with 64 points when a win at home and draw away would give you 63 points. If you did that it was accepted you would win the League, but we got more than that and still came second. The following season Derby won the League with 58 points.

'Don was at Leeds for 14 years and in that time Leeds won two championships, two Fairs Cups, an FA Cup, the League Cup and the Second Division. If someone had offered him all that when he arrived he would have taken it and everyone would have said it was incredible. The thing is, we did it over a long period of time whereas someone like Man City did it all in three seasons. They won the League in '68, the FA Cup in '69 and the League Cup and Cup-Winners' Cup in '70. It was a great period but, after that, they were gone and you never saw them again. They never got to another cup final or finished second to tarnish their record. If we'd finished in '72 people would have said, "What a record that Leeds team had." But we kept going. From 1965 to 1974 we were always there, challenging for everything, with basically the same players. Now a team like Liverpool changed an awful lot. When they won the League in '73 with Keegan and that lot, there was hardly anyone left from the team we played at Wembley in '65. But we were there, year in, year out, with the same players.'

Giles had more than justified his decision to quit Old Trafford and drop down a division. He had become respected throughout the game with many – including his team-mate Bremner – rating him as the greatest passer of the ball in the game. 'He could be compared with any footballer of his generation,' said Bremner. And Leeds and Giles were improving with every passing season. The only trouble was that Revie failed to see it. 'Don was an insecure guy,' Giles says candidly. 'That's why his attention to detail was so great: he was always so fearful. I talked to Don just before he died. As the team got older, wiser and better he just didn't see it. He would still pay a lot of respect, maybe too much respect, to the opposition. But he'd carried out one of the big jobs of football. He'd gone to a place which was not really a football area like Liverpool, Manchester or Sunderland, taken a team that was in danger of being relegated to the Third Division, and created one of the best sides ever.

'He also created a wonderful spirit. It's the thing I remember most about my time at the club. Whatever disappointments we had, and there were a lot, we took it on the chin. There were no public recriminations and we'd start again next year. And whenever we won something, which was quite often too, we never let that go to our heads either.'

Leeds' resolve in that respect was never more severely tested than in the FA Cup. In 1971 Leeds crashed out of the FA Cup fifth round at the hands of Fourth Division Colchester. Two goals from Ray Crawford and another from Dave Simms put a team that had been labelled 'Grandad's Army' 3–0 up. Belatedly, Leeds stirred from their coma and Norman Hunter and Giles made it 3–2, but Colchester hung on to secure a win that stunned the nation. Leeds were humiliated and humbled. Revie resolved to ensure that such a catastrophe would never happen again. He was not alone in viewing the defeat as a freak of nature.

However, two years later lightning did strike twice when Sunderland defeated Leeds in the FA Cup final. Many of Leeds' abundant critics decided this was the beginning of the end. Giles cringes at the memory. 'The Sunderland thing was one of the biggest embarrassments in football history. We knew we would get crucified by the Press and we weren't disappointed. God, we got some stick. Billy and myself were written off. We were too old. Leeds were over the hill. It was over. We never said a word. Generally, if you get a bad defeat like that, everybody cracks up and starts blaming each other. We didn't. There was no bickering in the changing-room afterwards. We knew we'd been no good and that nobody had played well. We just took it and, as soon as the match finished, we determined to set new standards. What happened? We went 29 games unbeaten and 12 months later we're champions and Sunderland are still in the Second Division.'

Ironically, the end of Leeds crept up almost imperceptibly on a Press that had been eager to pen the club's obituary. Revie had reinstated himself and the club as champions and Giles had summarily dismissed the dissenters questioning his own talent. However, according to Giles, it took just three months to undo 14 years' good work. 'Don leaving was a great shock,' he explains. 'We were close, but nobody knew he was going to take the England job. Suddenly, our leader was gone. I'd been with him 11 years and some of the other fellas a lot longer. A lot of them had never known another manager. In fairness to Don, the England job does not come around too often and it was obviously a step up. I don't agree with those who say he left because he couldn't bear to break up the team. I mean, we'd just won the League, so we were hardly on our way out. Of course, when Don then left to go to Dubai, he made it very hard for his friends to defend him. It is probably why a lot of people have never appreciated his talents. He was seeing these other guys while under contract to the FA. It was wrong.'

Giles, who had been managing the Republic of Ireland on a part-time basis for almost a year, was in Germany for the 1974 World Cup finals when he heard Revie was leaving. 'I'd signed a new contract when Don told me he was going and that he was recommending me to take over from him. I thought it was all fixed up, but then the board turned it down and appointed Cloughie. I think they did that because they wanted to flex their muscles. When you have a very successful manager, there is very little for the directors to do. So when Don finished I think they saw it as an opportunity to reclaim some power. Their attitude was "It's our turn to make a decision now, we'll do what we like." So they deliberately went against what Don suggested.

'I don't regret it, but it would have been the best thing for Leeds because there would have been continuity. I was put in a very difficult position because I was turned down for a job I'd never applied for. It didn't break my heart, but Cloughie came in and was the wrong man at the wrong time. He was a great football man, Cloughie – still is – but his approach was all wrong. If he had his time again I'm sure he'd do it all differently. He never had the players on his side. He was rude, arrogant and stupid. He insulted us and told us we were cheats. Now we had just won the League and had a lot of strong-minded individuals – people like Terry Cooper, Paul Reaney, Paul Madeley, Billy, Norman and myself – so a bit more respect would have worked a lot better.

'By the time Jimmy Armfield came in, we'd lost everything. That period between Don and Jimmy broke our spirit. We were out of the League championship almost before it started. Things would never be the same. Whatever magic there had been had disappeared. Those few weeks ruined everything.'

When Clough was sacked, the Leeds board voted 3–2 in favour of giving the job to Giles. Their irresolute vacillations left Giles distinctly unimpressed. Having been turned down once, he turned his back on the dithering directors and opted out of the managerial race before it had begun. 'I thought, three to two? If there's two of them against me from the start there's not much point in bothering.' Like a true son of Revie, Giles expected nothing less than a clean sheet.

So it fell to Armfield to steady an unhappy ship. One of the great enigmas of Leeds United is the fact that in this state of trauma, transition and cataclysm, they made the European Cup final. 'We got to the final because we were still outstanding players, who were able to raise ourselves for the big games, but it was over. It had taken years to build up the confidence, the attitude, the atmosphere. It's indefinable what we had during those years; but whatever it was, it was broken that summer. It should still have ended in glory in the European Cup final, but the referee was terrible and how he didn't give a penalty when Beckenbauer fouled Allan Clarke I'll never know. They were there for the taking, but it went wrong for us. It was the last hurrah of the team. I never played for Leeds again. I left to join

West Brom in the summer and the team broke up shortly afterwards. Billy went to Hull and Norman went to Bristol.' He chuckles to himself. 'They still talk about Norman in Bristol, you know.'

Like Bremner and Hunter, Giles pursued a career in management. He was successful at it too, getting West Brom promoted to the First Division, but he didn't like the inherent pressures. 'The job should come with a health warning,' he said after resigning from The Hawthorns. 'It's a precarious job. There is so much fear in the game, it spreads like a plague.'

Giles preferred patrolling the midfield to controlling the players, and his heart lay in playing the game he loved. He continued to do that at Shamrock Rovers and earned the last of his record-breaking 60 caps for the Republic of Ireland in 1979 aged 39. He coached in America and Canada before returning for a second spell in charge at West Brom. This time he would not get the opportunity to resign and was sacked within two years.

Time is getting on. Night has fallen and the flickering blue light of the television set in the neighbouring room dances on the wall. I wave to Giles's wife, thank her for my toast, and shake hands with a 60-year-old legend. He wishes me well and then gives me detailed directions to help negotiate Birmingham's unfathomable road system. I feel slightly sad as my meetings with the Revie team are almost at an end. They have all been very accommodating, responding to my phone calls and letters with good grace. I cannot help contrasting this with the hoops I have been required to go through to set up interviews with today's stars.

Now Leeds have their own press officers, but I am told I have to go through agents to arrange interviews with the current players. And so I ring London and even Israel to organise my trips to Leeds. It's a bit like ringing the Welsh tourist board to plan your Spanish holiday. I mention this to Giles and he smiles knowingly. 'Different world now,' he says. Of course he is right. And casting an eye over his framed photographs from his Leeds days, I can only conclude it's not necessarily a better one.

I ring my wife, tell her I'll be home soon and hang up. Then I drive into Birmingham and get hopelessly lost around the one-way system.

* * *

The following morning the procrastinators at UEFA announce that they are banning Turkish fans from the return leg of the UEFA Cup semi-final. Some Turks say they will come anyway. They are daft.

My friend the journalist rings me and tells me his efforts to talk to Cantona have been fruitless. Eric was mobbed and treated like a superstar by the fans at the ground, he says. 'We tried to talk to him, but he just kept saying "non, non, non",' he adds. He'd have got more joy out of that weird monkey in the zoo, he says. I tell him not to worry.

In the *Yorkshire Post* there is a message from Kevin Speight's children:

Forgive us Dad if we cry,
Why was it you who had to die?
Others have lost their Dads we know,
but you were ours and we loved you so.
Night Night Dad.
Lots of love and kisses,
George and Holly.

There really are more important things to think about.

NORMAN HUNTER & JACK CHARLTON
– The (Hard) Case for the Defence

> Leeds were the only team I ever wore shinpads
> against.
>
> GEORGE BEST

I ring Fulham Football Club. I have read in the paper that Max Clifford, the public relations guru now working for Fulham, has had lunch with Eric. There is speculation that Eric might even be set to take over as the manager of the Craven Cottage club. It is a comical situation. Bankrolled by Al Fayed's millions, the *bête noire* of French football and movie star wannabe is going to coach a bunch of journeymen plodders in the First Division. The girl on reception puts me through to the man in the press office. I ask for Max Clifford. Of course, he is not there. The man in the press office says he will ring Clifford's office on my behalf. I tell him I will save him the bother if he gives me the number. He says he is not at liberty to give it out. This puzzles me. A man whose whole *raison d'être* is to create publicity is ex-directory.

Except he is not.

Ten minutes later I find the number for Max Clifford Associates, friends of the Royals, the stars and second-rate footballers. I ring it. Of course, Max Clifford is not there. Only his associates. They assure me they will pass on my message and he will ring me. Bollocks. Max Clifford is too busy arranging a photo shoot for some albino gorilla to bother with me. I find myself getting quite annoyed. 'Press officer' is clearly a misnomer. I mean what is the point in having a press office which is incapable of advising the Press? I find this to be the same elsewhere. A press officer appears to be a person appointed with the sole objective of obstructing the Press. If the Met Office had the same attitude the weather forecast would take a hiding. You'd be there, sitting in anticipation, wondering whether the Bank Holiday picnic was a goer or not, and you'd have Michael Fish scowling at the camera, giving you the V-sign and putting you on hold as Beethoven's Fifth drives you to the point of madness.

I would like to set Norman 'bites-yer-legs' Hunter onto Max 'soundbites-yer-silly' Clifford. Some people cannot be put on hold. Norman Hunter is one of these. In the history of Leeds United, Hunter has been pilloried as the man who epitomised the thuggery which people claim was the club's hallmark. His nickname became a millstone round his neck and people now forget the sweet left foot and the unparalleled consistency. What they remember is the infamous brawl with Derby County's pocket battleship Francis Lee, when both men were sent off for fighting. As they walked off the pitch something snapped and they began to pound into each other again. Lee's arms were a blur as he flailed at Hunter like an overweight butterfly. The taller and thinner Leeds man jabbed and hooked. It was classic Hunter, according to Leeds' critics. It was one of the biggest regrets of his footballing life, according to the man himself.

'I'm very embarrassed about the Francis Lee thing,' he says. 'Unfortunately, these things happen. Because of the nature of winning and the team you are in, you do things you wouldn't normally do. You have that desire and the edge comes with it. The one thing I will say about that Leeds team is that the will to win was unbelievable. Nobody would lie down. But there's a few things I regret in football and the Francis Lee business is one of them. I shouldn't have done that. It was a loss of control. Nobody should do that on a football field, no matter what had happened beforehand.' Years later Lee would visit Elland Road as chairman of Manchester City. Hunter was working for radio. 'Let's finish it now in the car park,' quipped Lee. The older and wiser Hunter declined.

The reputation that has clung to Leeds has exerted a limpet-like grip on Hunter. Shortly before I met him at his attractive home in the Horsforth part of Leeds, Hunter had been savaged by Pat Collins of the *Mail on Sunday*. 'Did people really pay to see football played by the likes of Norman Hunter, Ron Harris, Tommy Smith and Peter Storey?' he said with a degree of pomposity. 'Football took its values from the destroyers, from teams like Don Revie's Leeds, who demeaned their own extravagant talents by adopting a code of choreographed cheating and intimidation by rota which was both witlessly admired and widely copied. Thuggery was cherished.'

'Yeah, we overstepped the mark,' admits Hunter. 'There's no doubt about that, but everybody did. We did it to win the game. What people choose to forget is that we could play and you don't win all the things we did without having world-class players. All good sides will do whatever they can to win. Look at Manchester United now. There's not one player in that side who will shirk a challenge. They don't mind getting physical if they have to. Take Roy Keane. He'll mix it with anyone. The players at Manchester United are in there fighting for each other and that's one reason why they are so successful. All the good teams, Leeds, Arsenal and Manchester United especially, do the basics first. They stop the opposition playing and then, when they get the ball, they go and play. No team, whoever you are, can win things with ten ball-players. It's physically impossible to compete without a physical edge, but what I can say is I never went out with the intention of hurting someone. It's all or nothing and if you pull out of tackles you will end up in trouble; but I've never tried to injure someone.'

Hunter would form the backbone of *the* great Leeds team with Jack Charlton, who is happy to act as a character witness for Hunter when we speak on the phone. 'The centre-half is meant to win the ball and if he starts giving fouls away around the penalty area he'll soon have the manager on his back,' says Charlton. 'Norman was a great tackler, but occasionally he would mistime one. People laugh when I say that and think it's a joke, but nobody should have picked on Norman. We were both Geordie lads and they always teach you how to tackle right, up there. We were a good partnership. My strength was in the air and Norman's was on the floor. We got on well enough and played for a few years, and then he came to me one day and said, "I'm sick of listening to you telling me what to do all the bloody time." I said, "Good lad, you'll be all right now, then."

'There was a lot of stuff that went on that I didn't agree with, but I never got involved. I'd watch other people do it and it would drive me mad. People deliberately went out to hurt people, but it worked both ways. We took a lot of stick. It was just that we did it better collectively than the rest. It was a case of "Cross us and the whole team will get you back, so watch out!"

'Me and Norman were never dirty, though. In all my time at Leeds I can only remember giving two or three penalties away. A couple of times I handballed it to stop an open goal. I'd have been sent off now, but things were different then. But neither Norman nor myself ever went out there to hurt someone.'

If Hunter was singled out as the benchmark by which the Leeds thugs set their studmarks, Charlton caused an almighty furore himself when he claimed to have a little black book filled with the names of those players he was intent on getting back for past crimes. He made the quip in a Tyne Tees television interview, the remark was taken out of context and the Press had a field day. They insisted Charlton be kicked out of football for saying he would kick his victims five yards over the touchline. Charlton still maintains he was only being honest. 'If someone nearly breaks your leg you don't forget it,' he says. 'There were vendettas. But I didn't mean it to be taken literally when I said I had a black book.'

Nevertheless, the hue and cry that followed woke the gin-soaked officials at the FA and Charlton was called before them to explain himself. At first he was incredulous and angry. But after being placated by Don Revie he offered an insincere apology which satisfied the FA, who cleared him. The incident, not surprisingly, turned Charlton against many journalists and it is with a great sense of relief that I find him to be such an amiable and helpful (albeit from a long distance) interviewee.

Both Charlton and Hunter came from the North-east and used football to escape a life down the pits. Charlton actually spent 16 weeks training to be a miner when he was 15, but disliked the work intensely and was thinking about joining the police when he was offered a trial at Leeds. He made his début as a 17-year-old, but then found his football career stonewalled by having to do two years' national service in the Royal Horse Guards. He would later recall how he inadvertently tried to cadge a light off Prince Philip as he sloped off for a sly fag at a polo match. 'I didn't know who it was,' he protested. The story is typical Charlton, the plain-speaking pit man showing scant regard for the pretences of the power-brokers.

After his national service, Charlton returned to Leeds but, by his own admission, was something of a pain to everyone. Part of the trouble was the fact that Charlton, under the influence of ex-Leeds player George Ainsley, had become interested in coaching. He took his FA coaching badge at Lilleshall and started to work in the schools in Leeds, Castleford and Bradford. 'I had a lot of ideas,' he says. 'I thought I knew a thing or two because I'd been away and I'd suggest things; but they'd just say, "Stop moaning and get on with it – this is how we do it." The thing is, we didn't have any coaching at Leeds in those days. A day's training would consist of turning up, running the long side of the pitch and walking the short side. For variety they'd say, turn around and go the other way. Then we'd go on to the tarmac car park and play seven-a-side. Nobody taught you anything and nobody learned anything. It was ridiculous and I got bloody fed up with it.'

In addition, Charlton admits he had become 'a bit of a Jack the Lad'. He adds: 'I was boozing, staying out late and there were girls. I had a bit of a chip on my shoulder and I was causing a fair bit of aggravation at the club.'

When Don Revie took over as manager, Charlton's life was about to undergo an inexorable change. From being the loud-mouthed rogue with the famous brother, Charlton would ascend to the status of World Cup winner himself. However, he reveals things were far from rosy at the start of the Revie era. The two had played together at Leeds and, though Charlton admired Revie's talents, he was irritated by his criticism. 'I used to charge about all over the pitch, which was a bit unprofessional,' he says. 'Don said to me once that if he was manager then he wouldn't pick me. I said I was glad he wasn't the manager. Of course, before I knew it, he bloody well was!'

At the time Charlton could scarcely have imagined that one day he would dedicate his memoirs to Revie for 'changing the direction of my life'. Those early years were blighted by a perditionable battle of wills between the two. 'One day he was bollocking me at half-time in a game against Rotherham for something which wasn't my fault,' Charlton recalls. 'I had a cup of tea in my hand so I hurled it at him. It missed him by a few inches and smashed against the wall. Everyone went quiet apart from me. Don just walked out. Later he said we would not discuss games on a Saturday in future. We'd wait until the Monday so everyone had a chance to calm down, because we were too full of adrenaline right after a game. You're on a high and not thinking too clearly. It was a good decision.'

The antipathy between the two would prove to be a storm in a shattered teacup, however. Charlton came to appreciate Revie's ways and respected the new-found professionalism he instilled in the club. 'Nobody knew how Don would be as a manager, but the first thing he did was to bring in qualified people. Les Cocker and Syd Owen arrived and they knew how to teach you the game. I began to enjoy my football more. Don was also a stickler for detail and we'd go over every free kick and corner, how to tackle, how to shovel people, how to defend. Things got more professional.'

Nevertheless, there was one final bridge to be overcome before Charlton would commit himself to the Revie regime. In 1962 Leeds finished 19th in Division Two and only avoided relegation via that last-day 3–0 defeat of Newcastle. One day Revie called Charlton into his office and told him he was prepared to sell him. Charlton was furious, as Revie had been playing him out of position at centre-forward. 'I was no John Charles,' he says. He stormed out of the office and thought he would soon be leaving the club too.

There was no shortage of salubrious takers for the bellyacher. Bill Shankly rang Charlton to tell him he was interested, but felt Leeds were holding him to ransom. Shankly was happy to pay £28,500, but would not be pushed to the £30,000 Revie was demanding. Then there was Matt Busby and the chance to join up with 'our Robert'. Manchester United went on a summer tour of America and when they returned, the elder Charlton found himself sitting across the desk from Busby at Old Trafford. 'He said he wanted to leave it until the start of the season, because they had this young lad and they wanted to see how he got on,' he recalls. 'I said, no chance! I'd caused a hell of a lot of aggravation at Elland Road by not signing and now here was Matt Busby telling me he wanted me to hang on until the next season just in case they needed me. I was sick. I left him there and went back to Leeds. I apologised to Don and told him I wouldn't cause him any more trouble. He offered me a new contract and I signed.'

A little more than a year earlier, Norman Hunter had made his Leeds début as an 18-year-old. Nine years younger than Charlton, he had cut a waif-like figure when he was signed as an apprentice. An ardent Newcastle United fan, he was as unsure about Leeds as they were about him. Revie ordered Hunter to consume raw eggs and sherry for breakfast in an effort to boost his skeletal physique, while the teenager wondered whether his sojourn south would ever amount to anything. 'Luckily, I met Billy Bremner early on and we lodged together in Mrs Leighton's house,' he remembers. 'It wasn't the grandest place around, but she'd iron our shirts and keep us fed. Her husband, Cornelius, was a strict man and he'd be standing at the top of the stairs to make sure we weren't late home. If we weren't back by a quarter to ten, or eleven at weekends, we'd be in trouble.'

Revie's predecessor, Jack Taylor, was utterly unconvinced by Hunter, but Revie had no doubts. He made him his second signing after Albert Johanneson and Hunter would go on to spend 15 years at Elland Road. However, it could all have ended before it had begun had fate not taken a hand in his fledgling days. Hunter and his great friend Terry Casey were getting a lift off a young goalkeeper called

Alan Humphreys. 'We both wanted to sit in the front, but Terry was very quick and he beat me to it,' says Hunter phlegmatically. 'I ended up squashed between two other lads in the back. We went round this corner and skidded into a truck and the car just crumpled on Terry's side. He was badly hurt. There was a lot of internal damage and he was lucky to live.'

Casey's career was over, while Hunter, shaken but uninjured, was ready to leave his back-seat role and take centre stage. 'I went five years without missing a single game,' he says proudly. 'And the gaffer would pick the same side nine times out of ten. There was never any resting. It wasn't like today where you have enormous squads and rotas. It was a problem for us. We were always involved and the backlog of games we'd get would end up costing us. The games all rolled into one. One year we were going for four trophies but lost the lot. Nothing was special. Finals and semi-finals should be something great, but we'd have one on the Saturday and another on the Wednesday. It was a blur. We didn't get bored, but you'd end up with tired minds and tired bodies. When we beat Arsenal in the 1972 FA Cup final it wasn't a classic by any stretch of the imagination and I remember this great feeling of anti-climax at the end. My mate Terry Cooper came hobbling into the dressing-room on crutches, because he had a broken leg, and I can remember just sitting in the bath, exhausted, thinking "bloody hell, I've waited and waited for this, now what?" I felt totally flat.'

Nevertheless, Leeds did win a lot and the Hunter–Charlton axis was the igneous foundation on which the Leeds dynasty was built. The line-up which Revie would pick nine times out of ten became the stuff of legend. Sprake, Reaney, Charlton, Hunter, Cooper, Lorimer, Bremner, Giles, Gray, Clarke and Jones. It was an eclectic mix of artists and artisans, the magical and the Machiavellian, a silk-wrapped sledgehammer which would pound its course to infamy and glory.

Both Charlton and Hunter are adamant that the vilification of Leeds has been a result of a deep-seated prejudice. 'The London press were very jealous,' says Charlton. 'It was the same when I was at Middlesbrough and we went to the top of the table for a while. They didn't like that one bit.'

Hunter dismisses the geographical argument. 'I don't think it's a North–South thing so much as the British dislike of success. For ten years we were never outside the top four, but Don Revie never got the credit he deserved and that's the one thing that disappoints me. The fact is it is the British mentality to knock those who do well. Now at every ground you go to you hear people chanting that they hate Manchester United. It's the same thing.

'Our image didn't help us either. People highlight the cynical side of that Leeds team, but it doesn't bother me. I know who I played with and I know what great players they were. There were a lot more great players all around the League in those days and you'd have to be on your mettle every single week. There were no coasters.'

Revie would struggle to understand the hatred his team inspired. He regarded himself as a consummate professional and was deeply hurt by the allegations which would follow his team wherever they played. In 1974 he wrote an extensive article, detailing the exacting standards of behaviour he expected from his players:

> On arrival at Elland Road, any new boy, be he a young apprentice professional or an already established star, is quick to appreciate that he should combine courage, hard but fair play and complete confidence on the field, with courtesy, good conduct, manners and humility away from it.
>
> To assist with this, we hold our own educational classes at United with members of the staff as the tutors and the incoming teenagers as pupils. Augmented by advice from outside professional and trade organisations, we inculcate into the lads a knowledge of dining out, checking into and out of hotels, how to travel in comfort, even how to reply to toasts and many other things. In addition there is the emphasis upon religious advice, if they want it, and talks on girlfriends, male and female fans etc.
>
> We have the situation in which any club and its players are faced with the dual problem of winning games and doing so with dignity. I could be said to be particularly conscious of this, because of what I believe to be a totally unfair impression given abroad about Leeds when we first started to chase honours. I refer of course to the suggestion that we were more physical than skilful. I have never subscribed to any such view, neither did I to any suggestion that we were more a defensive side than anything else. While winning matches is of vital importance, the manner in which successes are achieved must also be considered. The other vital factor ancillary to winning matches, and winning them in the right spirit, is that the boys who obtain these honours for a club and its city, and in turn are fêted by them, should be honourable representatives of that club and that city.

To go to such lengths to defend himself, his methods and his team goes to show how strongly Revie felt that he was wronged. In the same article he concluded: 'I recall George Best saying, when asked how he rated Leeds, that "their strength is that they have no weaknesses. They also possess a tremendous team spirit and players of great individual skills." I'd like to think George was echoing the thoughts of most people in football, but for a long time we had to suffer other things being said about us and bear it with dignity. And that is what being champions is all about, really – wearing a crown with dignity.'

The great irony and sadness of Don Revie is that he will be forever be remembered as a man who sacrificed his dignity at the altar of the filthy lucre. His departure from the England job for big money in the Middle East was the final nail in his reputation's coffin. For the anti-Leeds media the defection was a gilt-edged opportunity. They put two and two together and got 666. However,

Charlton insists that even in his moment of weakness, Revie was misjudged. 'Don left the England job under a cloud and it was purely self-inflicted. But Don was a very honest man and every journalist in Britain soon had it in for him because he kept a promise. The thing is, Don's job with England was very tenuous. He had an almighty row with Harold Thompson at the FA and said if they paid him up he'd leave. Now England were going on a tour of South America, but Don had a meeting with a guy who worked in the Middle East. So he decided to fly out and have a look at the place and then join up with the England party a few days later. The trouble was, there was a journalist on the plane. He approached Don and asked why, when the England squad was flying in one direction, he was going in the other? Don said that if he didn't print the story then he'd give him an exclusive if he did leave the England job. And he kept that promise, but he upset every journalist in the land apart from the fella at the *Daily Mail* who got his story. He did it wrong. He should have held a press conference and told everybody at the same time. But he kept his word and was tainted with it forever. The Press never forgave him and he never worked in football in this country again.'

That was the end of the Revie story, but it had been a page-turning thriller. Hunter, Charlton and the rest of the great Leeds team are blessed with a fabulous pot-pourri of memories thanks to the son of a Middlesbrough joiner. It had all started on 15 March 1961: Leeds chairman Harry Reynolds was writing a reference for Revie, who was seeking to move into football management at Bournemouth. Suddenly, Reynolds had one of those light-bulb moments. He binned the letter and offered the 33-year-old former Leicester, Hull, Manchester City, Sunderland and Leeds player the vacant manager's job. It was a wonderful whim.

Revie's vision would take a while getting off the ground, but he was brimming with ideas. 'I remember him telling us that he was going to change the kit and we were going to play in white,' says Hunter. 'He wanted us to be like Real Madrid. Nobody said anything. We just went along with it. He had that drive that sucked you in.'

Revie's faith in Hunter, and Charlton's decision to walk out of Matt Busby's office and pledge himself to Leeds, finally paid off in 1969 when Leeds got their 0–0 draw at Anfield to secure the First Division crown. 'It was an awful game,' recalls Hunter. 'We played Billy Bremner in front of the back four. I'll never forget the gaffer saying to us beforehand that if we're the champions by the end he wanted us to go to the Kop. We all looked at him as though he was mad, because the Liverpool fans are as passionate as anybody about their football. Well, we were the champions and I can still see him pointing at us and telling us to go to the Kop. So we approached it and suddenly the place went deathly quiet. It was incredible. I wondered what was going to happen. And then somebody hoists this fella onto his shoulders and this one voice starts chanting "Champions". A single voice in this almighty hush. Then the whole place erupted. "Champions, champions, champions". It was absolutely unbelievable, but there was always a lot of respect between those two clubs. There still is. No animosity whatsoever.'

Leeds would make five finals in the next four years, but claimed only two trophies. For Hunter, the hardest defeat to come to terms with was the 1970 FA Cup final loss to Chelsea. 'There was always feeling between Leeds and Chelsea,' he says. 'You can't deny that. It was the build-up to the North–South divide. The Press was trying to whip that up at the time. There was a programme on the television before the final. It was all about how they were all downtown in Soho with their trendy clothes, while we just a bunch of northerners with our cloth caps and whippets, playing bingo. I still can't work out how we lost. We were by far the better side and Eddie Gray tormented the life out of David Webb; but Peter Bonetti was outstanding for them in goal.

'It wasn't hard to pick ourselves up. We had a lot of disappointments, but Don would always tell us to forget it and go harder the next season. It got to you when there were things going on beyond your control like the referee in the European Cup-Winners' Cup final against AC Milan. As soon as we landed in Greece there were rumours going around, but you say to yourself, "This is a European final, surely not." By half-time it was obvious. But sitting in the changing-rooms, we thought we could still win it regardless of the referee.' They couldn't and Hunter was sent off for the first time in his career.

'That was sad because we thought it was Don's last game,' he says. 'He was meant to be going to Everton and had actually broken down and cried in the dressing-room before the kick-off. To think it had ended like that, with a referee who would get banned for life for taking bribes, was very sad.'

Revie eventually decided to stay for another year, but while one era was given a stay of execution, another had ended. Some 22 years after arriving at Elland Road, Jack Charlton was leaving. From being a dissentient teenager, Charlton had matured into a man who respected Revie and would take much that he had learnt into his own highly-successful managerial career with Middlesbrough, Sheffield Wednesday, Newcastle and, most famously, the Republic of Ireland.

'I picked up a lot from him,' says Charlton of Revie. 'Don would leave no stone unturned in his efforts to make his players understand what he wanted. When I said I wanted to leave, he offered me a two-year-contract even though I was 38. When I made it clear I wanted to go into management he told me to ring him if I ever needed any advice. I appreciated that.

'If you had to put Don Revie on some scale of great managers he would be very, very high up. He had his quirks, all right, and was incredibly superstitious, and that did rub off on the rest of us. I'd always go into the toilet to read the programme and then put my left boot on before the right. The time we nearly broke the record for the number of games unbeaten, it was taking us nearly an hour to get changed. Once he even brought in this medium fella from Blackpool because he'd heard there was a gipsy curse on the ground.'

Charlton laughs at the memory of such eccentricities. 'After that rocky start we got on fine. He was my biggest influence and I don't know what might have happened to me if I'd never met him. He loved his players. People would write to him and tell him that they'd seen me and Billy getting drunk in the pub on a Thursday night. It was rubbish. We used to go to the local and have a pint of beer and play dominoes, but we'd never have too much. Don called us in a couple of times and told us what he'd heard, but then he'd say, "Oh, all right then, go ahead, as long as you're not drunk." He trusted you to do it the right way and it never did us any harm. My mother's cousin was Jackie Milburn and he'd tell me never to drink bottled beer because draught was better for you. He'd say it goes through your system better and has plenty of calories: "You'll never be an alcoholic drinking beer."'

Charlton cackles down the phone line. He is good company even when he is a few hundred miles away. By no means the most talented footballer to play for Leeds, he was still the most successful. Apart from his triumphs with Leeds, he was lauded by Pelé and is the only player in the club's history to possess a World Cup-winner's medal. Writing about the 1970 World Cup victory over England, Pelé said: 'The English team has some outstanding players – people like Bobby Moore, Terry Cooper, Bobby and Jackie Charlton. They can play for any Brazilian team at any time and that is no light compliment.'

Charlton's memories of the momentous day of 30 July 1966 when England beat West Germany 4–2 after extra-time are typically colourful. He remembers the Germans equalising in the last moments of the game and his brother Bobby crying in disbelief and repeating 'Fucking hell, fucking hell' like a mantra. Then he remembers Geoff Hurst's controversial strike, which would send a Russian linesman into footballing folklore. 'I asked Roger Hunt, who was on the spot, if it was over the line and he just grinned at me and said, "Oh yeah, easy."' He missed Geoff Hurst's third goal because he was looking at Bobby Moore, who had calmly taken the ball down and played a killer pass into space for Hurst to run on to and score. 'I looked over at him and thought, Christ, I'll never be able to play this game.' He also remembers his mother scolding him the next morning for staying out all night partying!

Charlton was not the only one to be in awe of Bobby Moore. Charlton earned 35 caps in a five-year spell. Norman Hunter gained seven fewer, but had a much longer international career, spanning nine years. Why, then, did he end up with so few caps? The answer is Bobby Moore, who was capped 108 times between 1962 and 1974. 'Some people seem to think Bobby cheated me out of more caps, but he was a better player than me for England's style,' said Hunter. 'At club level I was probably more consistent, but once he slipped on that number six shirt for England, he was absolutely brilliant.'

When the 33-year-old Moore finally bowed out of international football, it left Hunter with the tantalising proposition of playing in the 1974 World Cup finals in Germany. However, with a perversity of fate which is exclusive to the tragi-comedy of sport, Hunter would be the architect of his dream's downfall. When England played Poland at Wembley they needed a win to make it to Germany. Hunter's error close to the half-way line sparked the Polish breakaway which saw Domarski shoot past a lame effort from Peter Shilton (doing his best Gary Sprake) to score after 58 minutes. Allan Clarke equalised six minutes later but, try as they might, Tony Currie, Martin Peters and Mick Channon could not beat Jan Tomaszewski, the man Brian Clough had myopically labelled a clown.

'I messed it up against Poland,' said Hunter. 'That's my other big regret.' He looks out of the large plate glass window and gazes at his tidy lawn. 'These are personal things,' he adds, drumming the tips of his fingers together. 'The ball just went under my foot, they scored and England did not qualify for the World Cup. The saddest thing for me was that in not qualifying, Alf Ramsey got the sack. I felt sorry for him. For my own part, it was nearly my turn too. Alf had rested Bobby Moore and was trying a bit of a changed side. If we'd qualified I think I'd have gone to play alongside the other centre-half, who would probably have been Roy McFarland. I took it very, very hard because I realised the enormity of the situation. I'd waited all these years to get a chance and had blown it. I knew I was never going to replace Bobby Moore, never in a month of Sundays; but I was his understudy for nine years! Still, you don't make mistakes on purpose and Peter Shilton could have thrown his cap on the shot and saved it nine times out of ten, but there you go. That's life.'

Charlton's departure left Revie with the sobering thought of facing a new season without his defensive colossus. He turned to Gordon McQueen, a £30,000 signing from St Mirren in 1972, and the young Scot proved a stylish replacement for the veteran sassenach. Hunter was far from finished, however. He would stay with Leeds for another three years, winning the championship in 1974 and then playing in the European Cup final in 1975. When the referee blew the whistle for the end of that game, he sunk to his knees, numbed by the defeat and perhaps subconsciously realising it was the end of more than a game. He had played in all ten of Leeds' finals between 1965 and that day. He would not play in another. And since that day a quarter of a century ago, the best Leeds have managed is the 1996 Coca-Cola Cup final when they rolled over and died somewhere on the coach trip up Wembley Way.

As Leeds slowly disintegrated post-Paris, Hunter left to join Bristol City. In 1979 he joined up with Allan Clarke at Barnsley as player-coach and would succeed his former team-mate when he left for Elland Road. Hunter took Barnsley into Division Two before being sacked in 1984, after which he had spells at West Brom, Rotherham and Leeds. He returned to his spiritual home in 1988, but scarcely had time to unpack before Howard Wilkinson arrived with fresh faces and fresh ideas. As Wilkinson insisted on taking down the pictures of the Revie heroes from the Elland Road corridors, he was hardly likely to appreciate the physical presence of one such figure. Hunter left, but joined up with another Leeds old boy, Terry Yorath, at Bradford in 1989. Now he commentates for Radio Leeds, does the after-dinner speaking circuit and makes the odd appearance on Sky.

Hunter is impressed by David O'Leary's young Leeds side and waxes lyrical about one of the few old heads in the side, Lucas Radebe. He says the current team has the same togetherness that knitted the Revie side together. What they have not got, though, is a combination like Charlton and Hunter. Steely and steelier. Charlton played 773 times for Leeds, more than anyone else before or since, and it is impossible to see anyone ever breaking that mark. He scored 96 goals, making him the ninth-highest goalscorer in the club's history. Hunter made 724 appearances, scoring 21 goals. Almost 1,500 appearances between them. That equates to around 94 full days playing for Leeds United. They were a class act. In 1967 Charlton was named Footballer of the Year. The only other Leeds players to have won the award are Bobby Collins, Billy Bremner and Gordon Strachan – though Revie, Syd Owen and Jimmy Adamson were also awarded the accolade during their playing days elsewhere.

Seven years after Charlton's award, Hunter became the first PFA Player of the Year, voted by fellow professional footballers. No other Leeds player has ever won it. If we are truly to believe, as Pat Collins suggests, that Hunter was a cynical bully, there were an awful lot of people who disagreed. One of them was Kevin Keegan, who voted for Hunter in 1974. 'He did not get enough credit for his skill,' he said later. 'He could flight the ball beautifully with his left foot. He was skilful and hard, but if he lived by the sword he was also prepared to die by it and that earned him a lot of respect. A great player.' Keegan also recalled how he travelled from his home in Wales to play in Hunter's testimonial in May 1975. 'I drove 100 miles and the first thing he did was chop me down!'

Keegan bore no grudge and appreciated that the sum was greater than the malignant part that the media were happy to magnify (to the extent that future generations now have distorted views of the 1970s). As I shake hands with Hunter, and he puts his golf clubs in the back of his car and contemplates his opening tee shot, I remember the words of Johnny Giles. 'Being Leeds United, we always have to defend ourselves,' he said.

The combination of Hunter and Charlton made a cast-iron case for the defence.

A BIT OF BATTY

People often ask me how you find the North Star. Well, it's quite easy. First of all, it's always in the north.

PATRICK MOORE

To understand the importance of David Batty, you really have to come from Yorkshire. He is the perfect synthesis of Briggate, Tetley's Bitter, sooty black buildings, Alan Bennett and a time line of hard-men in white including Bobby Collins, Billy Bremner and Johnny Giles. Batty is a Leeds boy who has matured into a leading man; yet it is more than a parochial faith in the local-hero phenomenon which makes him so loved. Batty is steeped in Yorkshireisms. He has that brusque honesty and transparent sense of perspective which is part of the Leeds psyche. His game matches the Yorkshire personality. Short, no-nonsense passes. An inherent lack of flair. This is real Yorkshire. This is the Yorkshire of Harvey Smith and his two-fingered salute, not your Harvey Nicks and six-figure price tags. 'The world had better watch out for Leeds United,' claimed chairman Peter Ridsdale after Batty signed for Leeds from Newcastle in 1998. He was home and, after the days of Rush, Hateley and Palmer, the world made more sense again.

My first and only meeting with David Batty came about ten years earlier when we were both starting out. I was taking a year off from university and decided to masquerade as a sports reporter, so I rang up several teenage sports magazines and asked if they wanted any articles on Leeds players. I lied and said I'd already arranged an interview with Gordon Strachan. They weren't interested, so I said, what about Batty? One mag said yes. So I rang Elland Road and they quickly set up a time and date. It was a million miles away from the long-winded process I have had to wade through in order to meet the current players. I turned up to Elland Road and walked into the reception at the agreed time. To my surprise Batty was already there, chatting away to John Lukic, forever the oversized Beatle with that basin hairstyle which would prove the most consistent feature of his career.

We sat down and Batty, who would have been 20 at the time, told me how he had stood on the terraces and idolised Billy Bremner. 'I dreamed of being out on the pitch when I was a kid and sometimes I have to pinch myself. Billy was me hero and it's unbelievable to be following in his footsteps.' Later Batty would receive the number four shirt, an honour he appreciated and which championed the comparison between the two midfield battlers; it was also an act which Vinnie Jones would recall spelled the beginning of his own messy end. Batty was the right man for the shirt, though. No question. If you wanted someone to take up the mantle of Bremner and adapt it for the last decade of the twentieth century, Batty was the obvious choice.

It was less than a year since Bremner had been sacked as Leeds manager, which I imagined must have been difficult for Batty to take. Years later he would say Bremner had been a father-figure to him. 'I think he saw something of me in him,' he said. 'And I thought the world of him. I couldn't have had a better teacher.' Bremner would reciprocate those sentiments. 'He was absolutely fearless,' he said of Batty.

To be quintessentially Leeds, you have to be misjudged in the eyes of the rest of the world. When Batty broke into the Leeds team as an 18-year-old in November 1987, he was hard and unfair. What his tackles lacked in accuracy, they made up for in intent. Bremner called him a Yorkshire terrier, but many thought he was more like Cujo, the rabid Saint Bernard from the eponymous Stephen King novel. His reputation was sealed in that fleeting period. Batty, from the beastly city – as Charles Dickens would have Leeds – was a dirty, grimy urchin.

My enduring memory of Batty in the early days is of the way he could take punishment as well as dish it out. People would claim Batty was a hothead, but I disagreed. If someone dumped Batty on the floor then he would get up, brush himself down and get on with the game in hand. To me this was the hallmark of the true hard-man. Now people talk about Denis Wise in that respect, but that is a laughable claim. As the poet Simon Armitage astutely pointed out, if Wise was not playing football he would be the short one in East 17 or working in a fairground. Norman Hunter dismissed him as a 'minor irritation', a bit like pins and needles. Wise is forever squaring up to the bellybuttons of taller players, snarling like a malevolent hamster and making a general nuisance of himself. I think he is actually an underrated footballer, but with those narrow rodent eyes and a face which smacks of vitamin deficiency, he is the taxi-driver's nightmare and the taxidermist's dream. He is not hard. He's just a poisoned dwarf with a chip on his shoulder.

Batty would soon clean up his tackling and rise through the ranks. But that image, of a limited midfielder with a nasty streak, stuck for years. When he was at Blackburn he was involved in a farcical spat with team-mate Graeme Le Saux during a European Champions' League game at Spartak Moscow. Le Saux took the ball off Batty and conceded a throw-in, whereupon the England full-back aimed a punch at Leeds' finest. The tabloids made a mountain out of the comical incident, which highlighted Blackburn's stunning post-title implosion, but overlooked the fact Batty had not thrown a punch back. Maybe it was the fact Le Saux was the darling of the media because of his stance as a self-styled outsider, a *Guardian*-reading, indie music fan. He wasn't the first to be called an anomaly. Previously, it had been Pat Nevin, an intelligent Scot with, God forbid, political concerns. Maybe it was that. Or maybe it represented a microcosm of football's class warfare, as one columnist laughingly suggested. More likely it was the fact that this was entirely the sort of graceless confrontation that they liked to think had followed Batty around since he was plucked from Tingley Athletic.

Batty joined Leeds from the marvellously Yorkshire-sounding Tingley in July 1985 and after the championship win of 1992 he seemed set to stay put forever. However, in October 1993 he was sold to Blackburn for £2.75 million. Howard Wilkinson had been reluctant to let him go, but the board needed the cash. His hands were tied and, though he did not know it at the time, his feet had been set in concrete. The Leeds fans were furious. Switchboards were jammed as radio phone-ins offered therapy. Having witnessed a pathetically lame title defence the previous season, the man with whom they empathised more than any other was going from Yorkshire to Lancashire. There were angry protests. Some 18 months after being the cream of the crop, Leeds had flirted with relegation and finished 17th, failing to win a single away game all season. And they had sold Cantona and Batty, two of the most popular players of recent times. Some insiders sympathised with Wilkinson, saying it was a board decision which Batty was quite happy to go along with. 'Sometimes you need to move on, have a change of scenery,' said Gordon Strachan.

Blackburn had been promoted via the play-offs the year Leeds won the title, but with Jack Walker throwing money at manager Kenny Dalglish, their ascent was a sudden one. The Premiership team would be almost unrecognisable from the one which ground their way to promotion courtesy of a controversial penalty against Leicester at Wembley. The strength of the side was undeniably the SAS strikeforce of Alan Shearer and Chris Sutton, but Walker funded quality recruits in almost every position. In 1995 Blackburn won the title as Manchester United failed to beat West Ham at Upton Park. Their success only served to underline Leeds' dwindling status. Suffering from injury, Batty only played five games for Blackburn that season and, as a result, did not get a second championship medal.

He almost got one the following season following his £3.75 million switch to Newcastle United. However, Alex Ferguson's mind games famously hit the target and Kevin Keegan exploded during a live television broadcast. Ferguson suggested Leeds had been 'cheating their manager' because of the way they fought against Manchester United in the title run-in. When Newcastle squeaked past Leeds soon afterwards, Keegan let rip: 'He went down in my estimation when he said that. I'll tell you this, honestly, I will love it if we beat them. Love it!'

They didn't. Newcastle choked and Batty was deprived of that medal. Newcastle were runners-up the year after too, but when Keegan abdicated in

January 1997 saying he had taken the club as far as he could, the decline started. Batty was reunited with his old Blackburn boss, Kenny Dalglish, but the marvellously gung-ho football which had thrilled a nation was replaced by a safety-first funeral dirge. The Geordies were unimpressed. It was like going from being entertained by Sinatra to a bloke with the spoons.

By this point Batty's international career was in full flow. He made his début as a substitute against the USSR in 1991, but it took Batty some time to establish himself. In fairness, that was as much to do with Graham Taylor's metamorphosis into a vegetable as it was his own form. England qualified in some style for Euro 92, but they would flop badly and finish last in their group. Draws against Denmark and France had been unremarkable but for the butt which bloodied Stuart Pearce's nose in the latter, and England needed a win against host nation Sweden to guarantee a semi-final place. Taylor decided to employ Batty as a right-back for the game, which smacked of desperation. To be fair, England were without Lee Dixon, Rob Jones and Gary Stevens – all natural full-backs – but the selection of Batty even as an interim measure had the scribes sharpening their poisoned quills. Batty did reasonably well in the circumstances, helping create the opening strike for David Platt; but a late goal from Tomas Brolin, the lost member of Hanson and later a spectacularly unsuccessful Leeds player, sealed England's fate.

The gamble on Batty was seen as a failure. Had it worked, it would have been a turn up for the books. In failure, Taylor became a turnip for the history books in a merciless newspaper campaign led by *The Sun*. The fact Taylor had substituted Gary Lineker half an hour from time was also held against him. Lineker would never play for England again and was thus deprived of a chance to beat Bobby Charlton's goalscoring record. As well as everything else, Taylor was accused of being vindictive.

Worse was to follow for Taylor, Batty and England. In 1993 they lost 2–0 to the USA. Then defeat against Holland in Rotterdam effectively ended their chances of qualifying for the 1994 World Cup. Having been subjected to the most personal newspaper assault of any England manager in history, Taylor belatedly bowed to the pressure and resigned.

Batty made just three appearances in the next three years, but, free from injury, he became a fixture under Glenn Hoddle. He was a substitute in Hoddle's first game in charge in 1997 and became a regular, playing in the epic 0–0 draw in Rome which sealed England's passage to the 1998 World Cup.

Since the bunting was taken down and the last ticker tape was washed away in 1966, England's international story is one of massive expectation unfulfilled. They have made no major final since, they have slipped down the world rankings and they have fuelled the nation's love of the unlucky loser. It is part of the British psyche to applaud glorious failure and frown upon unabashed success. You only have to look at the way Prince Naseem Hamed is reviled. A fantastically talented boxer, he is disliked for his arrogance, razzmatazz and killer streak. He is a clown.

Who do we prefer? Some flawed fall guy called Bruno whose prostrate form would see him rise to prominence. A perennial failure who now specialises in dressing up in tights and playing Widow Twankey.

It is a similar thing in football. Nobody much cared for Gazza until he started crying in Italy, and Stuart Pearce's penalty miss at the 1990 World Cup endeared him to everyone. When he went on to score a penalty in the shootout against Spain in Euro 96 it was a cathartic moment for us all. We revelled in those veins spreading like a spider's web across his neck as he rejoiced like, well, like a psycho should, really. One game later and Gareth Southgate replaced Pearce as our favourite duffer. His penalty miss in the semi-final against Germany – who else? – sealed our fate and meant Terry Venables would fail to dissociate himself from the nearly men who preceded him. Southgate would play on his failure by making a pizza advert: a triumph of expedience and anchovies over adversity.

Two years later and Batty would be added to this list. England's game against Argentina in the second round of the 1998 World Cup was a classic that had everything apart from a result. It finished 2–2 and so it came down to penalties again. The previous week a journalist had asked Batty, whose lack of goals for club and country had become a source of fun, whether he would fancy taking a penalty if the opportunity arose. 'Not a chance,' he said with characteristic forthrightness. After all, this was the man who had to wait nigh on four years to score his first senior goal (in a 3–0 defeat of Manchester City on 7 September 1992).

Batty was the fifth man to take up the challenge. Paul Ince, the self-styled Guvnor, who had been ridiculed for not taking a spot-kick in the Southgate shootout, had already missed. It was all or nothing for England when Batty stepped up. Brian Moore, commentating on his last match, asked co-commentator Kevin Keegan, 'Yes or no?' Keegan had little option but to say, 'Yes.' Gary Neville, the England and Manchester United full-back, said: 'I expected him to score. But five minutes from the end I was looking around the pitch thinking I can't see any natural penalty-takers out here.' At least Neville, who was down on Hoddle's list as the sixth penalty-taker, was spared a go at Russian roulette. Back in England, Batty's father had no doubts about his son's capabilities as he watched the drama unfold on television. 'I knew he would miss even before he took it,' he said. Miss it he duly did. England, who had played for 75 minutes with ten men following David Beckham's sending-off, were glorious failures again.

Batty took his miss stoically. He failed to live up to the way we wish our much-loved losers to react. There was no collapsing to his knees like Pearce, no tears like Southgate. Batty just poked out his tongue, winced a little and walked back to the half-way line. In the post-match press conference, as journalists sought a shattered figure, Batty fended questions with that bluff honesty Leeds fans so loved. 'Glenn asked me if I would take one and I agreed. I'd have volunteered anyway. All I could see was scoring and taking us into the next round. I was really confident, even though it was the first penalty I have taken since I was a kid. It hasn't sunk in. I'm upset, but I'm really proud of the way we played.'

We wanted Batty to be battered and broken, to need our sympathy to restore him. We would follow him until he released the demons, just as Pearce had in scoring from 12 yards against Spain six years on from his demise. But Batty was different. He just got on with things. There was no need for an exorcism or a pizza advert, no World Cup diary exploiting his misfortune. We should not have suspected anything else. This was the man who smiled and waved to his twins at home when the cameraman focused on each player during the national anthems. He had his priorities right. Do what you can, but there's no point killing yourself over spilt milk. And so, with Batty failing to fit into the stereotype, the Press turned from the heroic failure to the treacherous pariah and Beckham was crucified.

That December, Batty returned home to Leeds for £4.4 million. 'I'd left with tears in my eyes five years ago,' he said. 'I thought Newcastle were asking too much for me and I wasn't sleeping. If I'm not enjoying my football it affects me in different ways and I'm glad common sense prevailed.' Having made his first signing as manager, David O'Leary hit the nail on the head. 'I don't think he should have been allowed to leave in the first place,' he said.

O'Leary saw Batty as the experienced anchor for his exuberant young charges, but his first season back was plagued by problems. In his début, against Coventry, he picked up a rib injury which sidelined him for three months. The season just completed has been equally frustrating. Early on he damaged an Achilles tendon, and a calf, which has caused him to sit out the majority of a season where his nous and calmness would have been of enormous benefit, and then it was revealed he was taking tablets to control a heart condition. As the 1999–2000 season came to an end, the more pessimistic Leeds fans wondered whether they would ever see Batty in a Leeds shirt again.

Batty's agent tells me the man is writing a book and so is not doing interviews at the moment. Undaunted, I send a letter to Batty via Elland Road asking if he would be willing to meet one day. Soon afterwards I receive a reply. He has scrawled a brief but courteous note declining my invitation.

Dear Rick,
Many thanks for your letter. As you can imagine I am trying to keep
my own thoughts on what has happened in my career to myself with
my own book due to be started on soon.
Thanks,
David.

I imagine Batty will need the help of a ghostwriter to talk up his achievements. Leave it all to the man himself and you will probably get the most self-effacing memoirs of all time. This is biography Leeds style. 'Played well, played for England, missed a penalty, big deal, came home, got a heart problem, nothing serious, the end.'

To the Leeds faithful, if there is one thing David Batty – ex-Tingley Athletic and doyen of the Gelderd End – does not have a problem with, it is heart. He is the life-blood of the side, his clever linking passes diverging as though through capillaries over the great body of Leeds United. Vinnie Jones may have a Leeds tattoo, but Batty needs no such tacky trappings of allegiance. He is Leeds.

We are Leeds.

And that really is the heart of the matter.

MICHAEL BRIDGES, STEPHEN MCPHAIL & HARRY KEWELL — Babybabble

You'll never win anything with kids.
ALAN HANSEN

A study in *The Independent* in April 2000 states that the average Premiership footballer aged above 20 earns £409,000 a year. It adds that 39 per cent earn more than £500,000, while an élite nine per cent rake in a cool million. Just under 600 players from all divisions took part in the confidential survey which also concludes that there are around 100 Premiership players earning £1 million every year. And then there are endorsements and sponsorships, bonuses, subsidised houses and company cars. Alessandro Del Piero is widely thought to be the highest-paid player in world football on a staggering basic wage of £6.4 million a year. When Norman Hunter became a first-team player at Leeds, his weekly wage was £13. Little wonder the *Independent* survey causes much breast-beating. This is free-market free-fall. The survey gives ammunition to the sizeable lobby who view twenty-first century footballers as overpaid prima donnas, a bunch of pampered pubescents with bad attitudes and fantastical bank balances.

The Thorp Arch car park is a barometer of change. When Norman Hunter gained promotion with Leeds, he received a £1,000 promotion bonus and bought a Vauxhall Viva with the money. 'It was my pride and joy,' he said. Now the car park at Leeds' training ground is populated by an array of Mercs, BMWs, Porsches, the odd Subaru, a black Ferrari and a beautiful Aston Martin. The latter is a Jeremy Clarkson wet dream, its metallic, pastel blue paintwork gleaming in the sunshine, the cream leather interior kept immaculately clean by the pair of valets who parade the car park with pride.

The owner of one of these dream machines is Michael Bridges, a 21-year-old who became Leeds' record signing when David O'Leary plucked him from Sunderland's substitute bench for a staggering £5 million. He is one of Leeds' magnificent crop of young talent which includes Stephen McPhail, Ian Harte, Alan Smith, Lee Bowyer, Jonathan Woodgate, Eirik Bakke, Matthew Jones and – the most highly-rated of them all – Harry Kewell. They are all young and rich. When Bowyer and Woodgate were charged with assault, many cynics hung their heads, convicted the duo without hearing any evidence and said such incidents were the inevitable result of adding too much money to too young people and multiplying by massive media exposure and too much time.

Michael Bridges has had a good season. He joined Leeds in July 1999 and was looking forward to playing alongside the experienced and proven Dutch striker, Jimmy Floyd Hasselbaink, until the man who sounds like a cross between a Chicago gangster and an offshore bank quit for even bigger money. The ego landed in Spain. It left Bridges, who had been kept out of the team at Sunderland by the partnership of Kevin Phillips and Niall Quinn, under no little pressure. After a fourth-place finish the previous season, there was a groundswell of optimism at Elland Road and nothing – not even the departure of the hugely talented Hasselbaink – would dim the fires of expectation.

Bridges scored a hat-trick at Southampton in the second game of the season. By October he had managed to win over some of the media, a feat many of his predecessors at Leeds had never managed. After an epic 4–4 draw at Everton, Guy Hodgson wrote in *The Independent*: 'The 21-year-old striker looked expensive when David O'Leary paid £5.5 million [sic] for him, but he has become the focal point of an attack that appears to have endless options.' David O'Leary was similarly impressed with a player who constituted a major gamble: 'He has the potential to be someone . . . I expect him to score goals and create them.'

Despite a superb first season at Elland Road, immense wealth, a car to die for and a £5 million-plus price tag, Bridges is the antithesis of the stereotypical soccer starlet. If there is any arrogance about him, it is consigned to his football. He even apologises because there is to be an afternoon training session which means our meeting must be more truncated than expected.

'Five million quid,' he exclaims as he recalls his move to Leeds. 'It was hard to deal with. I mean, no wonder Sunderland snatched their hands off. It was a hell of a lot of money for someone who'd not played many games. I was thinking, "Hang on a minute, I haven't done anything yet, I haven't proved myself."'

He was also well aware that there had been other big-money signings who had fallen by the wayside, derailed by an inflated fee and unfeasible presumptions. 'There was a lot of pressure,' he says as we chat by the side of the training pitch on a glorious spring day. 'I'd seen what had happened to Kevin Davies and that was nerve-racking for me. I felt sorry for him because it hadn't worked out at Blackburn. I just thought I hope I'm not next. Luckily, I got off to a good start by getting a hat-trick down at Southampton. That got the fans behind me, which is so important.'

Bridges has a soft Geordie accent and an engaging manner. In his short career he has already been likened to Dennis Bergkamp and Allan Clarke. Both are unfair comparisons: he is the first to acknowledge as much. Bridges is modest and realistic. He knows he is good, but presents the image of a young man who has fallen on his feet and appreciates his good fortune. Whereas many of the Revie side had an infallible belief that they would succeed, Bridges admits to having had more than a little self-doubt in his early years.

I ask him when he knew he was going to be a professional footballer and he says: 'I didn't. I was at Newcastle's School of Excellence when I was 12. I was there when Keegan arrived and he got rid of all the reserves and youth team. I got released and I was devastated. I went back to school and played for Wallsend Boys Club and Whitley Bay Boys Club. Then Stan Nixon took us down to Middlesbrough for a two-week trial, but I didn't get picked so I was let go again. I was 15. I did my GCSEs, but didn't get the grades I wanted, so I stayed on and did a GNVQ in leisure and tourism. After about a year, Sunderland's Jack Hickson came to watch another lad play called Simon Foster. He spied me and turned to this fella and said, "Who's the number ten?" That was my dad, who said, "It's my son, actually." So I went to Sunderland and it worked out really well. I was faced with the gamble of finishing my course or signing for Sunderland, but we came to an agreement where I'd go to college once a week for another two years. So I got my pro contract and my results. I was delighted.'

Nine months later, Bridges began to travel with the first team. 'I was absolutely crapping myself on the way down,' he remembers. 'I kept getting put on the bench to start with, but I was still delighted. Then we were playing against Port Vale at Roker Park and Peter Reid says, "Get warmed up, you're going on." The butterflies were awful and I thought I was going to be sick on the touch-line from the nerves. I was scared stiff, especially being in front of the Sunderland fans. I came on for 40 minutes and got the Man of the Match award. I just couldn't believe it.'

Bridges clearly understood the precarious nature of football as a profession and was adamant that he would get his qualifications as a safety net. 'I thought I'd be staying on at school, doing my GNVQ and maybe getting into some sort of coaching or sports teaching. But it all worked out brilliantly. Six months after signing my YT, I signed my first pro contract. It was a great feeling. To be on £40 a week to seeing your first wage packet – well, you just think, "bloody hell, what's going on?" I went out and shopped. I bought my mum and dad something. That first pro wage wasn't much, but it was better than £40 a week and it made me realise how lucky I was.'

This self-deprecation and lack of pretension makes you realise these superstars are not so different from the rest of us. I play Sunday League, Michael Bridges plays Premier League. We are all dreamers; they just have the talent to realise their dreams. The only difference is in the varying degrees of talent and rewards. Bridges scores a beautiful curler against Sheffield Wednesday and is fêted. I get an opposing centre-forward sent off in a bottom-of-the-table Sunday League scrap and am chased into a nearby housing estate by a psychotic striker wielding an axe. Bridges worries about groin strains, I worry about decapitation and getting home for my Sunday lunch. These are subtle differences.

Harry Kewell is heckling Bridges from the centre of the training pitch where the Leeds players are beginning to assemble for that afternoon's training session. Kewell has gained a reputation for keeping the media at arm's length, which is probably a wise move considering his good looks, long hair, celebrity girlfriend (Sheree Murphy from *Emmerdale*) and sublime talents. 'He keeps himself to himself and people should respect that,' says Bridges as he ignores Kewell. 'We get on really well. We live in the same street. He comes across as quiet, but once you get to know him and he lets his guard down he's a tremendous lad. He could be followed around like Beckham if he doesn't watch it, especially with the situation with his girlfriend, so I think he's going the right way about it.'

Unimpressed by Bridge's diffidence, Kewell turns his attention away from his neighbour and strike partner. Bridges returns to explaining his rise through the ranks to his current status. 'After my Sunderland début I knew that I could make a career from the game somewhere or other, whether it be First Division, Second Division or Premier League,' he says. 'I never imagined that it would come to this, though: playing in the semi-finals of European football and things like that.'

With Phillips and Quinn barring his way at Sunderland, it would have taken a psychedelic imagination to envisage such things happening so soon. 'Kev came from Watford for £250,000 and a few journalists were saying, "He's not going to do anything, you've still got a chance." I turned round to them and said, "Listen, I've seen him in training, just you wait and see." I saw one of those journalists about a year later and he said, "You were right, lad." Initially I was happy enough sitting behind Kev, but when it started to get towards the end of my contract and there were other clubs wanting us, I thought it would be a fresh challenge.'

Leeds were not the only ones to come calling, however. 'Tottenham were interested and they were the team I'd idolised as a boy from the time Waddle and Gazza went there,' he says. 'Chris Waddle was my boyhood hero. I used to take a lot of stick at school because I tried to grow my hair like his, with the long perm at the back. But Waddle was my hero along with Glenn Hoddle – apart from when they did that song 'Diamond Lights', which was minging.' So why Leeds? 'I knew a lot of the lads here, I'd watched them on TV and liked what I'd seen, and they were all young, around 21 or so. It just seemed right.'

It is early days, but it seems to have been the perfect move for Bridges. With three games of the season to go, he has notched 17 goals, has the Clarke-esque swagger and pipe-cleaner physique, plus a silky touch. He is a fan's favourite and is relishing his fortune. I put it to him that players cannot have the same hunger as the Revie team, considering the disparity in wages. I remember Billy Bremner saying in 1974 that players then had it too easy and I wonder what he would have made of it all now.

'I disagree,' says Bridges with characteristic politeness. 'I think the wages have gone a bit like the Italians, with ridiculous figures, but if they're willing to pay you that much for doing a job then you'd be daft to turn it down. I don't see how you can lose your enthusiasm for the job. If I wasn't playing for Leeds United, I'd be back home playing Sunday League with my mates. People who have got jobs want to play football, no matter whether they get paid or not. Yes, I think it's gone a bit crazy. Roy Keane has been the first to smash it, but it's relative and he's on £50,000 a week, while Del Piero's on £80–90,000. The players don't talk about it with each other. I mean, there must be a massive wage gap here, with some getting a lot more than others, but nobody's bothered. We're winning and playing football. That's what matters. I don't care about money.'

Bridges makes a convincing case. The tabloid press have milked the *Independent* survey for all it is worth, citing the financial chasm between footballers and noble professions like teaching. It is a parlous argument. The bare fact is that there are far fewer people able to do what Bridges can do than can take geography lessons. It is a case of supply and demand and, let's be honest, nobody ever paid £20 and got deliriously absorbed by a 90-minute sermon on limestone pavements.

A more meaningful comparison is to juxtapose football wages with those earned in other sports and showbusiness. In his prime the basketball player Michael Jordan earned $78 million a year. We live in an age when snooker players drive Ferraris and journeymen tennis players are multi-millionaires. Film stars get £10 million a film. Noel Edmonds, the bearded irritant and genius behind Mr Blobby and Crinkly Bottom, can name his price from the BBC. Vanessa Feltz, the perfect union of a bulimic walrus and Matt Le Tissier in drag, can do the same. Are footballers overpaid? Of course they are, but surely that is better than the sad way in which their skills were exploited in the '60s and '70s.

One trend that might more readily resemble the Revie era is the longevity of the players' Leeds careers. Bridges believes there will be a return to players staying at a single club for the bulk, if not all, of their careers. 'I think that's the way it will probably go,' he says. 'My long-term ambition is to stay here as long as I can. I think the club is going places with the academy and new pitches here out the back. This is my first season and I've signed a five-year deal. I'm hoping David O'Leary gets me in at the end of the season so I can extend it.'

As Eddie Gray emerges from behind a door carrying a sackful of balls like a soccer Santa, I wish Bridges all the best and he saunters off to join up with his coach. The sorcerer and the apprentice, two generations working together to create a glorious future by rekindling past glories.

There is a genuine feeling that this team has the potential, the youth and the cash backing to become the nearest thing to Revie's Leeds since the glory days ended, 1992 notwithstanding. Bridges' assertion that he and his team-mates are looking for long-term contracts is encouraging. 'They're not there yet, but they could be,' said Norman Hunter. 'They're exciting,' Johnny Giles told me. 'They've the same spirit,' mused Peter Lorimer.

That spirit has no doubt been honed from the fact that many of the team have grown up together. Just as Revie trawled Britain picking up prodigiously talented teenagers and developing them, so too O'Leary is reaping the benefits of a much-envied youth system for which Howard Wilkinson deserves much of the credit. On a previous visit to Thorp Arch, I heard 20-year-old Irish midfielder Stephen McPhail explain how the modern system works. 'I played for the Ireland Under-15 side in Dublin against Norway and Paul Hart, the Leeds youth team manager, asked me to come over. A fortnight later I was here. I was homesick and it was very hard going home in the summer and then having to come back here. It really got to me then. I lived in digs for over a year and then I came to the complex, here, where they have accommodation for a lot of young players. That was the hardest part, because it's really boring. After training there was absolutely nothing to do and it would get to you. It was like a prison and we were in the middle of nowhere.'

I managed to get in touch with McPhail via a friend of my mother's who was his landlady in her early days. She later took Harry Kewell and still looks after some of the young interns. In his laconic manner, McPhail readily agreed to an interview. This was very different from trying to track down Michael Bridges and Harry Kewell. Arranging an interview with Bridges took some time. I should point out that Simon Bayliff, his agent, was charming and helpful, but I was given the third degree by others at his office. I was told not to mention Galatasaray, the pending court case of Bowyer and Woodgate, lifestyle issues (whatever they may be), and so on. 'We don't want anything going in that may portray Michael in a bad light,' said one woman. Of course agents are happy to use the Press, feeding them stories about their clients in an attempt to bump up their market price or strengthen their negotiating stance come contract time. It is the perverse world of PR. Criticise the media for its biased, sensationalist views, while insisting it portrays the world through your similarly jaundiced one eye – and the irony of it all, regarding Bridges, is that he is eminently likeable and unassuming. If ever a man did not need a PR brigade, it is him. Having met Bridges, I am sure he is bright enough to determine what he would and would not like to talk about, but such is the paranoid nature of the modern player's protectors.

McPhail does not need to consult an agent. He does not strike me as confident or an extrovert in any way, but he has experienced enough in his brief life to cope with a few questions from the likes of me. 'When I was four we moved to the Bronx,' he says. 'My dad was a carpenter and had a big job to do. I was a bit too young to realise what was going on, but we lived right in the middle of the Bronx so I suppose it must have been rough. We were right beside the hospital and it was mayhem, noise going on all through the night, but I never saw anything that really scared me. It was just another thing you had to do. We stayed there until we were seven. I remember the fact my brother and I were the only white faces at our school, but it was OK. There was a big Irish community over there.'

Having survived the Bronx and homesickness, McPhail settled in Leeds and started to earn some plaudits through his role in the 1997 FA Youth Cup-winning side. 'There are five or six of us from that team who are now in the first team squad,' says McPhail. 'We all got on together and seemed to crack it at the same time. The likes of Woody, Smithy, H, Alan Maybury and me were all in the same block at the centre. The first one to make it was Harry. Howard Wilkinson tried him for a few games and I was just delighted to see him doing so well.'

In 1997 Leeds seniors were awful. They scored 28 goals and kept 20 clean sheets. They were Mogodon United. Carlton Palmer was still around and so was Ian Rush. A parody of scouseness, Rush was Liverpudlian through and through. He was 34 when Howard Wilkinson signed him. In striking years, that made him a pensioner. Of course we instantly made him captain. Leeds finished 11th and people credited Graham, who had succeeded the sacked Wilkinson in September, for preventing the club from plunging to relegation. Nevertheless it was the sort of football which made Artexing your nether regions with cat litter seem an attractive proposition. Graham failed to endear himself to anyone, apart from perhaps Nigel Martyn, who had never been busier and romped the Player of the Year award as a result. In June 1997, just weeks after helping Leeds win the FA Youth Cup, director of youth coaching Paul Hart quit, saying: 'I find it astonishing that George Graham has only watched our youth team three times since he arrived.'

Former chairman Bill Fotherby remembered that, after the 1997 FA Youth Cup win, he told Graham the club should get the youngsters tied up on long-term contracts to fend off the avaricious advances of others. 'He wasn't enthusiastic,' said Fotherby. 'He didn't think they would break through. After George had gone they all blossomed.'

'George never would come to a youth team game himself, but he knew what was going on from training,' insists McPhail. 'He'd play the first team against the reserves and see from that who he thought might make it. He wasn't ignoring us. He'd always include us. For instance, he'd take the young lads aside to go and play against the first team back four. But we were doing really well in the youth team and thought things might happen quicker than they did – but they just went on and on and on.'

Perhaps it is the fact that Graham once compared McPhail to Irish legend Liam Brady which tempers his view of his former boss. 'People kept comparing me with him, which was ridiculous,' he says. 'I was in the reserves and hadn't done anything, whereas he'd won everything. It added to the pressure.' Yet there are obvious similarities. Both are Irish, both are left-footed and both champion the passing game which passes so many by in the hurly-burly of modern football. I used to love Brady, even though he was an Arsenal man and therefore, by the nature of his mercurial and subtle skills, a freak. A 'poet of the left foot' is how Nick Hornby recalled him in *Fever Pitch*. Some people believe McPhail needs to toughen up to be the complete midfielder, that his poetry does not always scan properly, but the potential is there and Harry Kewell for one thinks he is the greatest natural talent at the club.

It was another Gunner-cum-goner who gave McPhail his début in a 1–0 defeat at Leicester. 'I was told I was coming on and the excitement as I warmed up was just tremendous. I wasn't in awe of the situation at all. We were a goal down and I was just trying to work hard to get us back in the game. Then we got a penno in the last minute and I thought great, but Jimmy [Floyd Hasselbaink] missed and it was a real body-blow. It was great to be playing, but the result didn't help.'

He would get another chance as a substitute, but Graham seemed unsure about his young charges and was concerned by what he considered to be McPhail's fragility. Silky skills were never likely to be enough on their own for a manager who once rejoiced in the likes of John Jensen and Steve Morrow. However, when Graham left the following season, McPhail was thrust into the action in Leeds' UEFA Cup clash with AS Roma in the Olympic Stadium. Although Leeds lost 1–0 in what was O'Leary's first game as caretaker boss, the performance of the young Leeds team would be a benchmark in the club's history.

'It was a real surprise when George went, but the boss took over and he gave the young lads a chance straight away,' recalls McPhail. 'He just threw us all in. Woody and I made our full League débuts at Forest and then Alan Smith came through. George would have done it a lot slower, but David just put everyone on. He knows we're very young, probably a bit too young to be going out and winning things at the moment, but we'll give it a shot. The next couple of years we will be looking to win things, but you can't do it with all young lads. We need to be, not exactly protected, but have someone who's been there and done it – someone like David Batty, talking you through every game. It helps you a lot with your confidence when you know there's someone there who's going to look after you. Now we're striving to do what Manchester United have done. We want to get as many young players through as we can and win things consistently. That's what we're trying to emulate. This season we just want to improve on the fourth place we got last year, but there's a lot of ambition.'

Like Bridges, McPhail feels blessed by his natural ability which enables him to live a life most can only fantasise about. 'You can't have a better life than being a professional footballer,' he tells me. 'But it's not an easy life by any stretch of the imagination. It's not pressure, it's the fact it is a strenuous job. If you get injured, you get depressed. It's different from normal living. But then there is no better feeling than going out and playing in front of 40,000 fans, and you'll be able to look back at your career one day and have memories that not many people have.'

When we meet in the same Thorp Arch Portakabin where I'd met Radebe, the furore surrounding Woodgate and Bowyer is still dominating the papers. Leeds' form has begun to dip a little, too, and it is impossible not to link the two things. McPhail is adamant the much-publicised incident has not harmed morale at all. 'If anything, it's brought us closer together,' he says. 'It's not affected the way we've been playing. These days, you know you get hammered if you step out of line and anything you do will come out in the papers. So you have to be careful. It's what you have to live with.'

David O'Leary believes as much himself. 'I don't think they should be in discos,' he told the *Leeds, Leeds, Leeds* magazine, his word selection marking his age and making it sound as though Leeds players like hanging around the youth club with a bottle of cider. 'They are places where they are vulnerable, people with too much drink inside them, things go silly. They're leaving themselves open.'

McPhail does not strike me as a big nightclubber (or even a disco king), though I may be wrong. Before I met him I bumped into an old family friend, who runs a highly-successful fish-and-chip shop in Wetherby. She is a die-hard Leeds fan. 'They all come in our shop. Steve McPhail, Harry, Michael Bridges, Lucas Radebe,' she says. 'They're lovely lads.' It is hard to imagine the likes of David Beckham tucking into their pie and chips with curry sauce, but the image of McPhail doing so is somehow more believable. I actually met a Leeds player in a fish shop once. It was a wet and windy night and I found myself behind Chris Fairclough. He ordered chips. Open. No vinegar. I remember being impressed. It was the sort of prosaic order which suited his style. If a player can be judged by what he buys in a chip shop, McPhail would be something mildly exotic with a hint of class. Something like red snapper and chips.

When McPhail arrived at Leeds aged just 14, Paul Hart noted that he 'treated the ball as if it was gold dust'. In 1997 Leeds seniors more often regarded it like dandruff, crudely despatching it in any which way. Now that an Irishman has replaced the Scotsman, there is a chance that Leeds may be going places once again. In Revie's era, it was a diminutive Irish midfielder who held the team together. Now the Irish connection is no less great. 'There's David obviously, myself, Gary Kelly, Ian Harte and Alan Maybury,' says McPhail. 'With the youth teamers, there's 16 Irish lads altogether and it's great to have people who know where you're coming from. Gary and Ian really helped me when I first came over, because they'd been in the same boat. Now Gary's 24. He's the grandad of the team.'

I ask McPhail what he knows of the old Leeds team, but it is an unfair question. He is 20, after all. When he was born the Revie era had long since ended. Allan Clarke was the manager and Leeds were heading for the Second Division. Back in Ireland, the London-born McPhail was raised on John Barnes, Kenny Dalglish and Ian Rush. 'I've been a Liverpool fan all my life,' he says. 'When you're brought up in Ireland it's a toss-up between Liverpool and Manchester United. I've watched videos and seen bits on TV about the old Leeds side, though. We know how good they were and we're trying to get the club back there. Even now Eddie [Gray] is still a great player. Judging by his pre-season he's probably got a couple of years left in him, too.'

Like Bridges, McPhail has had a fine season at Elland Road. At Sunderland he flicked a casual left-foot pass into the path of the on-rushing Jason Wilcox, who scored. The vision he showed belied his youth. It was a deft touch and much admired by the fawning Sky commentators. At Stamford Bridge he scored twice as Leeds beat Chelsea's cosmopolitan mix of high-rolling imports. The future is bright for McPhail. O'Leary says he has the potential to be great. He is already the best passer of the ball Leeds have had since Gary McAllister. 'I take it all as it comes,' he says. 'I'm enjoying every second of it. There's always talk of someone going, and because H has been playing so well it usually concerns him; but if you asked the lads I think they'd say they want to stay here for as long as they can. Everyone loves the place and it's an easy club to come to as a young player. Five or ten years together would be great.'

A couple of months later I am back at the training ground. It is the Friday before the last game of the season at West Ham. Leeds have long since blown their title chances. When they lost 2–1 to Slavia Prague in the second leg of the UEFA Cup quarter-final, it was the start of a six-game losing run. Had they lost the second leg of their ill-fated UEFA Cup semi-final against Galatasaray, it would have been the worst sequence in the club's history – and this in a season when they had scarcely been out of the top two and chalked up a record-breaking run of ten straight wins. It has been a good season on the pitch, then, even though the murders in Turkey have cast a shadow over everything else. This is my final visit to the training ground. I have already interviewed Nigel Martyn, after much discussion with his agent, and am now looking for Harry. After weeks of trying and endless phone calls to his agent, Harry has agreed to meet me for a chat. The only trouble is, he has gone. Other players are lounging around and being interviewed for the end-of-season club video, while David O'Leary gives his pre-game thoughts for the last time this season.

'But I'd arranged to see him,' I tell the gateman. (He has replaced Jack, who has had a quadruple bypass operation since he mistook me for Henry Winter.)

'Sorry, he's gone.'

This irks me a little. Harry might be the truest star in this side, with an estimated market price of £25 million, and be the newly-crowned PFA Young Player of the Year, but I've driven 100 miles. I ask a local journalist if the players will be back later on to get the bus down to West Ham.

'Who are you after?' he asks.

'Harry Kewell,' I reply.

He lets out an exaggerated sigh and shakes his head. 'No chance,' he says. 'Harry doesn't like talking.'

I knew this already. When I told Stephen McPhail I was after Harry, he had said, 'Harry's hard.' I'd also read a quote from Kewell, himself, saying how he wanted to keep himself to himself when he finishes work. That is fair enough, I thought, but I'd have appreciated his agent just telling me that rather than having me take part in some wild goose chase. I know he is a star and I am a nobody, but good manners cost nothing. Of course, there could be some perfectly plausible explanation. At a crowded training ground it is feasible we just missed each other. Or perhaps there was some genuine reason why he had to shoot off early. Maybe he just forgot. Fair enough, but there was no explanation forthcoming.

I can fully understand Kewell wanting to keep a low profile. He is a rare talent and, along with Nigel Martyn, one of only two twenty-first century players who could have walked into Revie's side. As well as picking up his PFA Young Player of the Year award, he came third in the senior category behind Roy Keane and Kevin Phillips. He is arguably the most exciting talent to have ever played for the club. With the demands of the media at an all-time high, his decision to cultivate a Garbo-esque stance is shrewd and may well save him an awful lot of grief. The Press know it is pointless asking for Harry. He has got it sussed at an early age. David Beckham is forever biting the hand that feeds him – bemoaning the intrusiveness of the Press while he simultaneously flogs his wedding pics to *Hello* magazine, goes out dressed in a skirt, and lets his wife tell the world he wears her undies. This is the double-cross of the cross cross-dresser. Kewell, meanwhile, does not want publicity and does not cultivate it. For such a high-profile footballer, precious little is known or written about him.

Others are happier to talk. Terry Venables, who coached Kewell for Australia, says he is outstanding. David O'Leary says he is the best young player in the country by a mile. The list of former Leeds players enamoured of the 21-year-old Australian is a who's who of Elland Road. 'Fantastic,' said Norman Hunter. 'Could be one of the world's best,' added Eddie Gray. '*The* star,' commented Gordon McQueen. 'Worth a king's ransom.'

With such outrageous talent, Kewell knew he was destined for the top at an early age. One of his rare appearances on television was on a programme called *Football's Foreign Legion*, in which Alan Hansen spoke to numerous overseas players. Kewell's comments were routine enough, but what was most illuminating was footage of Kewell as a young boy. A crackly home video showed him tearing down the left wing in a boy's match in just the same way as he does in the Premiership. An Aussie voice was heard asking Kewell if it was true he could do 50 keep-me-ups as a two-year-old. 'So they say,' he replied.

Michael Bridges may say he never knew he would be a footballer, but Kewell is different. It was as if he was predestined to be a star. In an article in the Australian paper *Courier Mail* in 1999, Kewell said: 'I had one vision, there was no Plan B – it had to be soccer.'

Born in Sydney on 22 September 1978, Kewell decided he was going to be a footballer at the age of six and would use tin cans for target practice. His potential was obvious and his desire almost unnatural. As a teenager in a country where rugby, cricket and Aussie Rules were the favoured sports, Kewell bucked against the trend by deciding he would play professional football in England. He had been a regular at the New South Wales Soccer Federation's programme by the time he won a scholarship at the age of 16. Part of the deal was to spend four weeks in England. It was the chance Kewell had dreamt about for most of his short life and he was not about to waste it. Several clubs were interested, but Leeds got in there first. His opening trial match was at Rotherham and Kewell played at left-back. Woefully out of position he may have been, but it made little difference. Youth team coach Paul Hart, now with Nottingham Forest, estimated it took around two days to sign him. In 1997 he told *The Times*: 'From the moment he stepped off that plane, Harry knew what he wanted. He is the best of a group which has the potential to become the best young players in the country. He has great self-confidence and won't be budged from doing what he thinks is right for his career. It was difficult for me to leave these kids because I know they will all make it.'

Once at Leeds, Kewell impressed the coaching staff, not only with his ability, but with his fierce determination and faith in his future. Eddie Gray recalled that while some boys who lived two miles from the accommodation complex at Thorp Arch would grow homesick, Kewell, thousands of miles from his family, never complained. He made his début as a 17-year-old under Howard Wilkinson in the 1995–96 season, but at the time fans were more excited by the wing wizardry of Andy Gray, son of Frank and nephew of Eddie. Gray was the only solace to be gained from the Coca-Cola Cup humiliation against Aston Villa and many predicted a bright future for the youngster. Wilkinson's departure and George Graham's coronation put an end to all this youthful exuberance. Had King Herod been given the job, there would have been a better chance of Leeds' young guns being given their head. Gray would never realise his potential at Elland Road and would leave, while Kewell made just one appearance as a substitute, as Graham steadied the ship and sacrificed flair for security.

Necessity would promote Kewell the following season when Lee Sharpe broke down during the pre-season. Kewell slotted into the side as a left winger and began to show glimpses of his ability, scoring eight goals in 32 starts and even keeping Hasselbaink out of the side for a while. The teenager was making his dreams reality. Others could bide their time and contemplate escaping the strict regime, but Kewell was on a fast track to fame and the accompanying fortune. 'Nothing was going to stop me,' he remembered. 'There's no point in being a wuss about it. I came over here to do a job.'

Under David O'Leary, Kewell has blossomed further and has found his best position. For much of his time at Leeds he has been employed as a left winger, but he has proved most effective as an out-and-out striker, drifting wide when and if he fancies. The season that has just closed has been his best as his development continues. On 3 January 2000 Kewell was playing against Aston Villa when he picked up the ball close to the half-way line. He broke forward with that lustrous pace before shooting from more than 35 yards. It was an hugely ambitious effort, but the ball seemed to gather pace as it arrowed its way towards goal – beating the despairing dive of David James and nestling in the left-hand side of the net. It was a glorious, gorgeous goal that made you remember why you paid your money. Leeds lost the game 2–1, but Kewell's strike rose like a phoenix from the mediocrity of a poor game and two scrappy Gareth Southgate efforts.

On 9 March 2000 Kewell hit a thunderous shot from 25 yards which ricocheted off the keeper and into the net to settle the UEFA Cup tie with Roma. Then, on 30 April 2000, he surpassed himself again. Leeds were already 2–0 up against a Sheffield Wednesday side for whom resistance meant saying no to a second slice of orange at half-time. Leeds had not won for six weeks but were rampant against this tepid Wednesday effort. When Kewell received the ball some 30 yards from goal, he arrogantly tapped the ball forward and then flicked the ball with the outside of his left boot. His curling caress looped over Kevin Pressman and bounced in off the underside of the bar. Kewell turned with a look of 'so what?', cocked his hand like a gunslinger and let out a dazzling grin as his dumbfounded team-mates approached.

Three snapshots of Kewell the Jewell. Each one a lilting moment of genius with the ability to lift the heart of the most embittered cynic. The game is beautiful again.

It has not all been a blissful experience, however, and Kewell has already suffered his share of setbacks and injustice. With Venables in charge, it seemed as though Australia would qualify for the 1998 World Cup finals in France. It came down to a two-legged play-off against Iran. Kewell scored in the first leg to put the Aussies in pole position with a 1–1 draw and the home leg to come. 'The whole stadium went deadly silent. I just thought, there's something wrong here. One minute there were 130,000 Iranians screaming their heads off and the next there was nothing, not a sound.' Before the decisive second game in Melbourne, Kewell said: 'I never get nervous before a match. Never have done. I guess that's just me. The bigger the crowd the better, as far as I am concerned.' Australia were 2–0 up thanks to goals from Kewell and Aurelio Vidmar and seemed to be coasting towards France, but two Iranian strikes meant they missed out on the World Cup on away goals.

If that was disappointing, what followed left a bitter taste in the mouth. In March 1998 Kewell was selected for the Australian Under-23s for a series of games against Brazil. Just before he was due to join up with his compatriots, Leeds claimed he was unfit and that he would not be travelling. Soccer Australia did not believe Leeds and, employing FIFA regulations, banned Kewell from playing club football until after the Brazil games were completed. The mutual contempt between the two parties has continued to fester, with Leeds angry that their most charismatic player is periodically lost to them for international games of dubious merit.

Kewell is clearly a proud Aussie. When he arrived at Leeds, he said he would play at the club until his mid-20s and then go home. For someone so loath to talk, he has also been vocal in calling for a better league set-up in his homeland. 'It's sad so many of us feel the need to quit Australia to reach our goals,' he said in an Australian newspaper article in 1999. 'What we need is a fully professional national competition back home which will encourage players to stay and make a go of it in Australia.'

Nevertheless, it is hard to envisage Kewell playing in Australia until he is 'over-the-hill'. His performances for Leeds this season, especially in Europe, have alerted the Italian giants to his worth. Inter Milan's name has been mentioned several times, and Kewell is the sort of player you would expect to do well in Serie A. 'How you keep him is that, first of all, he respects me and enjoys working for me, and then you've got to have him in a successful side that is going places,' says O'Leary. He adds, with a degree of bluntness, 'And if a bid comes in, you turn it down.' The other way is to pay him a fortune.

As the 1999–2000 season stuttered to a conclusion, the top earners at the club were David Batty, Nigel Martyn and Lucas Radebe. They are all experienced thirtysomethings. The speculation, as I hunt in vain for Kewell, is that he is about to have his salary bumped up from £15,000 to £25,000 a week, to quell the temptation of Italy or Spain. This would make him the top earner.

In the current climate it would be money well spent. Kewell is getting better and better and, having had more Premiership experience than the other kids on the Leeds block, he is likely to hit full maturity before the rest. Some would say he is there now. The tragedies of Galatasaray and the shadow of Bowyer and Woodgate's court case has caused 'O'Leary's babies' to grow up quickly. Against Galatasaray, Kewell suffered the additional pain of being sent off. Gheorghe Popescu, once of Spurs, covered his face and rolled around on the floor in apparent agony when Kewell challenged him in the second leg at Elland Road. The referee was conned and sent Kewell off for stamping. O'Leary called Popescu a cheat. Popescu demanded an apology, claiming he was only holding his head for protection. UEFA finally cleared Kewell. It was a tacky ending to a tragic saga, but Europe will no doubt get more opportunities to see Kewell.

Kewell, McPhail and Bridges are peepholes to the future. All have the potential to go on and become huge stars. There are others too. Woodgate, Robinson, Harte, Bakke, Smith and Jones. Alan Hansen famously said, 'You'll never win anything with kids' and Leeds have proved him right this season. However, it is not the size of the dog in the fight that counts but the size of the fight in the dog, and Leeds are biting again. What they perhaps need is someone with a bit of experience to act as a pilot light, someone with the same mellifluous skills and attacking instincts, but with a worldly omnipotence. Someone like a Cantona. Now imagine that. Had he joined this team as a 25-year-old, with O'Leary in charge rather than Wilkinson, he might well have stayed. It is just fantasy of course. But then, isn't that what football is – from its salaries to its silent stars, from its ridiculousness to the rifling 35-yard screamer against Aston Villa? It is a fabulous freak show rooted in the ordinary. There is nothing like it. And Leeds are good at it again, thanks to their youngsters. Overpaid they may be, but they are also undervalued by people who just do not understand.

NIGEL MARTYN — Keeping the Faith

All that I know most surely about morality and the duty of man, I owe to football.

ALBERT CAMUS

I was 13 and playing for the school team. In those days I would spend most of my games hoping the ball would avoid me, and got quite good at finding myself in acres of space. The only problem with this technique was that other, more skilled players, unaware of my natural aversion, would then pass the ball to me. This is where the masterplan fell down. As time went on I moved into midfield and began to love playing. You see, you can make a mistake in midfield and nothing happens, but God help you if you are guilty of a lapse and you are playing as a sweeper. That inevitably gives some fleet-footed striker, probably a mouthy little upstart with his collar turned up, a free run in on goal. And what you also have to remember is that, when I was 13, our goalkeeper had a glass eye. I knew this because he was good at staring competitons and because it came out once. He was challenged at a corner and fell to the floor, clutching his face. His watching father ran on and clouted the player he judged to be the guilty assailant. There followed several anxious minutes as players and coaches jostled, while the rest of us scoured the six-yard box for his missing eye. It was then that I realised goalkeepers were different from the rest of us.

Albert Camus, the novelist and philosopher, played in goal for Racing Universitaire d'Alger in the 1920s and later claimed his entire sense of ethics was gleaned from his time between the posts. In 1956, former German prisoner of war Bert Trautmann played in the FA Cup final with a broken neck. He inspired a Manchester City side, including one Don Revie, to a 3–1 win over Birmingham. In 1995 Rene Higuita enlivened a dull 0–0 draw between England and Colombia with a quite audacious piece of showmanship. As the ball looped towards the goalkeeper, he shunned the simple catch in favour of leaping forward and kicking up his heels behind him to clear the ball. He called it his scorpion kick. Clearly goalkeepers had something extra. Some said that they were a little mad, that you had to be crazy to put your head in among the flying boots and sharpened studs.

And then there is Nigel Martyn. Unashamedly sane, this Cornishman renounces his brethren of El Locos and defuses the argument in one succinct sentence. 'I used to be an accountant,' he says. Suddenly, risking life, limb and ritualistic humiliation in front of 40,000 people seems to make perfect sense. 'I was there for about six months, but I did lots of other jobs,' he says. 'I worked in the offices of the local council; then I worked for a car company for a couple of years; and finally I spent six months in a plastics factory. I never knew I was going to be a footballer and I never had any ambitions. I didn't want to be a footballer, it just sort of happened.'

I am talking to Martyn two days before the final game of the season, away at West Ham. Leeds are third in the table, which would be enough for them to qualify for the Champions League now that you don't have to be a champion to be in it. Liverpool are one point adrift, but have what looks like an easier game on paper at Bradford City, who need to win to stay up. Martyn has been in superb form this season, but ironically he made an almighty gaffe in the previous game against Everton which led to the Merseysiders scrambling a draw. Now it will go down to the wire. Nevertheless, there are many who believe Martyn now deserves to be the undisputed England number one in the forthcoming Euro 2000 championships in Holland and Belgium.

It is all a far cry from that plastics factory and Martyn knows that all too well. 'I didn't get a trial with Bristol Rovers until I was 20,' he says. 'That was quite late, but I think it was an advantage because I'd seen the other side of the fence and it wasn't too clever working in factories. It gave me a better perspective.'

They get players young these days and it seems only a matter of time before scouts will need to hold a qualification in midwifery. Clubs are spending fortunes on youth academies and the best players are monitored from junior school, so Martyn's late development is unusual. 'I always liked playing in goal, but when I was at school the teachers made me play outfield because they thought I was more use to the team there. They forced me to do that all through my school years, even though I wanted to be a goalkeeper. When I left school at 15 or 16 I gave up football and didn't play for about four months, until one day my brother said his works side were short and would I play. I said, "Yeah, why not?" I gave it a go and liked it. I stayed in goal then and had two seasons at junior level – which was the kicking-everyone's-head-off sort of level – and then two seasons at a more senior level. Then I got offered the trial and went to Rovers.'

After two and a half years with Bristol, Martyn made the move to Crystal Palace in November 1989 and began to make a name for himself. In 1992 he earned the first of his England caps, but the long-forgotten Chris Woods was then the regular choice and would be so until his eclipse by David Seaman in 1994. The chances were few and far between. Seaman established himself, promptly becoming a national hero during Euro 96, and Martyn went three years without earning an England cap. 'Palace getting relegated ruined things for me as far as England were concerned,' he admits. 'When Dave got his chance, he took it and became a fixture. He's a great keeper. I didn't get back until the end of 1996 when George Graham was Leeds manager.'

The summer of 1996 was a major turning-point in Martyn's life. It started with him playing for Palace in the First Division play-off final against Leicester City. Palace were the favourites for the game and looked well on course for a return to the top flight after Andy Roberts put them ahead in the first half. However, a late Garry Parker penalty squared matters and took the game into extra-time. As is often the way at Wembley, both sides were tired and cagey in the extra period, the fear of making a crucial mistake proving an antidote to adventure.

With a minute remaining, Leicester replaced their goalkeeper. Their manager, Martin O'Neill, later said he had hoped that substitute Zeljko Kalac, a 6'7" Australian, would intimidate Palace during the penalty shootout. It did not come to that and Kalac did not even get a touch of the ball. 'Steve Claridge had the ball and there were quite a few bodies in front of me,' recalls Martyn with the furrowed brow of someone reciting a bad dream. 'I remember looking to the right of somebody to try to see him shoot, but I couldn't see him. As I was looking to my right, he hit it to my left. The ball suddenly appeared when it had travelled about three-quarters of its distance. It was too late for me to even start moving across the goal. Then it just nestled there in the top corner. We literally kicked off and the ref blew his whistle. It was unbelievable. We didn't even have time to hack the ball down the field and have one last go. It was such a choker, a scandalous time for them to score. I think that's about as bad as it gets, losing to the last kick in extra-time at Wembley.'

In one of those peculiar twists of fate football turns up so often, that disappointment would kick-start Martyn's career after seven years with Palace. 'I think I might well have stayed with them had we gone up that year,' he says. 'They might not have been in such a rush to sell me and, though it didn't feel like it at the time, I can now look at it as a blessing in disguise. I was quite happy to stay put. I'd gone on the transfer list during that season at one point, because I was trying to get away and wanted to play in the Premiership, but there was no interest shown by anyone. I think everyone had settled goalkeepers and they were obviously happy with them. So I came off the list and signed a new contract at Palace in the March and then it looked as if we might be going up anyway. Then they sold me in July. It was a strange scenario.'

Leeds fans have much to thank Steve Claridge's shin for. In a glorious history littered with great players in almost every position, Leeds had struggled to produce any goalkeeper you would label a legend.

In the Revie era there was Gary Sprake, who will always be synonymous with calamities despite 37 Welsh caps. Then there was David Harvey, who spent the best part of two decades at Elland Road. He was the nearest thing Leeds had to a great goalkeeper in the pre-Martyn years. Born in Yorkshire, Harvey qualified to play for Scotland through his parents. Despite a hairstyle that was like a badger succumbing to middle-age spread, Harvey had a degree of class about him. His crowning moment came when he kept a clean sheet against Brazil in the 1974 World Cup Finals. 'Check the footage of me in the line-up against Brazil and you'll see the diarrhoea running down the back of my legs,' he later recalled. Such was Harvey's importance to Leeds that Peter Lorimer was once banned from taking shots at him during practice because Revie was worried about his keeper breaking a finger. Harvey, who earned 16 Scottish caps, left Leeds for Vancouver Whitecaps in 1980, but returned for two further spells before leaving for Whitby Town, Morton and Partick Thistle. He is now a farmer and postman on the Isle of Sanday in the Orkneys.

Sprake, meanwhile, had left for Birmingham at the start of the 1973–74 season for a fee of £70,000. Revie knew Sprake was talented and persevered with him in the face of his numerous errors. In the 1968 FA Cup semi-final against Everton, Sprake clashed with Joe Royle, and in a fit of pique he angrily kicked the ball out. He mishit it, however, and the ball bobbled straight to Everton's Jimmy Husband. He lobbed Sprake, Jack Charlton deliberately handled and Everton converted the decisive penalty.

Then the 1970 FA Cup final came along. It was not only Johnny Giles who felt Revie had stuck with Sprake too long, and many fans breathed a sigh of relief when Harvey was promoted after seven years as the Welshman's understudy. Though Harvey played in most of Leeds' great games during the glory years, he did find himself coming under pressure from David Stewart, a £30,000 signing from Ayr United, in the mid-1970s. Stewart won a Scotland cap himself (when he saved a penalty in a 1–0 defeat by East Germany in 1978), and notched up more than 70 appearances for Leeds in his four and a half years at the club. One of those was in the 1975 European Cup final, when he stood in for the injured Harvey, and he rarely let the side down. Stewart moved to West Brom for £70,000 in 1978 and is now a jeweller in Swansea.

When Harvey's knee trouble spelled the end of his 20-year association with Leeds, manager Eddie Gray turned to former West Ham legend Mervyn Day, who had recently fallen out with his manager Graham Turner at Aston Villa. Merv the Swerve – these days on the coaching staff at newly crowned Division One champions Charlton Athletic – became a huge crowd favourite. 'I only had to think about the offer for two seconds,' he said of his switch to Leeds, even though it entailed dropping down a division. 'Leeds were sleeping giants. Eddie wasn't given the time he needed to finish the job he started. He had to sell the players who could have won us promotion.' Day would play for Leeds in their two near-misses of the Billy Bremner era, when they lost the First Division play-off final against Charlton in a third game and then went down 3–2 against Coventry in the 1987 FA Cup semi-final.

Promotion eventually came in 1990, but no sooner had Day uncorked the champagne than Wilkinson re-signed John Lukic as his number-one stopper. Lukic had played for Leeds in the early 1980s and had a lot of promise. However, a shocking display in a 5–0 home defeat by Arsenal seemed to shatter his confidence and he eventually joined the Gunners in 1983. He was a good keeper and won two titles – at Arsenal in 1989 and then with Leeds three years later – yet he never inspired total confidence.

Few would disagree that Nigel Martyn is the best we have ever had.

'The first I heard about the Leeds move was in the papers,' says Martyn. 'It was Leeds and Everton and after a while they got in touch with my agent and he said "Right, let's go and talk."' Martyn had already become the country's first £1 million goalkeeper when he joined Crystal Palace, and the £2.25 million Leeds paid for him was another record for a keeper. He says the fees did not bother him in the slightest. 'The thing with fees is they are not your own valuation. It's other people's. Now, if they are prepared to put this or that figure on your head, they are the ones who should worry about it. It makes no difference to me.'

Wilkinson was the man who had paid that money, but he had other things to worry about and was sacked in September. 'He was the man who had bought me, so for him to go after only five games was strange,' recalls Martyn. 'You just don't know what to expect when a new man takes over. It isn't so much worrying as unsettling, as you wait to see how things work out. George Graham came in and he did what he had to do. It wasn't attacking football, but I think we would have struggled more than we did that season had he not gone that way. I don't think it would have ended in relegation, but we'd have been down the wrong end of the table for longer than we were. George turned it around. He got us more organised, more disciplined, and we went on. The following season we qualified for Europe, so we made big strides while he was here.'

It is one of the curiosities of being a goalkeeper that the better the side you play in the less you have to do. It sounds like the perfect job for someone who is bone idle. At least that is the theory, but Martyn quickly knocks that one on the head. 'I am busier now in this team, which is better than the one we had in '96, than I was when we were more defensive. It's because of the way we play. We try to attack teams now and that means we get caught on the break a lot.'

Nevertheless, it is clear Martyn enjoyed working with a defensive guru like Graham. 'We had 24 clean sheets that year and his arrival was the reason I got back in with England. When he left to go to Spurs it was another surprise. It was in the papers, but you still don't believe it's going to happen. When it does, you go through that unsettling period again. It doesn't matter who you might want to take over, because the players don't get a say in it. It made it easier when they appointed David as manager, because we already knew him as George's assistant. There was talk of Martin O'Neill, but the way things have worked out has been fabulous. The team has gone from strength to strength. The aim now is to win something. We'd reached a stage before the start of the season and we've gone on from that. The next step is to go that little bit further and actually win something. It will be hard, because I think it's going to be much more difficult next season. Teams are getting better and better, more money is being spent all the time, everyone wants to compete and I think there will be more teams up there challenging. This season it has only been ourselves and Manchester United. Other teams are scared of Manchester United, but none of our young lads are in awe of them. When we fell away it handed the title to them because there was no one else. We got dragged back in with Arsenal, Chelsea and Liverpool.'

Martyn acknowledges that it has been an incredible season. 'At least it was for the first three-quarters of it,' he says. 'The last quarter has been very disappointing.' In the middle of March Martyn was quoted as saying: 'We'd be letting our supporters down if we settled for a Champions League spot. We don't go anywhere just looking for a point and there's no point saying, let's try to finish second.' A couple of months on and with just one game to go, Leeds cannot finish second and are clinging to the wreckage of a once-great season. The best they can hope for is third, the final Champions League spot, and the chance to play in the competition where Leeds made their mark in the 1970s.

'Why have we slipped down a bit?' he muses. 'I suppose it's fatigue. All the players have played a lot of games and we don't have an enormous squad. We played Arsenal and Chelsea towards the end of the season, when they were mixing their team around, and they were probably fresher.'

After West Ham, Leeds will have played 55 games this season, a sizeable total but still a long way short of the the days when Revie's side would top the 70 mark, play eight games in 18 days and have to play the Monday following the FA Cup final. Maybe it is fatigue, maybe it is luck, maybe it is inexperience or maybe other teams have just got wise to this precocious bunch of upstarts. What is clear is that if Leeds are to challenge the big guns they will have to start beating them. In eight games against the Premiership giants – Manchester United, Arsenal, Liverpool and Chelsea – Leeds have won one and lost seven, scoring four goals and conceding 15. 'That's been a problem,' says Martyn. 'We've hardly scored against them and, to be honest, hardly even looked like scoring. Once we're playing against the lesser sides we seem to do exceptionally well, but we need to develop a mental toughness to play against these bigger sides.'

In years to come the 1999–2000 campaign will not be remembered for a moment of genius from Harry Kewell, the impact of Michael Bridges, the solidity of Lucas Radebe or even the saves of Nigel Martyn. It will be remembered for what happened in Turkey on 5 April. Leeds had beaten Partizan Belgrade, Locomotiv Moscow, Spartak Moscow and AS Roma to make it to their first European semi-final for a quarter of a century. Although the team had suffered a loss of form and had fallen away in the title chase, hopes were naturally high that they could raise their game for a heady European night.

And then on the evening before the game, news began to break of trouble on the streets of Istanbul. It emerged that one Leeds fan had been killed. Soon reporters revealed that another had died. Leeds chairman Peter Ridsdale was called away from an official function and spent the night with the dead, the injured and the distraught at a Turkish hospital. On the breakfast news bulletins the following morning, the killing of Chris Loftus and Kevin Speight was the lead story. The hope and expectation regarding the semi-final was replaced by disgust and disbelief.

'It was an awful situation,' says Martyn, the memories still fresh in his mind. 'The players all knew what had happened. We'd seen it on the television late at night. One person saw it and knocked on another's door, the news spread and soon the whole team was aware of what had happened. It was incredible and the game should probably have not been played in the circumstances.'

The game was played and Leeds, almost incidentally, lost 2–0. The decision to go ahead with the first leg was condemned in some quarters. The *Daily Mail* ran a front-page headline comprising the single word, 'GROTESQUE'. Others agreed with the sentiment. Ridsdale, who handled himself with dignity and honesty throughout, was not impressed: 'There was a comment made that suggested the only reason that the game in Turkey went ahead was because I personally stood to gain financially, and I think that is the most distasteful comment I have ever heard in my life. We played the game because I'm not prepared for people to feel that the only way to progress through to the final of a competition is to go out and murder innocent people.'

At the game that night, insult was heaped on fatal injury. The Galatasaray players failed even to make a token gesture by wearing black armbands and there was no minute's silence. Leeds fans vented their own feelings by turning their back on the pitch for a minute prior to the kick-off. The Galatasaray supporters, meanwhile, were rampant and vociferous, seemingly oblivious to the significance of what had happened the previous night.

With the first leg done, dusted and lost, Leeds left Turkey as quickly as possible; but with a fortnight to go before the return leg, there was plenty of time for UEFA and Galatasaray to conspire to add to the feelings of incredulity and anger in Yorkshire. 'During the game in Turkey I could put it out of my mind,' says Martyn. 'It gave you something to focus on. But afterwards it was very hard. I couldn't really believe what had happened and it was a trying time for the team. It took time for it to sink in. We knew we had virtually the entire country behind us, but when you went to Elland Road and saw all the flowers and tributes people had put there, it really brought it home.'

Martyn went to Elland Road with his wife and children to lay his own floral tribute to the murdered fans. Other players did the same. However, such a vivid exposé of football's true status did not extend to all frontiers and many found the behaviour of Galatasaray in the interim between the two legs extremely distasteful. Fearing any emotive revenge bids by misguided fans, Leeds asked for all Turkish fans to be banned from the second leg. Galatasaray, showing a total lack of perspective, countered by saying if that was the case then the game should be played on neutral territory. In an unpalatable exercise in hypocrisy, they suggested a neutral venue was the only option if Leeds could not gurantee the safety of their fans.

With torrid tales of what had happened in Turkey filtering through and players admitting they had received death threats while in Istanbul, Ridsdale was incensed and spoke for most Leeds fans when he hit out at the Turks' behaviour. 'There were two people murdered, I saw the stab wounds and I never want to see anything like that again in my life,' he raged. 'I wish Galatasaray would take one step back and realise the impact that the events of Wednesday have had and at least show some respect. They seem to be trying to find every loophole and opportunity to get to the final without kicking a ball, and are undermining everything Leeds United have tried to do.'

UEFA, who had been conspicuous by their silence over the whole affair, then stuck their oar in by accusing Leeds of failing to control their players. Leeds had had four players booked in the first leg and whenever any side has that number yellow carded in a European game the club faces a mandatory charge. However, it was the dimwitted timing of the charge that was so galling and the *Yorkshire Post* ran a hard-hitting comment piece under the title 'The Sick Men Of Europe':

> While callously ignoring the murders of two United fans on Turkish soil, pontificating for an eternity on whether to cave into Galatasaray demands to switch the return to a neutral venue and ridiculously considering allowing 1,700 of their fans into Elland Road, they have moved swiftly enough to implement one of their obscure and lament- able laws. It is final proof, if ever any were needed, that European football is administered by a bunch of no-hopers. For eight days now they have been as ostriches, hoping that cold-blooded killings, seething tension, questions of leadership and top-level decision- making would quietly go away while their heads were buried in the sand.

The article shot from the heart and struck its target. UEFA finally bowed and banned Turkish fans from Elland Road and insisted the second leg would take place in Leeds.

On the day of the game Leeds spent thousands of pounds on full-page advertisements in the national Press. The personal message from Ridsdale was also printed in Turkish. In it Ridsdale spoke of how he and David O'Leary had attended the funerals of Christopher Loftus and Kevin Speight. He added that 'tonight must be about football' and denied being racist for asking for a ban on Galatasaray supporters. 'We totally accept the incidents in Istanbul were not directly related to the football club or Galatasaray officials,' he said. Ridsdale then pleaded with the fans to behave in a way which would ensure they all returned home to their families and 'had a memorable experience for the right reasons.'

The match itself, was not the most memorable. Leeds' hopes of overhauling the first-leg deficit lasted just a few minutes until the veteran Romanian, Gheorghe Hagi, scored a penalty. Eirik Bakke scored from two headers, but the game ended 2–2. Martyn sums up the feelings of the right-thinking majority when he says:

'We'd played better sides than them and beaten them on the way to the semi-final. Basically, we defended poorly in both games, but when you put things in perspective it didn't matter. The European campaign had been going brilliantly, but it all got ruined in Turkey. At the end of the day we're only a bunch of blokes kicking a ball around a park. It's not worth people losing their lives over. None of us will ever forget what happened over there, but it's the families you have to feel sorry for.'

After the emotional shredder of the UEFA Cup semi-final, Leeds actually found a degree of form and went into the last weekend of the season on a five-game unbeaten run. It had been a long season and the players wanted it over. Most would be enjoying holidays in the sun, but not Martyn. He was looking forward to going to Euro 2000 and, at the age of 33, accepted he needed to oust his long-term adversary, David Seaman – sooner rather than later. Seaman, the ursine Yorkshireman who ironically started his career at Leeds before being forced elsewhere by a curious lack of opportunities, is three years older and people have begun to suggest his talents are fading. Certainly, O'Leary has no doubts about who is the better: 'I wouldn't swap Nigel for any other goalkeeper,' he tells the hacks at his last Press briefing of the season. 'He'll go on until he's 40.'

Whether Martyn does that or not, time will tell. But this genial, laid-back Cornishman has already established himself as Leeds' greatest keeper, according to the panel who voted him into the dream team at the club's 80th birthday celebrations. 'God knows how I got in there,' he says, but this is a comment borne from modesty rather than honesty. I tell him Leeds don't specialise in keepers and he attempts to put up a defence. 'There was David Harvey, who played for Scotland for quite a few years, and then there was Gary Sprake. He gets remembered for the bad things he did, but he was a good goalkeeper.'

Good but not great. Keepers who are excellent shot-stoppers, at the same time as being able to command a defence and pluck whipped crosses from the air like apples from a tree, are rare. Martyn is one of them. The last line of defence is the first name on the teamsheet. Leeds' future is in safe hands.

Time is pressing on. Soon I must ask the question I have been saving up. The sun is relentless. A couple of the coaching staff saunter by, leaving a trail of sweat in the wake of their deformed footballers' calves. Martyn has been called for his role in the end-of-season video shoot. It's now or never. It's just, well, how do you ask someone if they are mad without being ever so slightly insulting?

'Do you have to be a bit mad to be a keeper?'

There. It's out. Martyn looks at me carefully. Too carefully for my liking. In my defence, I think it's a fair question. I mean, they are different from the rest of us, aren't they? For a start they can pick the ball up without penalty and can wear gloves without being called a big girl's blouse. They play football, but they use their hands. They are contradictions. It's like saying you want to be a soldier and then joining the catering corps. And some of them, quite clearly, are a couple of spanners short. It's not just football, either. In ice hockey the goalkeeper wears skates even though he doesn't skate anywhere, and wears a mask that was the chosen headgear of the psychopath in the *Hallowe'en* films. And what about Trautmann and Higuita and my mate with the glass eye? So it's a fair enough question.

'I don't think you have to be mad,' he says. 'You have to put your head in where the boots are all flying, but it's just part of the job. I don't do it because I'm being a glory-hunter like the striker who scores the winning goal. I'm just trying to help my mates out. It's a personality thing. You have to be that way.'

I suppose I should expect nothing less from a former accountant, who proceeds to tell me he never had any footballing heroes. 'I was a Liverpool fan when I was younger,' he says. And then, as we shake hands, he lets slip his guard and makes a howler to eclipse that one against Everton.

'At least, I was until I was old enough to go and watch Plymouth Argyle.'

I knew it. Proof. Mad as hatters, the lot of them.

ERIC IDOL – Waiting for God

*Has not the Count just told us that all human wisdom
is contained in these two words – Wait and hope'?*
ALEXANDRE DUMAS

High up in the rocky hills that look down over Marseilles lies the dilapidated suburb of Caillols. It is an ancient village, dissected by a snaking dirt road and aching with the ennui of rural Provence. There is a church, a bar and a *boulangerie*, but little else. It is almost picturesque. Had Peter Mayle pitched up here he would probably have stayed for an afternoon or two. Reddish-brown Mediterranean villas nestle unevenly above grim 1960s tenements, the wild colours of a rich fauna punctuated by walls that are heavily tattooed with political graffiti. It is an unremarkable place and yet it is here, on the boundary between the 11th and 12th *arrondissements* of Marseilles, that one of the most extraordinary football careers in history began. A career comprising scandal, corruption, poetry and art, six championships, three cups, a 'shitbag', a psychoanalyst and a puppet called Picasso.

The dusty shutters on the *boulangerie* flicker with the sound of hungry flies. The bar looks deceased. Caillols wears the image of village that rejoices in apathy. But a few score yards down the road there are signs of life. A diesel engine hums to life and alerts a passing dog. The car pulls up outside the Stade de Caillols and a father gets out. His son bounces out of the passenger seat and removes his sports bag from the boot. He is a *joueur* for Caillols Under-13s and they have a game that afternoon against Decuques. He walks through the wrought-iron gates, which are shedding flaky green paint, and enters the changing-rooms. He is the first to arrive.

Twenty-eight years earlier, the six-year-old Eric Cantona walked through these same gates for the first time. That is why I am here: to see where it all began and to see whether the people of Caillols, a stone's throw from the Côte D'Azur, remember Cantona.

Twenty minutes later the Stade de Caillols is bustling with people – players, coaches, parents, club officials. My wife and I pass through the gates and watch the teams limbering up on the red shale surface. The ground is enclosed by tall netting and neighboured by a field where a donkey does a passing impersonation of Tony Adams. As my French is awful, I have enlisted my wife to act as translator. We look around to see who would be the best person to speak to. She decides upon a white-haired gentleman wearing a blue SS Caillols tracksuit. It proves an inspired choice as he is none other than Yves Ciccullo, the club president who once coached the young Cantona.

Not in the slightest bit fazed by the fact that two foreigners have turned up in this backwater on a Sunday afternoon, Ciccullo merrily answers my wife's questions with a nonchalance laced with the odd Gallic flourish. 'Even when he was six, Eric stood out from the crowd and he always knew he would be a big star,' he says. 'I knew he would be a great professional. Lots of other players from here have become professionals, players like Jean Tigana, but Eric has superseded them all.'

From a rucksack I pull out a booklet on Cantona to show the president. He looks at the photograph on the front cover and stifles a laugh. The photo is a portrait of Cantona. He is looking down at the camera, a mixture of contempt, arrogance and mischievousness enlivening his face. 'He was the same when he was a six-year-old boy,' says Yves, who mimics the photograph by dropping the corners of his mouth and arching an eyebrow. 'Always very proud. This look is not an image, this is real Cantona. He did this same look when he was a young boy.'

I am mightily impressed with my wife's linguistic abilities. I stand and nod. The ignorant yes-man. But despite the unintelligibility barrier, Yves is a jovial raconteur. It is said that the people of Marseilles are friendlier than in the rest of France, and here is living proof. 'Eric is still a hero of the town, but he doesn't come back much. He is too big.' He laughs again as he trawls his memories. 'His family used to live behind the ground in a big villa, but they have moved to the Alpes de Haute-Provence now. His maternal grandfather was just like him. He had a big, droopy moustache and was very proud. He used to sit here alone and just say "bonjour" to everyone.' I have watched Eric on television. He is a superstar, but it does not surprise me. It was inevitable.'

The teams trot out. The number seven of Caillols has much to live up to. He is the tiniest player on the pitch. A muted ripple of applause is drowned out by the sounds of chickens, goats and geese. Yves invites us to stay and watch and we take our seats. This is the beginning. The best place to start.

*　*　*

About a month earlier I had sent letters out to as many French newspapers and radio stations as I could find addresses for. I may have been asking for a lot, but I was hoping someone would have kept in close contact with Eric since his days *en France*. I said I would meet anyone, anytime, anyplace, anywhere, realising I sounded vaguely desperate and strongly like a Martini advert. I'd given up hope until I received a letter from Raphael in Marseilles. He said he worked for a radio station and had heard that Eric was coming back to Marseilles for a players' reunion. He was sure he could wangle me an invitation. This was great news. So far my efforts to locate Eric had struck barren ground.

I knew Eric lived in Barcelona, but was told by journalists in Spain that he did not talk and it would be pointless for me just to turn up unannounced. Jean-Jacques Bertrand, his lawyer, had not returned any of my messages. The British journalists I'd tried had been unable to help. I'd written to all his former clubs but to no avail. And then when I heard he had blanked the Press pack in Madrid I began to give up hope of ever finding him. But then Raphael wrote to me in impressive English and I was filled with fresh optimism. At something as low-key as a players' reunion I figured I might catch Cantona with his guard down and fire a few questions. It may have been a long shot, but what the hell? I had nothing to lose. It was the best lead I'd got so far.

And so I booked Debs and myself on a flight to France. Even if I didn't find him, which I had to accept was a possibility, I would be visiting his home town. And if you cannot understand David Batty without being steeped in Leeds, it followed that you could not appreciate Eric without traipsing round Marseilles with a dictaphone, an instamatic camera and a ray of hope.

We picked up our car from the airport and drove into town to find a hotel. As I had not arranged to see Raphael until later that evening, I drove to the Stade Vélodrome, the home of Olympic de Marseille (popularly known as OM) where Eric had two spells before joining Leeds. It is an impressive stadium with an imposing main stand that is reminiscent of a gargantuan Venetian blind, fronted by a vast pedestrian area which was awash with rollerbladers when I arrived. I headed for the museum to see how Marseilles remembered one of its most famous sons – and soon realised the answer was that it didn't. On a wall was a mosaic of clay footprints, a variation on Mann's Chinese Theater in Hollywood where film stars would leave their mark in cement. Here Eric appeared to have left no impression whatsoever. I found Chris Waddle's footprint and Jean Tigana's. They were all represented. Jean-Pierre Papin, Amoros, Fabrizio Ravanelli. Everyone, it seemed, except Cantona. I asked the assistant and she shrugged. 'Cantona?' she said. 'He no so good.'

I flicked through a club history and found no mention of him there, either. Papin was clearly the club hero, with a comic book devoted entirely to him. This seemed strange. I knew Cantona had not been at his best during his spells at Marseilles, and that he had fallen foul of the infamous president, Bernard Tapie, but he was the local boy made good. Did that count for nothing?

On the way back to the hotel I saw a 50-foot image of Zinedine Zidane decorating the side of an apartment block. Zidane was also born in Marseilles and had become the hero of the nation by scoring twice in the 1998 World Cup final victory over Brazil. Maybe that was why Eric seemed to hold such a small place in the hearts of the Marseillais. He had been supplanted. Since Eric left town, Marseille had won the European Cup – although subsequently stripped of the title after a match-fixing scandal – and Zidane had achieved the ultimate without leaving a trail of devastation in his wake à la Cantona.

Perhaps it was the fact Cantona had often been at odds with authority that limited his appeal, or perhaps it was the fact he had shunned France for England. What is certain is that the story of Cantona's journey from Marseilles to Leeds is an incredible one and goes some way to explaining the peculiar attitude towards him in his homeland.

He was born on 24 May 1966. His family originally lived in a cave carved out of the side of the Caillols hills, the first sign that he was different. The young troglodyte enjoyed a blissful existence in the Provençal countryside, full of curious aromas and natural delights. And then there was football. At Caillols he began life as a goalkeeper before realising his talents lay in creating rather than stifling. By the time Eric was 12, the president had already earmarked him for a life of greatness. This was despite the incident when the colts side missed out on the chance of winning their league because he had his laces undone! During the crucial match Eric found himself faced with an open goal and knew that if he scored, Caillols would do the Double; but as he moved to shoot, the referee blew his whistle and told him to fasten his shoelaces. Such jobsworthiness would often light the blue touch-paper in the future.

At the age of 15 Cantona joined Auxerre. His decision to move hundreds of miles away from his family and shun the chance of joining Nice – a modest car trip along the Côte d'Azur – was partly due to the fact he felt the northern club had shown him more respect. They had also given him a shirt and a pennant, whereas Nice officials had come bearing no gifts. The manager of Auxerre was Guy Roux, an idiosyncratic figure who would vigilantly ride his moped around various villages at night to make sure his players were not out nightclubbing. I could scarcely imagine Howard Wilkinson doing the same in Leeds. Nor could I envisage Wilkinson using the same criterion for sending a player on loan as Roux apparently employed when farming out Cantona to Martigues. Roux had contacted Cantona's future wife, Isabelle, to test the strength of their burgeoning relationship and, according to Eric, sent the young striker into the countryside solely to be close to her. 'He wanted me to live on love and fresh air,' said Eric. It was a temporary measure, however, and soon Cantona was back at Auxerre and performing well enough to break into the French national side as a 21-year-old. His international début came on 21 August 1987 and he scored in a 2–1 defeat by West Germany.

The following year it became clear that Auxerre would not be able to hold on to their prize asset. The only question was where Cantona would go. As he strove to make up his mind, he had several sessions of psychoanalysis. He insisted he was not worried about his mental health, but was merely fascinated by the subconscious. Coming from any other footballer, such a claim would have been laughable: but this was a player who loved art, literature, philosophy and poetry. If he said he was interested in the subconscious, well, then it sounded far more feasible than, say, Gazza claiming the same.

In the end Cantona decided upon Marseille. As Batty would do more than a decade later, he was going home – but unlike his future team-mate, his return would see him hit the headlines for all the wrong reasons.

* * *

The game between Caillols and Decuques is hotly contested. After about ten minutes the little number seven takes a tumble in the box. The ball is cleared and the game continues, but the number seven stays down. Then suddenly he rolls over three times in elaborate fashion. I chuckle at his ironic humour, but attract a few Gallic glares and realise he is serious. The game stops, the shouts soften and we can hear the little number seven blubbing. He is carried off with a scraped knee. I cannot imagine a pre-pubescent English striker showing such incredible theatrics. Here in Caillols the memory of Cantona lives on.

* * *

Cantona's own descent into melodrama began shortly after his £2.3 million transfer to Marseille in the summer of 1988. He made a modest start, failing to score in his first five matches; but on 17 August he broke his duck, against Matra-Racing. Three days later, having been omitted from the French national squad, Cantona let rip and called manager Henri Michel a 'shitbag'. It was a defining moment in the life of *l'enfant terrible* and a one-year ban from playing for France ensued. Cantona seemed ambivalent about the ban, insisting his only problem was a need to learn the art of communication. Others felt his problem was he had no trouble whatsoever in getting his message across. His image was secured. *Guignols de l'Info*, the French version of *Spitting Image*, began to use a Cantona puppet going by the monicker of Picasso, a sarcastic reference to the self-styled aesthete. Cantona would have mixed views about his foam-and-latex double, believing the public came to view this parody as the real Eric. However, every stereotype begins with a grain of truth and Cantona was giving plenty of credence to his caricature.

The following January, having alienated the international hierarchy, he found himself a domestic outcast. When he was substituted in a friendly against Torpedo Moscow in aid of the Armenian Disaster Fund, he ripped off his shirt and hurled it to the ground. Bernard Tapie was distinctly unimpressed and threatened to send Cantona to a psychiatric clinic. He relented and sent him on loan to Bordeaux instead. Cantona had played just 22 games for his home-town club. The rift with Tapie was now an unbridgeable chasm, but Cantona, annoyed by the fact he was seen to have failed in the Velodrome, nevertheless vowed to return.

The following season Catona took a 50 per cent wage cut to go and play for Montpellier under the future World Cup-winning coach, Aimé Jacquet. In typically romantic fashion, Cantona claimed the team's mission was to interpret *The Magic Flute* every Saturday. Inevitably, problems continued to follow Cantona around. He would blame much of it on his non-conformism, but much of it had to do with an innate feeling of superiority. As Yves Cicculo told me, Cantona knew he was better than the rest. If others failed to see that then they were blind. Ignorance was no excuse.

One man who did not see it was Montpellier team-mate, Jean-Claude Lemoult. In a corridor after a game, Cantona overheard him decrying the team's strikers. That was a red rag to the bullfighting fan. He hurled his boots into Lemoult's face and a fight followed. Six players immediately signed a petition calling for Eric's head and he was banned again. However, for all his faults, Montpellier needed Cantona and he was recalled within two weeks. In June 1990 the decision paid off when Montpellier won the French Cup, beating Matra-Racing 2–1 in the final.

With Cantona's public profile enjoying a rare positive phase, his popularity grew and Tapie called him back to Marseille for the 1990–91 season. The antipathy between owner and employee could not be cured, however, and matured into a mutual hatred. Tapie expected his players to fall into line and work towards his own ends. Cantona refused to bow to pressure from anybody but himself. It was the excuse of the existentialist. He refused to join his team-mates in threatening strike action in support of Tapie when the millionaire businessman clashed with authority himself after making some outspoken remarks about a referee; nor would he add fuel to Tapie's well-oiled PR machine by going public with glowing references to Marseille's beneficent godfather. On the pitch things fared little better and a serious knee injury sidelined him for three months. By the time Cantona returned, the highly respected Franz Beckenbauer – a 'real gentleman' according to Cantona – had been replaced as coach by the Belgian Raymond Goethals – 'I never respected him and he didn't respect his players.' Once more Cantona failed to get on with his coach and, having made just 18 appearances all season, he was soon on his way again.

His reputation as a miscreant and a misfit seemed well earned. He was incredulous when Bordeaux spoke of his truancy from training. Cantona insisted he had missed only one session, when his dog had died. It may have been an honest and heart-rending excuse, but to the powerbrokers of professional football it was one step away from saying the same dog had eaten his homework. At Marseille, Tapie felt the fact he was bankrolling the team meant he was owed something more than mere footballing talent. Meanwhile, Henri Michel believed his position as national coach merited respect.

However, Catona would have the last laugh on both. His disdain of Tapie was frowned upon at the time, but he was ultimately proved right. In 1993 Marseille beat AC Milan 1–0 to win the European Champions Cup. Three months later they were barred from defending the trophy over a match-fixing scandal and the victory was expunged from the record books. Sixteen days later the French

Federation stripped them of their League title, suspended three players and relegated the club. Tapie initially appeared to have escaped punishment, but later stood trial for match-fixing and was jailed for corruption. Cantona no doubt felt slightly smug about the affair and would say he was glad he was suspended by a man whose methods were based on lies and trickery. As for Michel: within two months of being labelled a 'shitbag' by Cantona, he had been sacked. Cantona had questioned his ability, the fact he had used more than 50 players in two years, and accused him of being swayed by the media. Whether the French Federation went along with that or not, they certainly agreed that Michel needed to go. His replacement was Michel Platini, probably the finest French footballer of them all and a man Cantona respected more than anyone.

But Cantona was like a walking neon strip, attracting trouble like bluebottles from every quarter. They flew at him, collided and there were casualties, but Cantona was nothing if not resilient. He continued to shine and would tread his own path. In 1991 he started the season at Nîmes, but was soon clashing with authority again. During a game against St Etienne, Cantona's frustration boiled over and he threw the ball at the referee. He was sent off and summoned to appear before a disciplinary commission, which then banned him for a month. The fact he had called the commission 'idiots' had hardly worked in his favour. When asked to explain himself, he repeated the insult to each and every member of the commission.

Cantona asked to be treated like any other player, but of course he couldn't be. Eric was different. In his heart he knew that and so did the commission, whose president, Jacques Riolaci, told him that he left a trail of the smell of sulphur behind him. He then inadvertently paid Cantona a compliment, saying he could expect anything from such an individualist. This was intended as a reprimand, but to the maverick libertarian it was an acknowledgement of a life's work.

Outraged at the age of 25 by what he considered the injustice of the system, Cantona retired. He spoke of a noble sport being threatened by gravediggers and of a disappearing dream. When criticised for being a poor role model, he said children's heart and souls were not clay to be modelled into the established order. In short, Cantona was misunderstood and disillusioned.

And then he came to Leeds.

* * *

I walk to the OM bar on the Quai de Rive Neuve. On the way I pass a monument to the poet, Arthur Rimbaud, Eric's favourite. It looks remarkably reminiscent of a pile of rubble to me, like a reject from the Tate Gallery. I carry on walking through the old port, which is gridlocked with yachts and motorboats. On the other side of the road are the pavement cafés with their bold and bright canopies. A rickety-looking vessel is moored against the dock and half-dead fish are being flung on to the quay. Out to sea is the Château d'If. The sixteenth-century prison was the setting for *The Count of Monte Cristo*, by Alexandre Dumas, in which the hero is wrongfully imprisoned. In reality such miscarriages of justice were commonplace: one nobleman was famously jailed for six years for failing to remove his hat in the presence of Louis XIV. Somehow it seems fitting that Cantona, so often seen as the guilty party while protesting his innocence, should come from here.

I arrive at the OM bar, which is decorated with photographs, signed shirts, scarves and other memorabilia celebrating the city's football club. I take a seat and put my Cantona book on the table. Some people wear roses and meet under the clock at Waterloo station. Me, I say it with biographies of French footballers. There could be something in this. Book-club dating. Show prospective partners what you like. It would avoid a lot of trouble. You could just steer your way clear of all the Jeffrey Archer fans and go straight for the Jilly Coopers. A good night guaranteed.

I am not looking for a partner, however – just a radio journalist. He soon spies me and introduces himself. We order white wines and talk. In the street, impatient French drivers beep their horns if the reactions of the car in front are even just a fraction slow.

Raphael has bad news. He now thinks Cantona will not be attending the reunion. He also says invitations have proved harder to locate than he expected. Despite these bombshells, he retains a plastic grin and eyes up passing woman with a professional vigour. We drink away and Raphael gives me much background information about Cantona, Tapie and Marseille. As the alcohol kicks in, I forget my initial disappointment. 'Tapie is massively popular in the city,' says Raphael. 'Even with what happened, many people are grateful for what he has done. He is not a good man to fall out with.'

I nod. The wine is good and I feel slightly numb.

'I am not surprised,' I say. 'Some of those songs he wrote with Elton John were belters.' Raphael looks non-plussed and I feel guilty about my flippancy. 'Sorry, that's Bernie Taupin, not Tapie. I understand what you are saying. This is why there are no pictures of Eric on the walls?'

Raphael shrugs. He lights up another cigarette. Everyone in France smokes. They do it because it is cool. Style is everything. Raphael *wears* his fag rather than smokes it. He hails a friend, who is sitting at another table, and the man saunters over. After quick introductions and much back-slapping – plus a little book-slapping too, as he recognises Eric's face – this new man tells me he met Cantona the previous summer.

'He was promoting his latest film in my home town,' he said. 'He wasn't interested at all. I tried to speak to him about his football, but all he would say was "yes" and "no". There were loads of kids there, but he just couldn't be bothered. He gave a 15-second speech and then he went. I thought he was an idiot.' I had heard a similar report in England from a Norwegian fan. He recalled Cantona turning up at a charity football event, attended by Norway's Prime

LOOKING FOR ERIC

Minister, and refusing to take part. The fan claimed Cantona even refused to kick off the game, thus disappointing a crowd of 2,000. Maybe it is stories such as these which have caused Marseilles not to remember.

*   *   *

It was almost Sheffield instead of Leeds, South Yorkshire instead of West. Platini had talked Cantona out of retirement and suggested he move to England. With Jean-Jacques Bertrand (the man who never seemed to be in) overseeing his departure, links were soon made with Trevor Francis – who was then the Wednesday boss and a friend of Platini's. Francis agreed to take Cantona on trial, but the Frenchman deemed this to be beneath him and the deal fell through. Cantona blamed the agents involved and alleged they had failed to mention the prospect of a trial to him in fear of losing their commission. As the lure of Wednesday weakened, Leeds stepped in. Howard Wilkinson needed a striker, following an injury to Lee Chapman. After consulting Platini, Glenn Hoddle and Gerard Houllier, he took Cantona on loan. No trial required. The trials and tribulations were in the future.

Cantona's début was a forgettable affair. He came on at half-time for Steve Hodge in a 2–0 defeat at Oldham on 8 February. It was only Leeds' second reverse of the season. Wilkinson demanded Cantona be patient and he eased him into the side as a substitute, insisting it would take time to acclimatise to English football. When Cantona scored his first goal in Leeds colours, a ten-yard tap-in against Luton at Elland Road on 29 February 1992, there was no doubt he was ready. The fans loved him and chanted 'Ooh-aah Cantona' whenever he got the ball. Eric was similarly happy and would later claim Leeds had 'given me back my life'. Now he says he has forgotten nothing about Leeds, the fans, the applause and the generosity of spirit. This mutual appreciation society reached its peak on 11 April against the old enemy, Chelsea. In fairness to the rest of the team, the game was already won when Gordon Strachan played the ball to Cantona. But as he burst into the penalty area he juggled the ball on his right foot, first one way then another, totally wrong-footing the bamboozled defender, and then fired a stunning half-volley into the top corner. The crowd chanted his name for the remainder of the game. A legend was reborn.

Cantona explained his love affair with the Leeds fans by claiming they wanted players who could make them dream. He said his heart beat to the rhythm of the fans. He was right. There have been a host of more important players in Leeds' history, but none has been able to express the fan–player relationship so eloquently. Yet his individualism, grace and craft did not always sit easily with managers, who failed to view football as sporting opera. Cantona's heroes were the great artists because, he said, they were accountable to no one but themselves.

Like those managers before him, Wilkinson felt Cantona was accountable to him, and he continued to handle him with care. In retrospect, it is easy to mock

Wilkinson for failing fully to exploit the Frenchman's talents; but you have to remember Leeds were top of the table when Cantona arrived and Chapman and Rod Wallace had forged the most successful forward line since Clarke and Jones. If not Fish and Chips they were at least Chips and Gravy. Though Cantona's arrival is often credited with powering Leeds down the home straight in the 1992 title run-in, the facts of the matter are these. In the championship season, Cantona made only six starts, completing 90 minutes on five occasions. In addition, he made nine appearances as a substitute. He scored three goals. In truth, it does not sound much, but the statistics only tell part of the story.

With Manchester United breathing down Leeds' neck, Cantona gave Wilkinson's side an extra weapon in the form of a loose cannon. They had an unquenchable spirit and a unique individual to go along with their considerable collective value. Leeds duly won the title on that curious day in Sheffield and Cantona revelled in the success as much as his team-mates who had fought longer and harder for the triumph. A year earlier, he had been an outsider in his home town. It was only six months since he retired. Leeds had been the unlikely setting for one of the greatest players of modern times to fall back in love with football. Dickens may have seen it as a beastly city, but to Cantona it was beautiful.

In the summer of 1992 Cantona played in France's unsuccessful European Championships campaign in Sweden. He had served his time and was back in the international fold; but following that summer's failure his great friend Platini departed and Houllier replaced him. Like England, France failed to qualify for the 1994 World Cup, meaning Cantona never got to strut his stuff on the biggest stage of all. He scored seven goals in eleven qualifying games, but it was not enough. A tempestuous international career came to a close on 18 January 1995 when he played in a 1–0 win against Holland. Despite his ban, he had won 45 caps and scored 20 goals.

He returned from Sweden for pre-season training with high hopes of establishing himself as a first-team choice. He signalled his intent in the Charity Shield when he scored a hat-trick against Liverpool at Wembley. It was 18 years since the two sides had met for the same trophy. That previous game will forever be remembered for the red cards shown to Bremner and Keegan, but this game belonged to Cantona and his fantastic skills. He called it one of the greatest days of his career and, with a European Cup campaign to come, life looked good.

But the course of true love never did run smooth and Cantona was fast approaching a sudden split from the club which had breathed new life into him. Within four months of the start of the season Cantona was a Manchester United player. The reasons for his departure vary depending upon whom you wish to believe. Wilkinson explained it thus: 'Eric likes to do what he likes when he likes – and then fucks off. We'd all want a bit of that.' Not surprisingly, Cantona saw it differently and put the blame back onto Wilkinson. He claimed he had trouble decoding his manager's language, that Wilkinson did not like strong personalities and that he was jealous of the rapport Cantona enjoyed with the fans. Gordon

Strachan told me Cantona had made up his mind to go and there was nothing anyone could do to stop him – but the question is, why?

The answer is most likely in the clash of strong-willed personalities and obdurate natures. Though they may have seemed like chalk and cheese in terms of style and charisma, Cantona and Wilkinson may have been more alike than either would care to admit.

In the summer of 1992 Wilkinson had recruited David Rocastle from Arsenal for £2 million and old boy Scott Sellars had returned from Blackburn for £900,000. But with the uneasy alliance between the manager and Cantona deteriorating, Leeds began their title defence and European campaign in a state of flux. Strachan's persistent back trouble meant he missed out on the start of the season, which afforded Cantona a place in the side, but the season started poorly with only two wins from the opening seven games. As the shocking away record became a source of embarrassment rather than frustration, any hopes of another championship challenge were quickly extinguished.

Europe offered little respite. In their first game, away at Stuttgart, Leeds crashed 3–0. Things had gone well enough in the first half, but then Leeds fell apart. Cantona's status fell even further in Wilkinson's eyes when he played a careless pass into the path of a Stuttgart player who promptly started the counter-attack which saw Fritz Walter score the opener. It seemed that the European adventure would be a short story.

However, the return leg was an epic encounter to rival the magical nights of the Revie era. This was football as the beautiful game. For Cantona the artist, who said he could not renounce beauty, this was the masterpiece. For Cantona the footballer, who said sublime moments of sporting beauty could provide glimpses of eternity, this was the game that will live forever. It was billed as 'Mission Impossible'. No British side had ever come back from a three-goal deficit in Europe; but Leeds had the will and belief, even if many of their fans did not (only 20,457 turned up for the game). It was a night on which Leeds' key players all came up trumps. Gary McAllister was magnificent as he led the midfield, aided and abetted by Strachan and Gary Speed, while Cantona and Lee Chapman were immense up front. Strachan and Cantona created the opening goal for Speed, who tore into the box and connected with a sweet left-footed volley. It provided a glimmer of hope, but when Stuttgart scored on the breakaway, that appeared to be that. Leeds needed five goals and a third of the game had already gone.

A McAllister penalty then gave Leeds a 2–1 half-time lead and the second half saw them lay siege to the Stuttgart goal. Chances came and went with monotonous regularity, until Cantona bustled his way into the box and scrambled a looping shot into the net with the help of a German foot. Chapman soon added a fourth with a near-post header and the incredible suddenly looked feasible. The Germans hung on, though, and collapsed in a heap at the end. They had been demolished, yet they had still won. They breathed a sigh of relief.

Leeds were dead but not buried. A *Daily Express* reporter was told by the

German Press that Stuttgart had infringed the rules by fielding four overseas players when three was the maximum allowed. From black hole to loophole in 24 hours! Leeds attended a UEFA hearing and the game was awarded to them with a 3–0 scoreline, meaning a play-off was needed. The momentum was now with Leeds. Goals from Strachan and Carl Shutt gave Leeds a 2–1 victory in Barcelona and set up the Battle of Britain with Glasgow Rangers.

Leeds had a nation on their side. The tie was seen as a perfect opportunity to prove that English football was superior to Scottish. No away fans were allowed to attend the first leg and Leeds were told to expect a baptism of fire. Within two minutes they had drowned such talk in the font as McAllister struck a magnificent volley into the top corner. What followed was to magnify Leeds' capacity for self-destruction. With Leeds in utter control, John Lukic punched a high ball into his own net. Suddenly the crowd was a frenzied mass of blue-and-white: self-belief pumped through the Rangers players and the tide turned. Rangers won 2–1, but still Leeds were in a useful position going into the second leg.

Cue more frustration. Mark Hateley's wondrous strike and then a well-worked breakaway ending with an Ally McCoist header made it 2–0. Cantona's late goal was not enough. Leeds lost 4–2 on aggregate. It was a crushing blow. With Watford putting them out of the League Cup and the League campaign being over before it had begun, Leeds' season had turned into a bitter joke. Three weeks later Cantona was sold for £1.2 million. It seemed a paltry sum and suggested Wilkinson was happy to get rid of Cantona sooner rather than later, regardless of market values. Strachan sympathised with Wilkinson: 'Nobody had anything against the big fella personally, but there were a lot of places he didn't produce,' he said. 'I don't know what else Howard could have done.'

The reign of Eric Idol was over. He had made a grand total of 34 appearances in Leeds colours, scoring 11 goals. Compared to the other legends in this book it is a paltry total. His greatest achievements would come at Manchester United where he would win four Premiership titles, two Doubles, two FA Cups, four Charity Shields, the PFA Player of the Year award and the Football Writers' Footballer of the Year award. His greatest controversy would also come in a Manchester United shirt when he jumped into the crowd at Selhurst Park to assault a fan. Though there was media moral outrage at his crime, many were secretly glad that one of the thousands of low life, foul-mouthed upstarts who plague football matches had got his just deserts. Eric was banned for seven months. At a press conference he caused much mirth with his statement: 'When the seagulls follow the trawler it is because they think, perhaps, sardines will be thrown in the sea.' The man who believed the world was his stage had been reduced to the role of panto villain.

The Press claimed Cantona could not possibly return because he would be goaded into more terrible crimes by unsubtle defenders and unstable fans. They were wrong. Cantona returned in October, scored in a 2–2 draw against Liverpool and went on to inspire Manchester United to the Double.

Yet Eric deserves his place in this book, just as Leeds deserves a special place in his story. He is, without doubt, one of the most gifted players ever to turn out for the club; and it was the club which saved him, for his career had become a funeral pyre of the bridges he had previously burnt when he showed up at Elland Road. His obstinacy and contempt had forced him into premature retirement. But Leeds rekindled the passion in him and gave him the platform to mount, the chance to become a great icon instead of just a half-decent player who could never hold down a job in France. He deserves his place in Leeds folklore for different reasons to the rest, but that is fitting. Eric was different. It is why so many people reviled him. But as Micel Nait-Challal said in the French sports daily, *l'Equipe*, 'to condemn a person for the sole reason that he is different bears but one name – intolerance'.

* * *

A British warship has put into port and the old quarter of Marseilles, from the foot of Le Canebière to the cafés which kneel at the foot of the Basilique Notre Dame de la Garde with its resplendent gold virgin, are awash with sailors. Raphael has said he will ring me at the hotel with further news about the reunion, but I am losing hope. Back in my room I can see the ferries chugging their way to the Chateau d'If. Debs flicks on the television, which is showing highlights of yesterday's Premiership games. Bradford get thumped 3–0 at Leicester and look doomed, while Arsenal have all but wrapped up second place with a 2–1 win over Chelsea. And then the camera switches to Old Trafford where Manchester United romp to a routine 3–1 win over Tottenham Hotspur. It is the day they are celebrating the Premiership title, sealed a fortnight earlier against Southampton. I wonder about what might have been had Leeds just kept going a bit longer, if Batty had been fit, if Bowyer had not missed that open goal against the Mancs at Elland Road, if Hasselbaink had not been so greedy and had stayed put . . . And then the camera focuses on a face in the crowd. My jaw drops. I stare at Debs. She has seen it too. There, on the television set beaming pictures back from Old Trafford, is none other than Eric.

'I don't think he's coming,' says Debs.

'I'll kill that bloody Raphael,' I mutter.

Raphael calls later that evening. He too has seen the television and realises Eric has made an unexpected visit to England. He apologises. I tell him not to worry.

Instead of crashing a players' reunion, we end up in a tiny bar watching the French Cup final. Calais, a bunch of amateurs from the Fourth Division, are playing First Division Nantes. They are holding them at 1–1 until ten minutes from time, when they concede a dubious penalty. The barman curses. We are all on the side of the under*chien*. The striker shoots and the Calais keeper dives. This is a mistake. Had he stood still, he could have caught it. As it is, he still gets a good connection on the ball, but only manages to deflect the shot into the roof of the net. The barman curses loudly. At the final whistle the Nantes players celebrate in a ludicrously OTT manner, considering they have just squeezed past a team of part-timers. Calais have been inspirational and scarcely deserved to lose. There are tears before full-time. The Nantes skipper remembers himself and, in a fine gesture of sportsmanship, invites the Calais captain to lift the cup with him. I sup my beer and decide to give it one last go. I ask the barman who he supports and, with no little incredulity, he tells me Marseille. So I ask him about Eric. Surely someone remembers him, idolises him, appreciates him.

I am in luck. 'Cantona was *fantastique*,' he says, the memory allaying his frustration at the cup-final result. 'He was a magician with the ball and he come from here. He used to eat in my father's restaurant.' At last I have found a fan. 'And was he your favourite player?' I enquire.

He takes my money and frowns. 'Oh no,' he says, almost affronted by the question. 'Chris Waddle was my favourite.'

* * *

The Caillols number ten is the best player on the pitch. He stands out a mile. Whereas others kick and chase, he makes time for himself and has some party pieces to rival any tupperware king. After half an hour he latches on to a loose ball, plucks it out of the air with his right boot and fires in a shot with the outside of his foot. The keeper has no chance. The net ripples, as does the applause. Yves Ciccullo is on his feet. He looks across at me, does his Cantona impersonation and then points to the scorer. I get the message and nod enthusiastically.

Maybe.

The number ten stops, scowls and salutes the 30 or so fans sitting on the concrete steps with a thespian pomp. Then he puffs out his half-formed chest, turns his collar up and puts his hands on his hips.

Oh yes. Definitely.

THE FINAL WHISTLE – Journey's End

I didn't find Eric, but maybe that was just as well. Sometimes it is better to live with your preconceptions, to imbue your heroes with the qualities you admire rather than have reality drop its trousers and reveal the naked truth. That is what football is all about, the suspension of belief and knowledge. It is a surrogate life masquerading as sport.

I didn't find Eric, but I discovered a lot more. I found out that the legends of Elland Road were just ordinary mortals, flushed with rare talents and common failings. They were an accommodating bunch – warm, generous and honest. In an age when football has reached a trough of cynicism, it was invigorating to hear them recount events of another lifetime with such enthusiasm. For each of the players featured in this book, I was reassured to learn that Leeds United had been more than just an office with turf. Like the rest of us, the hardy souls who suffer perennial rejection, disappointment and heartache, they really cared. I can breathe easier now.

Leeds drew their final game of the 1999–2000 season at West Ham, but Liverpool's defeat at Bradford, which ensured the latter Premiership's survival, meant David O'Leary's side came third. Thanks to UEFA's rejection of tradition and sporting excellence for the sake of greed, this was enough for them to clinch the final Champions League place, worth an estimated £10 million.

On 17 May Galatasaray and Arsenal played in the UEFA Cup Final in Copenhagen. Both sides had started the season in the Champions League, but their failure in that arena meant they entered the secondary European competition at the third round stage. Their ineptitude had effectively given them two byes, another UEFA farce which devalued the tournament and highlighted the inadequacies of the decision-makers. Prior to the game there were running battles between the two sets of supporters. Three men, a fan of each club and a Dutchman, were stabbed. Five fans were seriously injured. Galatasaray won the cup on penalties. To many in Yorkshire it was an amoral victory. UEFA president

Lennart Johansson said he was saddened by the scenes of carnage. 'After the tragic incident where two English fans were stabbed to death in Istanbul, I truly in my simplicity believed violence would decrease,' he said. Such simplicity spoke volumes.

As another season shuddered to an ugly halt, Leeds United's future looked bright. Michael Bridges ended up as top goalscorer with 19 Premiership goals and 21 in total. O'Leary insisted Harry Kewell was staying put. No sooner had the season ended than Leeds smashed their transfer record by signing French midfielder, Olivier Dacourt, for £7.2 million. Another Frenchman with disciplinary problems. We awaited the fireworks.

My journey was at an end, but the joy of football is that there are always fresh starts. It's a beautiful cycle as we unfailingly allow our expectations to bring down our experience in the six-yard box. It is the same from Milan to Macclesfield. The fan who watches dross does so to reaffirm his dreams of a better place, a never-never land where strikers do not have club feet and home defeats are banned. We are all slaves on the chain gang, shackled to reality but free to dream of the great escape. And that is where football comes in. It is sport's answer to Steve McQueen's motorbike.

I will continue to watch Leeds, hope for the future and drift indulgently into memories of yesterday. I suppose we are all particularly fond of the players we knew as kids, when we were spared the bitterness and worldliness of adulthood and knew our heroes only for what we wanted them to be. We all live in hope that things will be like that again one day, that there will be another Bremner, another Currie, a Clarke and a Charles.

We all live in hope thanks to the legends, and for that they deserve our eternal gratitude.

RB 2000

PETER RIDSDALE – The Aftermath

Football hooligans? There are 92 club chairmen for a start.

BRIAN CLOUGH

Office workers and bohemians split benches in Golden Square. They eat oversized sandwiches from the neighbouring deli, drink designer water and read Ian Rankin novels. Down the road is Piccadilly, besieged by tourists, to the rear is Carnaby Street, that kitsch reminder of '60s teen spirit. Inside No. 21 Miss Nigeria grins at me in the hallway. Alongside her, more photographs of faded beauty queens create an ivory wall of feigned smiles. It is a fitting welcome party as I am here to look beyond the surface and find out what lies beneath. I have come to London to find out what really happened in West Yorkshire.

In the two years since I completed the original version of this book, Leeds United have descended into the maelstrom. The spectre of race hatred still remains at the club following the trials of Lee Bowyer and Jonathan Woodgate for their roles in the attack on Sarfraz Najeib. Bowyer was cleared and Woodgate convicted of the lesser charge of affray, but they were still vilified as amoral anarchists – the unthinking man's heroes. The favourable glances generated since the cynicism of the Revie era and the thuggery of the hooligan years were sacrificed for what David O'Leary called one 'boozy, boozy night'. Everyone hated Leeds again and who could blame them?

It took a few hours to decimate a decade and Leeds was again a bastion of bile. Although the Football Association suspended both players from playing for England while the trial progressed, O'Leary was told they were available for selection. He agreed that they should be viewed as innocent until proven guilty and picked them, thereby igniting a tension that had already been fuelled by Leeds' lack of public sympathy for the victim. Woodgate, perhaps appreciating the severity of his actions, faded to a pallid shroud, but Bowyer, showing either an indomitable will or inveterate arrogance, never played better than when making motorway dashes from Hull Crown Court. The subsequent collapse of the trial because of an article in the *Sunday Mirror* prolonged the agony of it all. In the piece, Najeib's father said the attack had been racially motivated. Despite the initial comments of the police back in 2000, the jury had been told to discount the race issue. Colin Myler, the tabloid's editor at the time, had shown an incredible ignorance of legal procedure and later paid the price. And so we had another multi-million pound trial. Yet for Asians throughout Britain and for the gossiping laymen in the pubs up and down the country, colour would not be whitewashed.

Initially, Leeds coped with their off-field problems with surprising ease. Football was a cathartic release after all the insinuation and innuendo. In the 2000–01 season they rekindled memories of the legends by making it to the semi-finals of the Champions League. It was a triumph of youthful precocity and verve over adversity, but sweet victories over Lazio, AC Milan and Anderlecht were soured by the stench of suspicion. Valencia knocked Leeds out of the semi-finals with a comprehensive victory and a mesmerising journey came to a satisfied end. Yet an achievement that flew in the face of expectation was not to signal the rebirth of the club and, instead, Leeds would be brought to their knees by self-inflicted wounds.

O'Leary signed Rio Ferdinand for a record-breaking £18 million at the start of the following season, but the public perception of the club was already tainted by the stain of outside events. The Majestyk nightclub, awash with Day-Glo billboards, stands in the centre of the city as a permanent reminder of football's dark side. Next to it is the Queen's Hotel ,where John Charles signed for Juventus in a hazy age of innocence. A thoroughly decent man with a working-class code of ethics, Charles's quiet dignity counters the vacuity of many who have followed in his footsteps. As a result of that chase through the streets on a wild night, a room was set aside at the training ground for solicitors. The exuberance of a European odyssey was lost amid a welter of speculation and knee-jerk reactions. Whatever happened in court, many had already determined Leeds United's guilt.

It was a year after Najeib was left bloodied and beaten that the trial of Bowyer and Woodgate began. Eleven months later it was over; at least we thought it was. Bowyer breathed a sigh of relief while Woodgate prepared to carry out 100 hours of community service. Paul Clifford, Woodgate's friend since childhood, was jailed for six years. The sense of disappointment from those baying for justice was palpable. Professional neutrality was discarded by the media as it railed against the result. Journalists, most of whom had probably not followed the daily events in Hull Crown Court, jumped on the bandwagon, accusing the Leeds two of a blood lust and then borrowing it for their own ends.

Yet just as shallow was the reaction of the pro-Leeds lobby. Bowyer was feted by the club's fans who instantly assumed the moral high ground and ignored all the discrepancies in his story by pointing to the verdict. They ignored the fact that the jury had not said that Bowyer was innocent, only that his guilt had not been proven beyond all reasonable doubt. Nobody connected with Leeds had any cause for smug satisfaction. Bowyer had lied to police, changed his story and had been identified by other defendants as being at the scene of the crime. The court heard that Bowyer had given a 'victory' hug to one of his co-defendants after the attack. In the aftermath the Najeib family received threatening letters from people purporting to be fans of the game, while similarly misguided fanatics warned O'Leary that payback was coming. Michael Duberry, the black defender who had shopped Woodgate, received death threats. Suresh Grover, the chairman of the

National Civil Rights Movement, denounced the all-white jury as 'perverse'. West Yorkshire became a melting pot of emotions. There was no winner.

'Being Leeds United we always have to defend ourselves.' Johnny Giles' words now had a prescient ring about them. The media condemnation of Bowyer, Woodgate and Leeds in the aftermath of the retrial was savage. The *Daily Mirror* called Bowyer a 'scumbag' and invited him to sue. His picture adorned a piece in the *Daily Mail* in which Simon Heffer spoke of 'young men too revolting to find a nice girl and too thick to hold down a decent job'.

It was Bowyer who bore the brunt of the attack. Although he had not been convicted of anything, the tabloids worked hard to dig up people with a grudge against him. Here was their timely chance for vengeance. The incident in a McDonald's some five years earlier, when Bowyer hurled chairs at Asian staff and was convicted of affray, was rehashed and twisted to fit the theory that the Najeib jury had got it wrong. It was pointed out that Bowyer once smoked cannabis. Sweeping assumptions were made. Even now you will struggle to find a journalist who believes Bowyer. Why? Because they have been fed Chinese whispers and hearsay for two years. And because Bowyer, with that hateful scowl, eyeballs popping and veins throbbing, is an easy target for those drained by years of footballers behaving badly and happy to justify the stereotype peddled by Heffer.

Woodgate and Bowyer are clearly flawed men with a dubious choice in friends, but the ubiquitous animosity that followed their trial was out of all proportion to the judgement. After all, English football is littered with miscreants whom the media have been happy to forgive. The fact that a self-confessed wife-beater like Paul Gascoigne can appear on *A Question Of Sport* does not excuse the Leeds pair, but it highlights the hypocrisy that coursed through the ensuing months. In a piece in *The Observer* in which Bowyer and Woodgate were described as being 'total arses', Gasgoine was said to combine 'fame and the finer qualities'. Bowyer got drunk, Gascoigne hit a woman. The gloves were off and blinkers on.

Woodgate paid his club fine. 'He has a heart of gold but is daft as a brush with it,' O'Leary said. With the Asian community believing it had been short-changed by the cult of celebrity, such comments were unhelpful. Nice-but-dim people did not do this sort of thing. 'The tea ladies love Lee Bowyer,' O'Leary added, but such bonhomie was soon to be jeopordised.

Bowyer fanned the flames of ignominy by refusing to pay his club fine. He said he was innocent, end of story, but such a simplistic reading of the situation overlooked the fact that he had breached club rules. His defence, that he was drunk and running through the streets because he was 'excited about meeting the ladies' at a lap-dancing club, scarcely put him in a good light. He had also compromised the club by lying. Now he refused to pay a fine and Leeds, to their credit, put him on the transfer list.

On 19 December 2001, Leeds was awash with Christmas shoppers. The brass band played on the Headrow. Across the city at Elland Road, Leeds played Everton. Bowyer watched from his self-made exile in the West Stand. When Leeds scored the players ran to Bowyer and saluted him. It was a show of solidarity and a V-sign to the club. Camaraderie, it seemed, rode roughshod over principle. The fans backed their man too, chanting his name and waving banners of support. 'Lose Bowyer, lose the title – it's your choice' declared one. It struck a chord with the majority and missed the point.

Bowyer did pay up but, by now, Leeds were sinking in quicksand. They were top of the league on 1 January, but subsiding beneath troubles of their own making. The jury delivered its verdict on a Friday. On the following Sunday extracts from O'Leary's book – *Leeds United On Trial* – appeared in the *News of the World*. O'Leary labeled Bowyer and Woodgate a disgrace and in the next breath accused the FA of political correctness for suspending them. Accused of cashing-in on the club's new-found infamy, O'Leary defended his right to write and the season plummeted into disappointment and confusion.

In the summer of 2002, O'Leary was sacked. He had hauled Leeds to a new level but paid the price for failing to qualify for the Champions League in successive seasons. His perennial defence of his transfer record smacked of paranoia and there were reports that he had lost the dressing-room. Just like Wilkinson had done, he had helped to destroy his creation. Leeds fans owed him a debt of gratitude, but that did not stop many celebrating his departure. And so to Terry Venables, the man whom Tony Currie had called 'the best'. After all their troubles the choice of a man whom the Department of Trade and Industry had investigated for 19 charges of serious misconduct and had banned from holding any directorships until 2005 was a bold move. After two horrible years, in which the club had been held up as the epitome of all that is wrong with football, a new season began with the jury still out.

* * *

Peter Ridsdale met me with a hearty handshake, a pink shirt and a smile to shame Miss Nigeria. He is not the sort of chairman to lock himself away in an oak-pannelled boardroom with his single malt and King Edwards. This is 'Publicity Pete'. He is a meeter and greeter *par excellence* and, despite the sneering monicker handed him by his fellow chairmen, a much respected figure. He has put his head above the parapet where others would have quivered inside their ivory towers. He has had to deal with murder, hate mail, severed alliances and two years of trials and errors. He has weathered it all with dignity and honesty, but there are questions and that is why I am here. Having met the Leeds greats I want to find out what it is like to be on the other side of the fence. I want to know how a club comes to make those cataclysmic decisions. I want to know why Leeds sacked the man that had put together the best sequence of results since Revie? And why do they still stand by Bowyer? How have they ended up £77 million in debt. And finally, the question all true supporters want answering: will things ever be the same again?

This small room above the Miss World offices is Ridsdale's London base. A cool breeze blows in through the half-opened window. Ridsdale sits down behind a large desk, orders me a coffee and begins.

'The problem with the trial was that the incident happened in the first place and everyone forgets that there is a victim,' he said. 'That is terrible. We were criticised for not saying much at the time, but we were advised not to because it wasn't just footballers who were in court. So we kept silent and were heavily criticised for that. Then the trial collapsed and that was the most mentally taxing situation of all. Everybody had geared themselves up for a resolution, whatever that may be, and there was just a sense of disbelief when it didn't come. I'm sure it was the same for the victim and his family. It dragged on for two years and there's no doubt it was completely distracting for the management and the players.

'The impact on the club's image has been to tarnish it for a long time. Can we repair it? With time, but there is a lot of work to be done. The hard work we'd put in and the good will we'd created disappeared overnight. For me personally, that was disappointing because we'd tried very, very hard to do the right things and say the right things. Now, something that was not directly the football club's making has put us back a number of years.'

Ridsdale understands his place. He was born and raised in the city. When the local education authority was falling foul of Ofsted, he took over as chairman. Like David Batty, he not only stands up for Leeds but is Leeds. His heart pounds to the rhythms of a complex club that draws on base emotions. Since seeing his first game at Elland Road in 1959, he has seen the club rise and fall at least twice. But never has the fall been accompanied by such naked hatred as this time. *His time*.

'The negativity we've had to live with for many years,' he admitted, 'but we'd started to change that. Now we've been put back and I don't think I was prepared for the anger that came at the end of the trial. The media were particularly disparaging towards the football club, but a lot came at me too. The letters I got were horrific, terrible, threatening stuff. You wondered about people's mental condition to be able to write what they did. It was disappointing because neither David nor I were personally involved. It was something that happened outside the football club, yet we were held responsible. I think the reason was people at large did not believe the outcome.

'The response from the public was vitriolic in the extreme towards me and other officials at the club because they felt justice had not been done. But I've always believed in the jury system. When we heard the original charges we said we'd stand by all our players and respond at the end of the trial. What were we supposed to do? Lee was found not guilty and Jonathan was found not guilty of GBH with intent. To some degree you could say it vindicated our decision to play them during the trial, but to the other degree it meant there was this huge outpouring of anger. But I believe in the jury system, we're a public company and what are we supposed to do with someone who is found innocent?'

Ridsdale had said that if either player was convicted then he would never play for the club again. He quickly changed that original statement to relate to the GBH charge alone. People seized on that as backtracking, but it was a totally reasonable response. It is unlikely that there is a club in the country that would sack players for a minor conviction. Rightly or wrongly, this is the way of the world. The flood of money into the sport does not change that. Players, some of whom are horrible, odious mercenaries and some of whom are decent, gentle family men, should not have to subscribe to a Utopian code of ethics simply because they are richer than ever. And while Bowyer was vanquished, the double standards remained. Just after I met Ridsdale, Leicester City were ordered by the Football League to reinstate Dennis Wise. They had sacked him because he had punched Callum Davidson, a team-mate, while he lay in bed following a row over a game of cards. Davidson suffered a broken cheekbone. And yet here was the Football League agreeing that the assault had taken place but criticising Leicester's actions. The story raised a murmur in the papers, whereas several forests had been felled to fuel the campaign against Bowyer. (On appeal Leicester later won the right to terminate Wise's contract.)

But what of Bowyer? His status as returning hero was nauseating. When the fans sang 'Jingle Bells, Sarfraz smells, Woodgate got affray, oh what fun it is to see Bowyer get away' it was impossible not to feel anything other than ashamed. He has been one of the club's best midfield players of the last 20 years, cutting a swathe through games with lung-busting surges from midfield and a healthy goalscoring record, and is a huge favourite of the crowd. Everyone hates him and that is an endearing trait for Leeds fans. He is the outsider, the outlaw and the outcast. No one likes him; Leeds don't care.

The irony is that Bowyer lost face with some supporters through refusing to pay his fine rather than cavorting through the streets as a drunken mess. Prior to my date with Ridsdale, Bowyer's prospective move to Liverpool had fallen through. The Merseyside club were prepared to double his wages, but Bowyer wanted more. So he is back at Leeds, still refusing to sign a new contract, overweening and overpaid, a perplexing mix of pride and Prada.

Speaking to Ridsdale it becomes clear that there is a rift between the two. A radio interview in which Ridsdale questioned Bowyer's character and said he would not countenance signing him were he not already at the club cut deep. 'I can understand how he feels,' Ridsdale says. 'Lee feels we shouldn't have fined him, I felt we should. He also feels let down by something I said and he's probably right about that. With the benefit of hindsight it would have been better left unsaid. I apologised to him for that. Has he accepted it? You'd have to ask him.

'Whenever you don't get your own way in life you can do one of two things. You can get emotional or you can say it's part of life's experiences. I wish he'd sign a new contract, but I have no control over that. I made him an offer that I thought was right and he has chosen not to sign it. I've apologised for my comments – not for the fine because I'd fine him again tomorrow – and can do no more.'

A resigned expression dulls Ridsdale's natural effervescence. Leeds United have taken its toll on him. 'I'd be very surprised if I'm still here in five years,' he says. 'This is not an easy job. I've never done a job where I get insulted so much and it's hard to cope with. The letters I got following Rio Ferdinand's departure have been appalling – they make you wonder about people's psychological state. It shocks me that people can be so vitriolic towards me and it's a reminder of how passionate fans can be in a negative way. You know you don't take any decision to get it wrong. You do your best and try to be honest. But for a club that has been through what we have and with our expectation levels, there is only so long you can do it.' One day, you suspect, maybe in the dim, distant future, the poison pen letters will be replaced by thank you notes.

* * *

He started watching games regularly in 1962. Gary Sprake was his hero. 'If you'd seen a lot of the away games you'd think he was a better player than his publicity suggested.' (As Ridsdale has rapidly discovered, you cannot trust the Press.) He loved strikers too. Allan Clarke was his favourite but he also had a soft spot for Jimmy Greenhoff, an oft forgotten part of the club's history. 'And I like people who could pass the ball. Tony Currie was majestic and John Sheridan could play that game. Now there's Stephen McPhail. I could watch him play with a ball all week. He went out on loan last year but he's back at the club and is in Terry's plans.'

McPhail highlights the ephemeral nature of football. When I met him in 2000 he had the world at his feet. Then he faded by the wayside, O'Leary questioned his fragility and he ended up at Millwall where he was sent off on his debut. Time has ravaged others. Michael Bridges, the top scorer two years ago, has barely played since I met him after a number of injuries. The same goes for Lucas Radebe. And, in their absence, Leeds signed Rio Ferdinand, Dominic Matteo, Robbie Fowler, Mark Viduka and Robbie Keane. (Keane was sold a fortnight after this interview took place.) Even Nigel Martyn, the best goalkeeper we'd ever had, lost his place at the start of the 2002 season. It is a cruel world where sympathy is routinely sacrificed at the altar of ambition.

Leeds could only dream of such luxuries or of playing in Europe when Ridsdale became a director in 1987. The club was still mired in the old second division then. A decade later, Ridsdale, formerly the managing director of Topman, graduated to club chairman. By then the goalposts had been moved and Leeds were fueled with grand plans.

'We invested a lot of money,' he says. 'It has been a clear passion to get our club into the top four or five. The top half dozen clubs in the country will become pan-European and if there is ever a European Super League we have to be one of those at the forefront of people's minds. We have qualified for Europe in every year that I have been the chairman. It is the best consecutive performance since the days of Billy Bremner and the rest. You have to have that vision in a city the size of Leeds. That is easy to say but harder to deliver and my biggest frustration is that we still have not won trophies. But people have short memories. They forget that this is a very successful period in the club's history.

'The European nights we have had in the past few years have been like a fairy tale. In David's first full season we got to the UEFA Cup semi-final. There were some fantastic performances. We beat Roma at Elland Road with a single goal from Harry Kewell and we got to see parts of the world we'd never seen before. That all ended horrifically with the events that surrounded Galatasaray, but the next year we were storming the Champions League. People forget we were not even seeded that season. Manchester United and Arsenal were, but we weren't and we had to play Barcelona and Milan. The thing that is stunning is that people in Leeds perceive us to have failed, yet most of those people have never seen a five-year period like it. The expectation has been raised because of our investment and European runs, but this is a very fickle game and people soon get on your back. Sometimes you don't realise how much you have to learn until things start to go badly wrong. Now, for the first time, I sense people are not believing in us as much. The pressure is off a little and maybe we'll all be better for it.'

It has been a glorious and spurious period of gold and grey. But if the team is one of the best the Leeds public has seen, as Ridsdale says, why sack the manager? The week I talk to Ridsdale sees O'Leary come out and declare his intention to sue Leeds for compensation. He wants around £1 million, but the deterioration in what was one of the closest bonds in the Premiership means more bad blood is likely to be spilt before a resolution is reached.

Ridsdale scratches his chin. The split with O'Leary has pained him. 'A manager's dream,' Eddie once called his chairman. O'Leary would punctuate many a tired press conference with talk of the 'good people' he worked for. Ridsdale himself once said, 'I don't think David has been given the credit he deserves for what he has achieved in a short space of time.' So what happened?

'There comes a moment in time when you have to take a decision that hurts but that you feel is right,' he says. 'I thought, and the board agreed, that given everything we'd been through, the last six months had been extremely disappointing. The attitude and motivation of the players was not what it should have been. We just felt that everything had taken its toll and a fresh start was needed. David did a very good job, but the spark had gone. I felt the decision was right to make a change and felt David and the players would benefit from it.'

O'Leary has suggested his stance against selling Ferdinand to Manchester United was partly to blame for his exit. He also claimed Leeds had already lined up his successor and that he was hurt by the brevity of the meeting where he was sacked. Ridsdale paints a different picture and it is clear that the publication of O'Leary's book was a contributory factor to his demise. 'I believe the book was a mistake and have told him that. I was told he was doing a diary of the season, but had no idea when it was coming out or what it was called. I was stunned by the title and timing, but it was outside my control. The first I heard about it was in the press conference after the trial. A journalist said, "You say Leeds United have not been on trial, so how come David's book is called that?" I said I was unaware of that. I was disappointed. I don't see the real need to write books when you are in a well-paid job. And it would be wrong to say that it did not have an impact on the team's performance in the second half of the season. We were top on 1 January and then had an appalling two months.

'As for the meeting, I don't know how else you can do it other than sit someone down and tell them. I have written to David and the author of an article that appeared at the time, talking about what happened, and pointed out the various inaccuracies in it. That was not the way it was. It was a face-to-face meeting and there was a lengthy discussion over a cup of coffee. Ultimately, we shook hands and said we hoped we'd stay friends. I'd like to think that's possible because he is not the first manager to change jobs. We did get on exceptionally well, but it was a professional relationship and the worst reason for someone staying in a job is because they are perceived to be friends.

'I think David thought we had got Mick McCarthy lined up. His perception was that we waited until after the World Cup so that Mick was back. But the reality was we waited until after the World Cup so that David had finished his TV stint and we could tell him face to face, not because we wanted McCarthy. We thought that was right, but with the benefit of hindsight it probably was not the best thing to do because we were then blamed for the timing of it [the sacking].'

Ridsdale rejects the notion that O'Leary paid the price for the board's impatience. The final six months of his reign had been disappointing, but the previous 39 had been hugely successful. It is hard to disassociate O'Leary's exit from the fact the club was £77 million in debt and had failed to make the Champions League by a single place. 'We have invested for Champions League football,' Ridsdale says. 'We've spent more than I'd like in terms of player trading.

Before we signed Robbie Fowler and Seth Johnson, we'd essentially said that was it. What we had to do thereafter is recoup some money.

'You have to remember that Robbie Fowler is an unique talent and we bought Robbie Keane because we never thought that Fowler would become available. Then we had the injury to Michael Bridges and so there was an issue there. Last season Michael Bridges and Lucas Radebe didn't play, and Lee Bowyer and Jonathan Woodgate faced uncertain futures. We had to bring in cover for those players. Now they are all back and I'm saying "let's stop covering and bring the squad down". We have got what I'd call 31 full-time pros and I feel it should be nearer 23. I have agreed with Terry that there is a size of squad in this day and age that we can afford. We have to keep a tighter hold on the purse strings. But I'm not talking about getting rid of the top stars, I'm talking about getting those players who are never going to get a game off the payroll. There isn't a player we're prepared to let go that Terry wants. I'm not naming any names, but there is a list of players who we've said we will take any acceptable offers for. We're set fair for the time ahead. We've got a great coach and a very good squad.'

* * *

It is August at Throstle Nest. Leeds United are playing Farsley Celtic in a pre-season game in Pudsey. Peter Ridsdale is happy to see Michael Bridges back in action. He is also pleased to see Sue Speight, the widow of one of the fans stabbed to death in Istanbul two years ago. Kevin Speight was the landlord of the local pub and used to sponsor Farsley's reserve team. The club will never forget him. Neither will Ridsdale.

'It was nice to see Sue,' he says. 'Her children are doing well and she was looking like her old self again. I don't see Mr and Mrs Loftus much because they, themselves, were not football fans and obviously found the whole period very distressing. But Kevin's son played in a schools game at Elland Road and I handed out some trophies at Farsley Celtic a year ago. You carry a responsibility as a chairman in any city. It's right that I remember it's the people of Leeds who pay the money for the players and for me to do a job.'

Ridsdale will never forget the Taksim Hospital either. He saw the stab wounds and sent his driver to a neighbouring hospital to pick up more blood. He was with Philip Loftus when he identified his brother's body. 'One minute I was talking to Galatasaray directors to promote the friendship between the two clubs and the next minute I received a telephone call telling me there had been some problems in town,' he said at the time.

He attended the funerals of both men and showed his diplomacy and reason in defusing the raging emotions that preceded the second game against Galatasaray at Elland Road. One tabloid ran the headline 'Grotesque' in response to the first leg going ahead, but nobody in possession of the facts could accuse Ridsdale of being anything other than a caring, humane fan.

'I find it hard to say it was a traumatic time for me or the club when you have families going through the worst experience of their lives,' he says. 'I tried hard not to say it had been traumatic because it looked like I was looking for sympathy, but the reality was I'd never been through anything like it before and responded in the way I thought proper and appropriate. Everyone has their own style, their own approach. I am a Leeds supporter and know the city and I was upset. It was hard to manage through that time, especially when the Galatasaray response to us wanting to play the return leg without away fans was slowing what I thought was an easy decision. I don't want to talk too much about Galatasaray though, because the incidents happened in the centre of Istanbul and there was no suggestion that it was Galatasaray supporters who were to blame; I am conscious that football clubs sometimes get blamed for the behaviour of their supporters.

'But I did think it inappropriate that it took so long to resolve. The tension that was created was partly hyped by that. It would have been easier if everybody had just said: "we're sorry for what happened, let's just get this game out of the way". You know, let's talk about the real things in life.'

This is Ridsdale. Despite the Publicity Pete nickname and the fact he has just done a Fulham and employed Max Clifford as the club's image consultant, he cares deeply. It is not surface fluff designed to massage an ego. It is not simply a quest to gain a favourable press. The real things do matter to him. Football is transient. Seasons merge into one another and messianic managers pale to footnotes in history books. As the media picks at the last flesh on the bones of a dying relationship, Ridsdale knows O'Leary will soon be forgotten. Instead, we have Venables. After all that wearisome blarney we have a man with the gift of the gab, a second-hand car dealer in a silk shirt. With his chugging Steptoe laugh and permatan, Venables is a breath of fresh air. And at a club where a fog of stale halitosis has hovered for months, that is no bad thing.

Perhaps mindful of how his relationship with O'Leary soured, Ridsdale is quick to point out that Venables went along with the sale of Rio Ferdinand to Manchester United. Eyebrows were raised when Leeds signed the defender from West Ham United for a staggering £18 million, but he proved his worth. With Old Trafford's defence creaking under the weight of a failed title defence, Ferdinand became the number one target. Ridsdale made public utterings about keeping Ferdinand, Venables endeared himself to Leeds fans with a sideswipe at Manchester United, but the outcome was inevitable. 'I spoke to my family about things like loyalty,' Ferdinand said. Presumably he decided against it and thus the impatience and avarice of the modern footballer was perfectly illustrated. Long-term contract be damned.

'Everyone forgets that we bought Rio because of Lucas Radebe and Jonathan Woodgate's uncertain futures,' Ridsdale says. (This same proclamation would make the tabloids a few days later with Ridsdale mocked for having the temerity to suggest that England's best defender had been signed as back-up.) 'We happened to be in a situation where Rio said he wanted to go. Jonathan and Lucas were back and we had a clause in his contract saying he could not even talk to another club unless they were offering £25 million. You manage it as you see fit at the time.'

The sale prompted more hate mail, but Ridsdale had little choice and effectively accused Manchester United of 'tapping up' his captain. 'I spoke to Rio when he got back from the World Cup and he said that if the offer came then he would like to go. It was pretty clear we were talking about Manchester United. I went on holiday and ultimately we got a written transfer request. I'm a pragmatist at the end of the day, but a lot of people who shout about the way things should be done don't play the same game. But it's like business, if you want to go and work for someone else you go and talk to them. As long as the club is properly compensated, and we were, you have to accept that.

'Rio has gone but Terry has still got a very good squad. Time will tell whether he is a success. You don't appoint someone you don't believe can do the job. When David went we drew up a short list and I think if you took a poll of people's views they would come up with the same names. I said we needed to get someone quickly and, secondly, that the person had to be available. People talked about Martin O'Neill but he was under contract and I did not talk to Celtic. Our view, considering everybody else's opinions, including people who'd played for various managers, was that there was one name that kept coming to the fore. That was Terry.

'We sincerely believe he is a great coach and working with a very good squad. I just hope his coaching skills can get the best out of a bunch of talented players. I want to win trophies. I want to get back into the Champions League. When I took over I said it might take five years. I have made it absolutely clear to Terry that there is no bad trophy, but psychologically the first trophy is the most difficult.'

And so it goes on. Venables became Leeds' 11th manager since the great days of Revie. Of those, only Howard Wilkinson and O'Leary could claim to have been successes. The fact O'Leary descended into self-parody and had his personality dissected by the likes of Tony Cascarino – 'He would win few popularity contests in the game. He was the kind of guy who would call you "top man", put the phone down and probably hammer you afterwards' – did not detract from what he had achieved at Elland Road. Dotted throughout this book are glowing references from the sons of Revie and there is no greater accolade for a Leeds manager.

But while that marriage ended in a messy divorce and a bitter compensation claim, the fans have moved on to Venables. To Ridsdale's delight, Leeds got off to a good start under their new manager. Some wondered whether El Tel had been seduced by his myth and would have been better working as a pundit, but he looked like he meant business. Then they lost a game at home to Sunderland, boos rang out and the honeymoon ended with the club in a state of flux. Who could foresee which way the pendulum would swing?

I thank Ridsdale, who has been typically generous with his time. I tell him that, as a fan, I think he has done a tremendous job. He sighs and says it has not been easy. 'I'd hate to think we'd have to go through more years like the last few,' he muses. He deserves an easy ride, but this is Leeds United and the course of true love never did run smooth.

DOMINIC MATTEO and ALAN SMITH –
Looking For A Hero

Football is a simple game – it's the players that make it difficult.

GORDON STRACHAN

Dirty, dirty Leeds. It is the same now as it was back in the days of Bobby Collins and Johnny Giles. The club has become a spittoon for the football populace. The past two years have hurt and it has become increasingly hard to put up a defence. But that is history. All that troubled water has long flown under the burning bridges and there is hope for the future. Crikey, even when Terry Connor was clogging up the strikeforce there was hope.

I make a final trip to Leeds' training ground two days before the start of the season. I sit in the corridor of the academy and wait. A door flies open and a guffawing orange haze bursts through. Terry Venables offers his hand and shows a magnificent tribute to the dental profession. Then he is gone, departed to do more interviews as he plots the rebirth of the club and his own reputation.

I am here to meet Dominic Matteo. He is the quiet man of Elland Road. Last season he did few interviews but, with Rio Ferdinand taking the road less travelled, he has been installed as the new captain and has accepted the need to act as a spokesman. Leeds have taken a battering in recent times. Bowyer, Woodgate and O'Leary fuelled a bonfire of enmity and the abrasiveness of Alan Smith and Danny Mills added a dash of paraffin. I need to know that the club is in safe hands as it attempts to step back from the precipice.

'It's brilliant to be the captain of such a big club,' he says reassuringly as we sit in one of the ante-rooms in this warren of offices. 'It's what you dream about as a boy. I know what it means to people in the city because they stop me and tell me. I know how people feel about Billy Bremner and Gordon Strachan. It is an honour to be captain. When I found out, I was inundated with phone calls, even from Liverpool and Everton fans, wishing me all the best.'

Matteo is a Scouser-Scot. Born in Dumfries, he spent 12 years at Anfield. His father, Alberto, is half-Italian and there was always pasta cooking in the family home. He championed the great Italian stoppers to his son. Cesare Maldini, the father of Paolo, was his hero. It was, perhaps, inevitable that Matteo would therefore become a defender. At Liverpool he played primarily as a full-back, but at Leeds he is a centre-half. With Ferdinand gone and Woodgate aiming to rise from the ashes of his charred reputation, he has a considerable weight on his shoulders.

'Rio will become the best defender in the world, but he's gone and I wish him all the best,' he says. 'He had to make a decision and you can't blame him. I hope that the fans don't give him too hard a time when we play them because he's a great bloke. But we have to get on with it. Woody had problems, but I don't think there's much between him and Rio. It won't surprise me if they end up playing for England together.

'Jonathan knows that this is a very big season for him. He has to keep his head but he knows that. Jonathan's discipline is unbelievable; he's hardly ever been booked. The abuse will come from the terraces – Lee gets it already – but he'll be prepared for it. It won't work trying to wind him up. He won't bite. He's very level-headed on the field and a very tough player to play against. I think he's learnt a lot. I think he's probably a stronger person for what he's been through.'

It is a nice defence. But Matteo, at 28, is mature enough to know that there is work to be done. 'I think we can repair the image of the club,' he said. 'Eventually we'll get out of it. People have made mistakes, but it's not my business. These things happen and we have to get on with it. As long as we are doing our job on the pitch and conducting ourselves off it then nobody can say anything against us.

'But things change when you become a footballer. You can't go out as much as you like. You're in the public eye and people are going to notice you. I go out for meals and nobody bothers me, but you know the slightest thing will be in the papers. You have to be sensible. I go out with my family and close friends; I know I can trust them.'

Matteo does not get in trouble. He is the sort of man who appreciates his good fortune. When Leeds signed him for £4.25 million, it was primarily as cover for Ian Harte, the most spectacularly sloth-like full-back in the club's history. However, injuries meant he played in midfield and then alongside Ferdinand at the heart of the defence. He excelled to such an extent that when he decided to play for Scotland, Tord Grip, Sven-Goran Eriksson's assistant, rang him in an effort to persuade him to reconsider.

So much has happened since I first turned up at Thorp Arch to meet Eddie Gray. At that time Lucas Radebe was the captain. Matteo was a Liverpool player. Ferdinand had yet to be signed by Leeds and the trial of Bowyer and Woodgate was still to begin. The mood has changed dramatically and so has the scale of the club. Since talking to Gray, Leeds have signed Viduka, Keane and Fowler, a £28 million trio of forwards that past generations could only have dreamt about. I think of Allan Clarke telling me that he never saw the £2 million he was promised for rebuilding. Poor old Sniffer. The arrival of Fowler, a boyhood friend of Matteo and Liverpool legend, was probably the most stunning signing in the club's history in terms of sheer eyebrow-canting, phone-a-friend repercussions. 'Things change very quickly in football,' Matteo agrees. 'But everyone around here is so nice that it makes it easy. With Robbie coming here it's like it used to be years ago when we were kids. It's great for me. Everyone thought I had an influence on it because we were so close off the pitch, but I didn't. Robbie came to play football.'

I attended the press conference at Thorp Arch when Fowler signed for the club. It was a media scrum. Fowler's glassy cow eyes had never looked sadder. This may have been the move designed to kick-start his career, but he looked like a bereaved man. As Batty is to Leeds, so Fowler is to Liverpool, an amalgam of Alan Bleasdale, Toxteth and run-down dockyards. 'Will you ever be able to have the affection for Leeds that you do for Liverpool?' came the question. It was unfair and the quintessential Scouser laughed. 'That's a terrible thing to ask,' he said. No mealy-mouthed platitudes or thinly-veiled lies from him. Everyone knew he would rather be at Anfield but he had fallen foul of the hierarchy. He had not signed a new contract because he had not been offered one, he said. Watching his performance made me realise how hard football can be. Your fate is often out of your hands and today's headline is soon yesterday's news. Every player is expendable.

Matteo went through similar feelings when he left Liverpool. He did not know if it would work out, but he was encouraged by O'Leary's faith. Eddie Gray recalled that when Matteo first arrived at Leeds he was touchy about receiving criticism. 'I can understand it,' he said. 'He had been at Liverpool since he was 14 and the adjustment to a new club, initially without a role or position that he could call his own, was bound to involve some feelings of insecurity.' Footballers need to be wanted. That had become clear to me from my conversations with the Revie greats and beyond. 'I don't stay anywhere where I'm not wanted,' was how Bobby Collins put it. So when O'Leary, the man who had bought Matteo was sacked, I imagine those self-doubts must have crept back into his mind.

'David told me himself,' he recalls. 'I was here at Thorp Arch, doing a bit of training to keep my fitness up. He explained what had happened and was pretty upset. It was very difficult to say something. I was disappointed for him and we wished each other the best in what we did. That was it. Yes it was unsettling. David was a big influence on the club, but he's gone and will soon be forgotten. The players were all apart because it was the summer, but everybody was ringing each other up that night. It's no different to any other job. Just people ringing and saying, 'the gaffer's gone'. I was surprised but it's between him and the club. He had a great time here, taking the club to the semi-finals of the Champions League and doing well in the League year in, year out. My football improved a lot under him too. But life goes on. You have to get on with it.'

The need 'to get on with it' peppers Matteo's conversation. It is an insouciant credo that all players must adopt to deal with football's capriciousness. Matteo may have been saddened by O'Leary's exit, but there is no time for self-pity or introspection in this cut-throat world. I doubt that many of the Leeds team experienced a sense of guilt over their manager's sacking, but it was they who had underperformed. A better finish here and a more creative effort there and they might have saved him. Whatever the real reason for the axe being wielded, it would have been a public relations disaster to sack a manager who had qualified for the Champions League and Leeds were only five points short.

'To not get into the Champions League was a nightmare,' Matteo admits. 'We were devastated with the end to the season but, to be honest, although we were top of the league at Christmas we weren't playing to the best of our ability. In the

New Year we didn't play well as a team. There were some good individual performances, but as a team we didn't do it. We've been working on that, striving together as a team.'

That has always been the Leeds way. 'Side before self every time,' said Billy Bremner. It is a maxim that still holds true. All the individual talent in the world will count for little if there is no collective will. You only have to look at Chelsea to understand that. They have adopted a selection policy that appears to have been honed from *The Magnificent Seven*. Anyone with a reputation is in. They generally beat Manchester United and then lose to Southampton as a result, but that is Chelsea. Ken Bates should watch more videos and realise that it even went sour for Yul Brynner in the sequel.

At Leeds there is a genuine spirit of affection among the players. A few months earlier I met Michael Bridges again as he neared a comeback from terrible injury problems. He said the support of his team-mates had helped him through his darkest hours. 'You think "what the hell have I done to deserve this?" but I wasn't ever going to tie a knot in the ceiling and put my head in it. I thought about people worse off than myself.'

One of whom was a Croatian skier who he met at the Colorado clinic where he went for a career-saving knee operation. 'He was in the bed next to mine and had his legs wrapped around his neck,' said Bridges. 'He could only move around in a wheelchair and told me he should have been going to the Olympics.'

Since our original meeting, Bridges had also suffered a meningitis scare – 'when you spend three days lying in bed, not knowing what is happening, it is very worrying' – snapped ligaments, a torn tendon, having a bone drilled and more depressed days than he cared to remember. In the meantime, Leeds have signed three international strikers. Like Lucas Radebe, Bridges had to draw on a deep well of desire to get him through. It is a torrid tale that provides perspective; it is the flip side of the coin for all those willing to jump on the Bowyer bandwagon and shout that footballers have it easy.

Matteo, too, is well aware of the vagaries of football. One minute you are up and playing in the Champions League semi-final in Valencia, the next you are down and dismissed as underachievers. Matteo accepts that criticism better nowadays. Gray felt Leeds might have avoided the second killer Valencia goal that night had Matteo closed down Juan Sanchez instead of retreating to his own box. When he broached the subject, he had barely got the words out before Matteo said: 'Eddie, I know. I knew as soon as I did it.'

Football is a great life but it is a hard life. The summer has been difficult for all connected with Leeds. The loss of the captain, the manager and last vestiges of good will have piled woe on woe. 'When a manager goes, you do start wondering what will happen now,' Matteo says. 'Most of the players rang him to wish him well and then it was wait and see. We read the papers like anyone else. Terry was mentioned and we thought we'd like him. All you hear is good things from players who've worked with him. He has his own style, likes to be hands on, shows you what he can do. The training is team based; it's about getting everyone to play to the best of his ability. Maybe after a couple of months under him we'll have a new way of playing and a solid base.

'We're all trying to achieve the same goals here. People talk about getting back into the Champions League, but I want some silverware. We need some. The club needs something, the fans need something.'

What they need is what they have always needed. People to make them dream and conjure up those days 'when you cry your eyes out and walk on air'. I wish Matteo well for the season and walk to the car. A peroxide figure is ambling along with a cocky swagger. I catch his eye and nod. For all the £94 million that O'Leary spent on new players in his 45 months, this is the one who plucks the heartstrings of the Leeds people. This is a walking memento mori of Revie's Leeds – an igneous core dressed up in innocent white. 'I don't care for reputations,' he once said. His public lapped up that devil-may-care bluster. 'I'm not dirty,' he added. A few people laughed on the inside and remembered Allan Clarke.

This is Alan Smith, a wrought-iron hero. 'He was mean and I don't like players who are like that,' said Frank de Boer after Leeds had been humbled by Barcelona in the Champions League in September 2000. 'Over-enthusiasm,' was Smith's phlegmatic response. When Leeds finally went out of the competition in Valencia (a fact not helped by UEFA handing Lee Bowyer a three-match ban on the eve of the game for an alleged stamp on Juan Sanchez), the red mist again descended on Smith. He made a scything two-footed lunge and was sent off. It was wrong, of course, and everybody, O'Leary included, told him so. Yet, deep inside many Leeds fans, there was a small glow of pleasure at seeing a player provide a vicarious release for their frustrations. Just as Howard Wilkinson had said he wished one of his players had taken a swing at the referee in the 1996 Coca-Cola Cup surrender, Smith's action, wrong though it was, showed he cared. Valencia had ruined his hopes of walking on air and he was damned if he was going to let them get away with it. And so he damned because he did not.

'I knew it was silly but it meant so much to me,' he said later. In the changing-room David Batty told him it was not worth it and that he would learn. But for a split second, with sense blurred by emotion, it was worth every ounce of anger. 'It was one of those things where the circumstances meant that everything had come to an end. It was more about disappointment than anything else.'

This is part of the Smith psyche. Five minutes after his introduction to a game at Arsenal in 1998 he was headbutted by Gilles Grimandi. The following April he rattled David Beckham's cage and then floored Peter Schmeichel with a robust challenge. When the Dane complained, Smith threw the ball at him. At the end of the 1999 season he cemented his infamy by provoking Tony Adams and Martin Keown, Arsenal's hugely experienced defensive axis, into red raw rage. The story goes that he lit the touch paper by asking Adams, a former alcoholic, if he fancied a pint after the game. Smith denies that, but was still concerned when he was called up for England and walked into the dining room to be greeted by the pair sitting at a table. 'I thought "Jesus Christ, what am I going to do here?"' he recalled. 'So I sat between them and Tony Adams said, "you're not going to kick me are you?"'

Yet, to be a true hero there have to be other qualities. Only a fool would worship at Smith's feet purely because he kicks Arsenal defenders. And Smith has that extra dimension. He scored with his first touch for Leeds after coming on as a substitute in a rare victory at Liverpool when he was barely 18. His namesake, the former Arsenal striker, positively fawned over Smith's qualities in a piece in the

Daily Telegraph and the player whose name kept coming up in discussion with the past heroes, even more so than Harry Kewell, was this small, angel-faced assassin whom O'Leary once labelled 'a thug'.

In the season recently finished, Smith's reputation in the wider world plumbed new depths. He was sent off against Aston Villa for elbowing Alpay, the Turkish defender. It was a blow that would have struggled to fell an inebriated gnat, but it was still daft. He was also sent off as Leeds crashed out of the FA Cup at Cardiff City and received a five-match ban. For a while it seemed he was rejoicing in his stereotype. Smith was a black heart with cherubic features, an oompah-loompah with a caffeine problem. When it came to keeping up with the Joneses, this manchild was part Aled, part Vinnie. O'Leary claimed Smith was becoming a victim of his image and that referees had an agenda, but Leeds fans were more realistic and knew that his reputation for mayhem was well earned. It was the very reason that they loved him.

'I've grown up,' Smith said last season but there was plenty of contradictory evidence. In one 11-game period he received five yellow cards and was sent off twice. 'When the red mist descends Alan is not aware that he is doing anything wrong,' said Eddie Gray. 'It can be so agonising. When he was sent off in the last minute against Valencia I could see it coming. There is an element of the daredevil in his make-up.'

Smith is an iconoclast. When his place came under threat following the arrival of Mark Viduka, Smith told O'Leary: 'I'm a better player than Viduka and Bridges put together and I'm going to prove it to you.' Gray says the fans love him for the same reasons they love Batty. He is right. This is why Smith sells more shirts than Viduka or Kewell. Leeds fans like their diamonds to have rough edges. It is a northern thing.

Yet, there is another side to Smith. As a boy he grew homesick when he went to the national academy at Lilleshall and so went home to Rothwell. Those close to him say he has a sharp wit. He is not precious either. When *The Times* asked him to get dressed up as a choirboy for a photo shoot, he did not even blink. 'I've worn worse on a lads night out,' he said.

Forget the pompous journalist who wrote a diatribe against him after being refused an interview. This was sheer arrogance, he claimed. More likely, it was the natural reaction of someone whose character has been routinely dissected by media moralists. What is truly arrogant is to expect a couple of juicy soundbites from someone you have just crucified.

His critics talk of him needing to grow up, but age will not distil him. In one breath he says he must stop the silly challenges, but in the next he says he finds it harder to ignore trouble when Leeds are losing. That is the core of Smithy. He cannot turn the other cheek because it matters to him. He is not in it for the win bonus. The fans know this and that is why they want to freeze him as a 22 year old. They do not want him to be sanitised by experience because he is one of them. You can see it in the act of wilfulness.

In some ways, this diminutive figure ambling through another sunny day is the personification of this club. Loved and hated, he lives, breathes, sleeps and eats Leeds United. He is a transmitter for fandom's visceral anguish. He is the passion and fury. They may try to soften him but Alan Smith will never be able to walk away. That is the beauty of the beastly city and its beastly football club. When it comes to heroes, only the faces change.